PLANNING THE PLAY
OF A BRIDGE HAND

BARBARA SEAGRAM • DAVID BIRD

MASTER POINT PRESS • TORONTO, CANADA

Master Point Press
214 Merton St. Suite 205
Toronto, Ontario, Canada
M4S 1A6   (647)956-4933

Email: info@masterpointpress.com

Websites: www.masterpointpress.com
                   www.teachbridge.com
                   www.bridgeblogging.com
                   www.ebooksbridge.com

Library and Archives Canada Cataloguing in Publication

Seagram, Barbara

Planning the play of a bridge hand / Barbara Seagram, David Bird.

Issued also in electronic formats.
ISBN 978-1-897106-51-8

1. Contract bridge. I. Bird, David, 1946– II. Title.

GV1282.3.S419 2009   795.41'53   C2009-901315-0

Canada | We acknowledge the financial support of the Government of Canada.
       | Nous reconnaissons l'appui financier du gouvernement du Canada.

Editor   Ray Lee
Copy editor/interior format Sally Sparrow
Cover and interior design   Olena S. Sullivan/New Mediatrix

7 8 9 10 11   22 21 20 19 18

PRINTED IN CANADA

PLANNING THE PLAY
OF A BRIDGE HAND

CONTENTS

INTRODUCTION

Any worthwhile book on bridge cardplay will emphasize the importance of making a plan. This should be done right at the start of the contract, before you play the first card from dummy. It is one thing to know that you should make a plan — quite another to discipline yourself to do it!

Most bridge contracts are relatively easy to plan, particularly those at the game or slam level. We will see in the next few chapters exactly how you set about the task. This might be the plan for a typical suit contract:

> **PLAN: I will win the club lead, draw trumps, and ruff the diamond loser in dummy.**

As you see, the plan is only fifteen words long. It doesn't give the details of what happens, from trick to trick, but is still sufficient to explain what you intend to do.

When you first start to play bridge, the mechanics of playing tricks and of moving from one hand to the other can seem daunting. It is much the same when you first learn to drive a car. If you asked an expert driver how to get to the nearest McDonald's burger bar, he might tell you:

> **Go North to the I-28 and make a right. McDonald's is a mile up, on the right-hand side.**

Suppose you were still learning to drive and desperate for a quarter-pounder. You would have to concern yourself not only with these basic directions, but also with gripping the steering wheel, operating the indicators, braking if any traffic light turned red, and so on.

So, don't worry if the mechanics of playing a bridge contract are new to you and you find our recommended 'plans' somewhat brief. The full details of the play will be given in the accompanying text. You will soon become familiar with the basic cardplay techniques and can then put all your efforts into determining the best possible plan for the contracts you play.

One note: bidding can be complicated, but the focus of this book is on cardplay. We have therefore elected to use only a few simple conventions in our example auctions, including old-fashioned Blackwood (not Roman Keycard), so as not to distract readers.

Barbara and David

PART I

PLANNING A SUIT CONTRACT

1

HOW TO PLAN A SUIT CONTRACT

The first step in making a plan for a suit contract is to count the potential losers in your hand, declarer's hand, looking at each suit in turn. You do this by taking into account the high cards in both your own hand and the dummy. Look at these three suits, for example, assuming that South (as always in bridge books) is the declarer:

(a) ♠ A 10 7 2

♠ 5

(b) ♡ Q 8 6 5

♡ K 3

(c) ◇ K 8 4

◇ 9 5 2

The South hand has only one spade in (a), so the maximum possible number of spade losers would be one. Here, your loser is covered by dummy's ace, so you have no spade losers. If dummy's top card was the king, or some lower card, you would have one spade loser.

You have two hearts in (b), so the maximum possible number of heart losers would be two. Since you have the king and queen between the hands, you have only one potential loser, to the ♡A.

In position (c) you have three diamonds in your hand and therefore a maximum of three potential losers. Dummy's king does not necessarily prevent you from losing three tricks, as it may be captured by the ace, so you must count three diamond losers. If instead dummy held ◇A84, you would have only two diamond losers. With ◇AK4 in the dummy, the number of losers would drop to one. With ◇AQ4 you would again have two losers, since if a finesse of the ◇Q failed you would lose two diamond tricks. Do you get the idea?

To test yourself, look at the 4♡ contract overleaf and see if you can calculate how many potential losers you have in each of the suits.

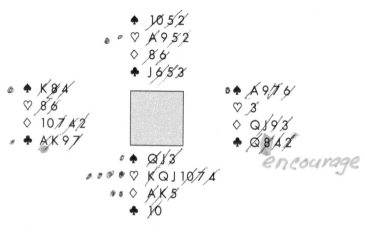

West	North	East	South
			1♡
pass	2♡	pass	4♡
all pass			

West leads the ♣A against 4♡; East encourages with the ♣8 and West continues with the ♣K. How many possible losers are there in each suit?

Spades: Two losers. You will lose to the ace and the king.
Hearts: No losers. The suit is solid.
Diamonds: One loser. You have three diamonds and the ◊5 is a loser.
Clubs: One loser.

For every suit contract in this book, we will summarize the loser situation like this:

Losers: ♠2 ♡0 ◊1 ♣1   Total 4

You have a total of four possible losers and the contract is 4♡, where you can afford only three losers. You must therefore plan to reduce the number of losers from four to three. Can you see how to do it?

There are three main ways in which you can dispose of a loser:

(1) You can ruff (trump) a loser in dummy;
(2) You can take a successful finesse in the suit containing the loser;
(3) You can discard a loser.

On the present deal, you have no chance of avoiding the three losers in the black suits, but you can ruff your diamond loser in the dummy.

How does the play go? You will ruff the second club and draw trumps in two rounds. You will then play the ◊A and ◊K and ruff your diamond loser in the dummy. Finally, you will drive out the ♠A and ♠K to set up one trick in spades.

You would express the plan in this abbreviated form:

> **PLAN: I will ruff the second club, draw trumps and ruff my diamond loser. Then I will establish the spade suit.**

As we mentioned, there are three ways to avoid a loser: ruffing, finessing and discarding. In the previous contract, you saved a diamond loser by ruffing. In the next two contracts we will see the other two methods of saving a loser. See what you make of this small slam in spades:

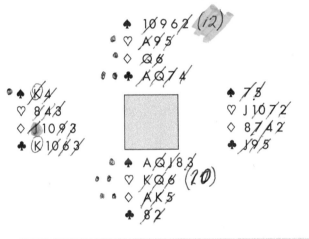

West	North	East	South
	1♣ *(12)*	pass	1♠ *(20)* forcing
pass	2♠	pass	4NT *(5♡*
pass	5♡	pass	6♠
all pass			

West leads the ◊J against your spade slam and you count the potential losers in each suit:

Losers: ♠ 1   ♡ 0   ◊ 0   ♣ 1   **Total:** 2

To make the small slam, you must reduce the total number of losers from two to one. Both the black suits offer you a chance to finesse against the king. If either of these finesses wins, you will save yourself a loser. *to push them*
   You win the diamond lead with dummy's ◊Q and lead the ♠10, running the card (in other words, you play low from your hand when East follows with a low card). For the moment, it is not your lucky day; the finesse loses to West's ♠K. It makes no difference what West chooses to return. Let's say that he plays his remaining trump and you win in your hand, the suit breaking 2-2. The time has come to take the other black-suit finesse. You lead a low club and play the ♣Q

from dummy. That's better! The finesse wins. You have managed to side-step your potential loser in clubs. The remaining tricks are yours and the slam has been made.

> **PLAN: I will win with the ◊Q and run the ♠10. If the trump finesse loses, I will need a subsequent club finesse to win.**

We have seen two contracts so far. The first was made by ruffing a loser in dummy; the second was made by finessing successfully. Let's see a deal where the contract can be made by discarding a loser.

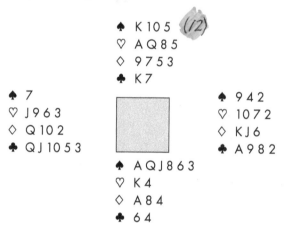

```
                    ♠ K 10 5  (12)
                    ♡ A Q 8 5
                    ◊ 9 7 5 3
                    ♣ K 7
     ♠ 7                            ♠ 9 4 2
     ♡ J 9 6 3                      ♡ 10 7 2
     ◊ Q 10 2                       ◊ K J 6
     ♣ Q J 10 5 3                   ♣ A 9 8 2
                    ♠ A Q J 8 6 3
                    ♡ K 4
                    ◊ A 8 4
                    ♣ 6 4
```

West	North	East	South
	1◊	pass	1♠
pass	1NT	pass	4♠
all pass			

West leads the ♣Q against your spade game. As always in a suit contract, the first part of making a plan is to count the potential losers in your hand:

Losers: ♠0 ♡0 ◊2 ♣2   Total: 4

West's opening lead of the ♣Q makes it perfectly clear that East holds the ♣A and that two tricks will have to be lost in clubs. So, you need to reduce the number of diamond losers from two to one. Do you see how this can be done?

One of the diamond losers can be discarded on the third round of hearts. Let's say that the defenders take their two club tricks and then switch to a diamond. You win with the ◊A and draw trumps in three rounds. You then play the ♡K, ♡A and ♡Q, discarding a diamond from your hand on the third round. You will now lose only one diamond trick and the contract is yours.

PLAN: I will win the diamond switch, draw trumps and discard one diamond loser on the hearts.

The deals in this chapter illustrate the three main methods of reducing the number of losers. You can ruff a loser, you can take a successful finesse in the suit, and you can discard a loser on a surplus winner in a different suit. In the next few chapters we will examine these three techniques in more detail.

Remember these points

- When you are planning a suit contract, you begin by counting the potential losers in your hand, looking at each suit in turn to see whether dummy can help you. If the total number of losers is more than you can afford, then in order to make the contract you must look for the safest plan to reduce that number.

- There are three main ways to avoid a loser: ruffing, finessing and discarding. When you need to avoid two or more losers, you may have to use two different techniques on one deal.

- Before you embark on the play, try to fix a brief plan in your mind.

① ruffing
② finessing
③ discarding

Now try these...

A.

       ♠ K 3
       ♡ 10 8 6 2
       ◇ J 9 7
       ♣ K 7 6 3

♠J led

       ♠ A 7 4
       ♡ A K Q J 7 5
       ◇ 6 4
       ♣ Q 8

West leads the ♠J against your contract of 4♡.
   (a) How many potential losers are there?
   (b) What is your plan?

B.

       ♠ Q J 4
       ♡ A 8 5 3
       ◇ A Q 2
       ♣ 10 7 6

♡J led

       ♠ K 10 9 6 5 2
       ♡ K 7
       ◇ K 6 3
       ♣ A Q

West leads the ♡J against your contract of 6♠.
   (a) How many potential losers are there?
   (b) What is your plan?

C.

       ♠ A Q 6 3
       ♡ J 10 5
       ◇ 10 9 3
       ♣ K 7 4

◇K led

       ♠ K 7
       ♡ K Q 3
       ◇ A 4
       ♣ A Q J 9 8 2

You reach 6♣ and West leads the ◇K.
   (a) How many potential losers are there?
   (b) What is your plan?

D.

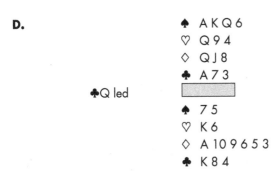

♠ A K Q 6
♡ Q 9 4
◇ Q J 8
♣ A 7 3

♣Q led

♠ 7 5
♡ K 6
◇ A 10 9 6 5 3
♣ K 8 4

You reach 6◇ and West leads the ♣Q.
    (a) How many potential losers are there?
    (b) What is your plan?

E.

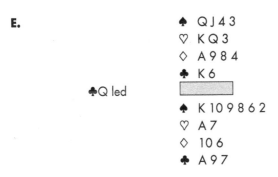

♠ Q J 4 3
♡ K Q 3
◇ A 9 8 4
♣ K 6

♣Q led

♠ K 10 9 8 6 2
♡ A 7
◇ 10 6
♣ A 9 7

West leads the ♣Q against your contract of 6♠.
    (a) How many potential losers are there?
    (b) What is your plan?

F.

♠ A J 6 3
♡ K 9 6 2
◇ 9 3
♣ J 7 6

♣A led

♠ 5
♡ A Q J 8 5 4
◇ A Q 4
♣ 9 8 2

You reach 4♡ and the defenders cash three club tricks, switching to a trump.
    (a) How many potential losers are there?
    (b) What is your plan?

ANSWERS

A. (a) You have one potential loser in spades, on the third round. The hearts are solid, so you have no losers there. In diamonds you have two certain losers. You have two cards in clubs but only one loser — you will lose one trick to the defenders' ace. This is the summary:

Losers: ♠ 1   ♡ 0   ◇ 2   ♣ 1   **Total: 4.**

(b) You can ruff your potential losing spade in the dummy. You win the spade lead with the king and draw trumps. You then cash the ♠A and ruff a spade in the dummy. Finally, you drive out the ♣A.

PLAN: I will win the spade lead, draw trumps and ruff my spade loser in dummy. Then I will play clubs to set up a trick there.

B. (a) You have one certain loser in spades, since the defenders hold the ace. You have no heart losers; the South hand contains only two hearts and these are covered by the ace and king. The diamond suit is solid, so there are no losers in that suit. You have one possible club loser.

Losers: ♠ 1   ♡ 0   ◇ 0   ♣ 1   **Total: 2.**

(b) After winning the heart lead, in either hand, you should immediately play a trump to drive out the ace. Suppose West wins with the ♠A and plays another heart. You will win and draw the remaining trumps. You can then cross to dummy with a diamond and finesse the ♣Q, hoping that East holds the ♣K.

PLAN: I will win the heart lead, draw trumps, driving out the ace, and then finesse the ♣Q.

C. (a) You have no losers in spades and one certain loser in hearts (to the ace). There is one loser in diamonds but none in clubs, the trump suit.

Losers: ♠ 0   ♡ 1   ◇ 1   ♣ 0   **Total: 2.**

(b) You can discard the diamond loser on the third round of spades. Win the diamond lead, draw trumps and play the ♠K, ♠A and ♠Q, discarding a diamond. You can then establish the heart suit.

PLAN: I will win the diamond lead, draw trumps and throw my diamond loser on the third round of spades.

D. (a) This is the loser position:

Losers: ♠ 0 ♡ 1 ◇ 1 ♣ 1   **Total: 3.**

(b) You must avoid two losers to make the slam. A successful trump finesse will save a loser there; the club loser can be discarded on dummy's spades.

Win the club lead with dummy's ♣A and run the ◇Q. If West follows with a low diamond, repeat the diamond finesse if necessary and draw all the trumps. Continue with the ♠A, ♠K and ♠Q, discarding the club loser. Finally, you can knock out the ♡A to set up a trick in that suit. You combine the techniques of finessing and discarding.

PLAN: I will win with the ♣A, finesse in trumps and draw trumps. I can then discard my club loser on the spades and set up a heart trick.

E. (a) This is the loser position:

Losers: ♠ 1 ♡ 0 ◇ 1 ♣ 1   **Total: 3.**

(b) Even this wonderful book cannot tell you how to avoid losing a trick to the ace of trumps, so you will have to dispose of the two losers in the minor suits. The diamond loser can be discarded on the third round of hearts and the club loser can be ruffed in the dummy.

You win the club lead with the king and play a trump to drive out the ace. When you regain the lead, you will draw trumps and play three rounds of hearts to discard the diamond loser. You can then play the ♣A and ruff the club loser. You combine the techniques of ruffing and discarding.

PLAN: I will win with the ♣K and play a trump. When I regain the lead, I will draw trumps, discard a diamond on the third heart and ruff the club loser.

F. (a) This is the loser situation:

Losers: ♠ 0 ♡ 0 ◇ 2 ♣ 3   **Total: 5.**

(b) You have already lost three club tricks, so you must avoid any losers in diamonds. You must hope for a successful finesse of the ◇Q to save one loser. You can then save another by ruffing the third round of diamonds in the dummy. You combine the techniques of finessing and ruffing.

PLAN: I will draw trumps, finesse the ◇Q (hoping that East holds the ◇K) and then ruff a diamond in the dummy.

2

MAKING A PLAN — TO FINESSE

In this chapter we will look in more detail at how you can make a plan that involves one or more finesses. Here is a straightforward example:

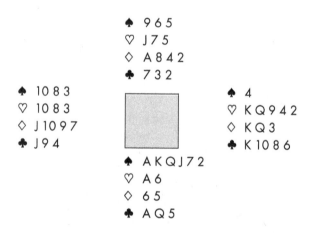

```
              ♠ 9 6 5
              ♡ J 7 5
              ◇ A 8 4 2
              ♣ 7 3 2
♠ 10 8 3                        ♠ 4
♡ 10 8 3                        ♡ K Q 9 4 2
◇ J 10 9 7                      ◇ K Q 3
♣ J 9 4                         ♣ K 10 8 6
              ♠ A K Q J 7 2
              ♡ A 6
              ◇ 6 5
              ♣ A Q 5
```

West	North	East	South
		1♡	dbl
pass	2◇	pass	3♠
pass	4♠	all pass	

West leads the ◇J against your spade game. What plan will you make?

Looking at the potential losers in the South hand, you see:

Losers: ♠ 0 ♡ 1 ◇ 1 ♣ 2   **Total:** 4

You must hope to reduce the number of club losers from two to one, by finessing the ♣Q successfully. You win with dummy's ◇A and must decide whether to draw trumps straight away. What do you think?

Drawing trumps would not be a good idea, since the ◇A was your only sure entry to dummy. Unless the ♠10 fell on the first or second round of trumps, which would set up the ♠9 as an entry, you would never be able to enter dummy again. You would not be able to take the club finesse.

After winning the diamond lead, you must take the club finesse while you have the chance. A club to the queen wins the second trick, as you rather expected after East's opening bid. All that remains is to draw trumps and claim the contract.

PLAN: I will win the diamond lead and finesse the ♣Q immediately, while I have the chance.

Leading toward the high cards

As you probably know, there are two main forms of the finesse. The most common one is where you lead toward a card in the hope that the missing higher card lies with the defender who will have to play second to the trick. Look at these combinations:

(1) ♠ K 7	(2) ♡ Q 6 3	(3) ◇ K Q 4
♠ 6 2	♡ A 8 5	◇ 7 6 2

In position (1), you lead a low card toward the ♠K, hoping that West holds the ♠A. In (2) you lead low toward dummy's ♡Q, hoping that West has the ♡K (it makes little difference whether you cash the ♡A first). Position (3) is slightly different because you have two cards that you would like to win a trick. By leading twice toward the dummy, you will score two tricks when West holds the ◇A.

Note how important it is to lead toward the high cards that you are hoping to score. If you lead the ♠K from dummy in (1), you will never score a trick with it. Similarly, it would be a poor idea to lead the ♡Q in (2); East will cover with the ♡K if he holds that card and you will never score more than one heart trick. Similarly, it would be hopeless to lead the ◇K in (3). The defender with the ace would win and you would score just one diamond trick, with the queen.

Leading a high card for a finesse

We saw in the previous section that it is normally right to lead toward the high card that you are hoping to score with a finesse. There is another type of finesse, where you do have to lead a high card. Let's see some common positions:

(1)

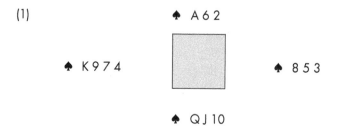

♠ A 6 2

♠ K 9 7 4   ♠ 8 5 3

♠ Q J 10

In position (1) you are assured of two spade tricks, however the cards lie. You can score three spade tricks when West holds the ♠K, by finessing in the suit. It would be no good to lead toward the ♠QJ10 because the defenders would then be certain to win a trick with the ♠K. Instead you should lead the ♠Q from your hand. What can West do when he holds the ♠K? If he covers your ♠Q on the first round, you will win with dummy's ♠A and score two more spade tricks with the jack and ten. Suppose instead that West does not play his king on the first round. You will play low from dummy and the ♠Q will win. You can then repeat the finesse by leading the ♠J. Whenever West chooses to play his king (or even if he never plays it), you will score a total of three tricks from the suit.

If you have a lurid frame of mind, you can think of the ♠QJ10 as an executioner's block. When the king's head appears, the axe (dummy's ace) will fall! These are equivalent positions.

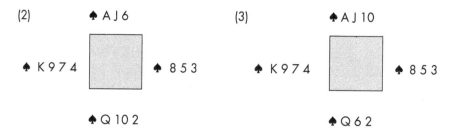

(2)   ♠ A J 6   (3)   ♠ A J 10

♠ K 9 7 4   ♠ 8 5 3   ♠ K 9 7 4   ♠ 8 5 3

♠ Q 10 2   ♠ Q 6 2

In both these positions you again hold two cards (the ♠J and ♠10) that are neighbors of the ♠Q. By leading the ♠Q, you can score three spade tricks when West holds the ♠K. Why would you start with the ♠Q, rather than playing a low card to dummy's ♠J? By leading the ♠Q, you will leave the lead in the South hand if West decides not to cover with the ♠K. You can then finesse the ♠J on the second round.

This type of finesse is most effective when you have two or more neighboring cards. As we have seen, all is well when you hold ♠QJ10 opposite ♠A62. If the queen is covered by the king and ace, your two touching cards — the jack and the ten — will score the remaining tricks. Look at this, less effective, position:

(4)

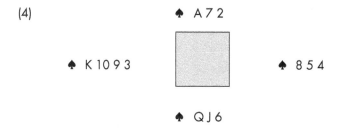

♠ A 7 2

♠ K 10 9 3   ♠ 8 5 4

♠ Q J 6

You cannot score more than two spade tricks (except in the freak position where spades break 6-1 and the ♠K is singleton). If you lead the ♠Q, this will be covered by the king and ace; you will make only the two spade tricks that were yours originally, however the cards lay.

It may still be worth leading the ♠Q for a finesse, because this gives you the chance of scoring two spade tricks without losing the lead. To have a chance of three spade tricks, though, you would need one extra touching card: the ♠10. It would make no difference whether you held ♠QJ10 in your hand or ♠A102 in the dummy.

When is it right to lead a high card?

If you are uncertain whether to lead a high card or a low card when taking a finesse, ask yourself this question: Will I be happy if I lead a high card and it is covered? This is an important topic and we will look at several combinations. Here is the first one:

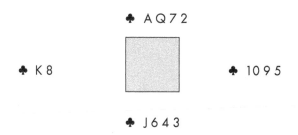

♣ A Q 7 2

♣ K 8   ♣ 10 9 5

♣ J 6 4 3

Suppose you need four club tricks. What chance is there?

It can be done only when West holds a doubleton king in the suit. You must lead a low card to the queen on the first round. When you continue with the ace on the next round, West's king falls and your jack will capture East's 10 on the third round.

The crucial point to remember is that you can never make four club tricks (against correct defense) if you lead the ♣J on the first round. West will cover when he holds the ♣K and you will win with dummy's ♣A. That will leave you with only one high card in the suit, the queen, and the defenders will be certain to win the third round.

Remember the question that you should ask yourself in these situations. 'If I lead the ♣J, will I be happy if it is covered with the ♣K?' The answer here is: 'No, because I will have used up the jack and the ace on the first round. The defenders will then be certain to score a trick in the suit.'

Here is a similar position:

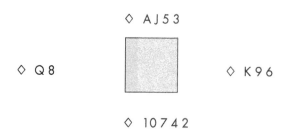

♢ A J 5 3

♢ Q 8   ♢ K 9 6

♢ 10 7 4 2

Let's say that you need three diamond tricks. One good chance of this is to find West with something like ♢KQ8. You lead toward dummy, planning to play the ♢J if West plays low. If instead West decides to 'split his honors', playing the king or queen, you will win with the ace and force out West's remaining honor with your remaining jack and ten combination.

When you play for this chance, you can benefit from another situation — when West holds a doubleton honor (as in the diagram). A low card to dummy's jack loses to East's king but on the next round the ace will drop West's queen; your ten will win the third round and three diamond tricks will be yours.

As before, you will waste this chance if you mistakenly lead a high card (the ♢10) on the first round. It will be covered by West's ♢Q and dummy's ♢A; East will then score two tricks with his ♢K and ♢9.

So, be wary of leading a high card in a finessing position. Calculate how you need the defenders' cards to lie in order to achieve your objective in the suit. Then determine whether all will be well (a) if you lead a low card and (b) if you lead a high card.

Let's end this section with a full deal where the success of a slam depends on the way in which you tackle the trump suit.

```
              ♠ Q 6 5 2
              ♡ K 7 5
              ◇ K J 5
              ♣ A 8 2
♠ 10 8 3                      ♠ K
♡ Q J 10 3                    ♡ 9 8 6 2
◇ 9 6 4                       ◇ 10 8 7 3
♣ 10 7 4                      ♣ Q J 9 5
              ♠ A J 9 7 4
              ♡ A 4
              ◇ A Q 2
              ♣ K 6 3
```

West	North	East	South
	1♣	pass	1♠
pass	2♠	pass	4NT
pass	5◇	pass	6♠
all pass			

West leads the ♡Q against your spade slam. What plan will you make? Looking at the potential losers in the South hand, you see:

Losers: ♠ 1   ♡ 0   ◇ 0   ♣ 1   **Total: 2**

There is no chance of avoiding the club loser, so you must give yourself the best chance of avoiding a loser in the trump suit.

Suppose you win the heart lead in dummy and lead the queen of trumps. You will soon regret it! East will cover with the singleton king, drawing your ace, and West will then score a trick with the ♠108.

The correct play is to lead a low trump from dummy at Trick 2. When the king appears, you win with the ace and can then draw West's remaining trumps with the queen and jack. Suppose instead that East follows with a low trump. You will then finesse the ♠J. The trump finesse has to win to give you a chance. If it does, and West follows with the 8 or 3, you will cash the ♠A next, hoping that the suit breaks 2-2. Once in a while, the suit will be divided like this:

```
              ♠ Q 6 5 2
♠ 10                         ♠ K 8 3
              ♠ A J 9 7 4
```

When you finesse the ♠J, West follows with the ♠10. You can then return to dummy, in one of the side suits, and finesse the ♠9 to pick up East's remaining ♠K8 on the second round.

> **PLAN: I will win with the ♡K and lead a low spade, planning to finesse the ♠J. By leading a low card, I will succeed against a singleton ♠K with East and a singleton ♠10 with West, as well as ♠Kx with East.**

Which high card should I play first?

When your holding in a particular suit includes the ace and king (and maybe the queen), you will normally want to cash at least one honor before taking a finesse. What's more, it may be important that you cash the right honor. Look at this diamond holding:

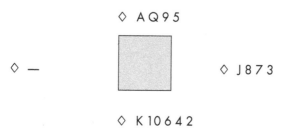

◊ A Q 9 5

◊ —   ◊ J 8 7 3

◊ K 10 6 4 2

If the suit breaks no worse than 3-1, you will score an easy five tricks. So, you must plan your play in the suit to cater for a 4-0 break, with either defender holding the length. Which diamond honor should you play on the first round?

You should play the ace, because that will still leave you with a top honor in each hand; if either defender shows up with four diamonds, you will be able to finesse against his jack. Here West will show out on the first round; you can then play a low diamond from dummy to the ten, scoring all five diamond tricks. If instead East had shown out, you could cross to the king on the second round and then lead low to dummy's ◊9, again scoring all five tricks. As you see, it would be a mistake to play the king first. East would then score a trick with his ◊J.

Here is a similar position:

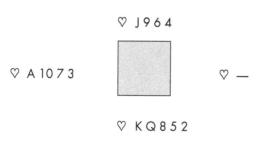

♡ J 9 6 4

♡ A 10 7 3   ♡ —

♡ K Q 8 5 2

Your aim is to lose only one heart trick. Again you should play a top card from the holding that contains two honors. You lead the king and West wins with the ace (it will make no difference if he chooses to duck instead). East shows out on the first round and you will then know that a finesse against West's ♡10 is necessary. When you regain the lead, you will play a low heart from the South hand and finesse dummy's ♡9. You can then draw West's remaining hearts with the jack and queen. This is the rule to remember:

Holding three honors of equal rank (AKQ or KQJ) between your two hands, you should normally begin with an honor from the hand containing two honors.

Now let's look at something slightly different. In the contract below, everything depends on your play in spades, the trump suit. Would you have made the right plan?

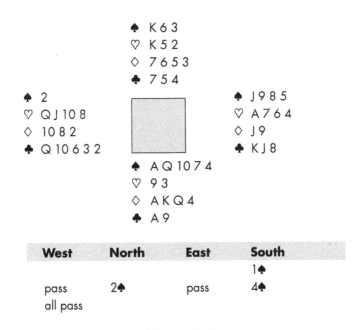

```
              ♠ K 6 3
              ♡ K 5 2
              ◇ 7 6 5 3
              ♣ 7 5 4
♠ 2                              ♠ J 9 8 5
♡ Q J 10 8                       ♡ A 7 6 4
◇ 10 8 2                         ◇ J 9
♣ Q 10 6 3 2                     ♣ K J 8
              ♠ A Q 10 7 4
              ♡ 9 3
              ◇ A K Q 4
              ♣ A 9
```

West	North	East	South
			1♠
pass	2♠	pass	4♠
all pass			

West leads the ♡Q against 4♠ and this is the loser situation:

Losers: ♠ 1 ♡ 2 ◇ 1 ♣ 1   **Total:** 5

Most of the time, you will have no loser in trumps (when the suit breaks 3-2, for example, or the ♠J is singleton). We show one possible trump loser in the summary, just in case the suit breaks 4-1.

You could avoid one of the two heart losers if West held the ♡A, but that is hardly conceivable after West has led the ♡Q. There is a possible loser in diamonds, if the defenders' cards break 4-1. Well, there is nothing much you can do about that, so you will have to hope for a 3-2 break. Nor can you expect to avoid a club loser. Everything is likely to depend on avoiding a loser in the trump suit.

Let's see how the early play goes. West cannot possibly hold the ♡A when he has led the ♡Q against a suit contract (it would be a very poor lead), so there is no point in playing the ♡K from dummy. By playing low on the first two rounds, you would set up a trick for the king if East had begun with ace doubleton in the suit. In our scenario, West's ♡Q wins the first trick and he continues with the ♡J, ducked again, and a third round of hearts. You ruff in your hand and must now decide how to play the trump suit. Any ideas?

You can pick up a possible ♠Jxxx with East by finessing the ten. So, at the moment when you lead from dummy toward your trump holding you will need to know whether to finesse or not. You can arrange this by playing the ♠A on the first round and then crossing to the ♠K. When the cards lie as in the diagram, West will show out on the second round. You will then know that you have to finesse the ♠10 on the next round.

Suppose instead that you make the mistake of crossing to the ♠K on the first round. You would then have no idea whether to finesse the ♠10 on the second round. If you continued with a trump to the ace, West showing out, there would be no way to recover the situation. If instead you guessed to finesse the ♠10 on the second round, you would go down when West held ♠Jxx or ♠Jx.

> **PLAN: I will play low from dummy on the first two heart leads and ruff the third round. I will then play the ace and king of trumps, so that I know whether to finesse on the third round.**

Here is a slam contract for you to try:

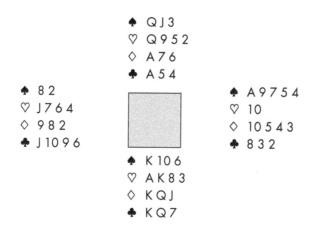

♠ Q J 3
♡ Q 9 5 2
◇ A 7 6
♣ A 5 4

♠ 8 2
♡ J 7 6 4
◇ 9 8 2
♣ J 10 9 6

♠ A 9 7 5 4
♡ 10
◇ 10 5 4 3
♣ 8 3 2

♠ K 10 6
♡ A K 8 3
◇ K Q J
♣ K Q 7

West	North	East	South
		pass	2NT
pass	3♣	pass	3♡
pass	6♡	all pass	

With his 3-4-3-3 shape, North might instead have raised directly to 6NT. You end in 6♡, however, and West leads the ♣J. This is the loser situation:

Losers: ♠ 1   ♡ 1   ◇ 0   ♣ 0   **Total:** 2

You cannot avoid the loser in spades, so you must look for the best chance of avoiding a trump loser. What would your plan be?

There will be no problem if trumps break 3-2. When trumps break 4-1, you may have the chance of a finesse in the suit when you drop a singleton jack or ten on the first round. In most situations like these, you do best to begin with an honor from the hand that contains two honors. After winning the club lead, you should play the ♡A. As it happens, the ♡10 falls from East. Since this card may be a singleton, you play the ♡K next, preserving the ♡Q9 sitting over West. East does indeed show out. You can then finesse the ♡9, draw West's last trump with dummy's ♡Q and establish the spade suit.

Suppose that it had been West who dropped the ♡J or ♡10 on the first round. You would then play dummy's ♡Q on the second round, preserving the ♡K8 over East and allowing you to finesse against a possible four trumps to an honor in his hand.

As you see, it would not be a good idea to play the unaccompanied honor (the ♡Q) first. You would not then be able to catch ♡Jxxx or ♡10xxx with West.

> **PLAN: I will win the club lead and play the ♡A. If the ♡J or ♡10 falls from one defender, I will choose my next play in trumps so that I can finesse against his partner later.**

Planning the entries for a finesse

Sometimes you have to repeat a finesse and must plan your entries accordingly. Suppose you have ◇AQJ in your hand and ◇873 in the dummy. You will have to reach dummy once, to finesse the queen. If the finesse wins, you will then need to return to dummy to finesse the ◇J. Let's see a full deal on this theme:

```
              ♠ 9 7 5 4 2
              ♡ J 3
              ◇ 8 7 3
              ♣ A 4 3

♠ Q J 10 8 3               ♠ K 6
♡ 5 2                      ♡ 9 6 4
◇ 10 6 2                   ◇ K 9 5 4
♣ Q 10 8                   ♣ J 9 7 2

              ♠ A
              ♡ A K Q 10 8 7
              ◇ A Q J
              ♣ K 6 5
```

West	North	East	South
			2♣
pass	2◇	pass	2♡
pass	2♠	pass	4♡
pass	5♣	pass	6♡
all pass			

South had forced the bidding to 4♡ on his own hand, so North was entitled to look for a slam with an ace in his hand. How would you plan the heart slam when West leads the ♠Q? You start with this loser situation:

Losers: ♠ 0   ♡ 0   ◇ 1   ♣ 1   Total: 2

You have a certain club loser and must therefore hope to avoid a diamond loser by finessing in the suit. Suppose you win the spade lead and immediately draw three rounds of trumps. You can cross to the ♣A to take one diamond finesse and, as it happens, the finesse will win. Much good will it do you! With no further entry to dummy available, you will be unable to repeat the diamond finesse. You will lose one diamond trick and one club trick, going down one.

Instead, you should make good use of dummy's entry in the trump suit. You win the spade lead and play the ace and jack of trumps. You finesse the ◇Q successfully and draw the defenders' last trump. You can then return to dummy with the ♣A and finesse the ◇J. Twelve tricks are yours.

> **PLAN: I will win the spade lead, play the ace and jack of trumps and finesse the ◇Q. If the finesse wins, I will draw the last trump and cross to the ♣A to finesse the ◇J.**

Remember these points

- In most finesse positions, you lead toward the high card that you are hoping will give you a trick. For example, you lead toward a king in the hope that the ace lies with the defender playing second to the trick.

- When you hold several cards of equal rank, you may be able to lead a high card on the trick where you perform a finesse. For example, with ♡QJ10 in your hand and ♡A63 in the dummy you would lead the ♡Q. Your aim then is to 'trap the ♡K', rather than to 'score a trick with the ♡Q'.

- If you are unsure whether you should lead a high card, when taking a finesse, do so only when you will be happy to see the high card covered.

- When you hold three honors of equal rank between the hands (such as ◇A10xx opposite ◇KQ9xx), you should normally begin with a top card from the hand containing the two honors.

- Plan carefully the entries that you may need to take finesses. When you hold AQJ10 in your hand, for example, you may need to finesse several times, perhaps using entries in the trump suit to reach the dummy.

A
10
x
x

K
Q
9
x
x

Now try these...

A.

                  ♠ 9 6 5
                  ♡ K 4 2
                  ◇ 9 8 4 2
                  ♣ A 7 3

♣Q led

                  ♠ A Q
                  ♡ A Q J 10 8 7 5
                  ◇ K 5
                  ♣ 6 2

Expressing your plan as concisely as you can, how will you play 4♡?

B.

                  ♠ A 7 6
                  ♡ K 6 3
                  ◇ 10 9 4 2
                  ♣ 7 5 4

♠Q led

                  ♠ K 4 3
                  ♡ Q J 9 7 4
                  ◇ A 3
                  ♣ A K Q

Once again you are in 4♡. What is your plan for the contract?

C.

                  ♠ A Q 3
                  ♡ A Q 3
                  ◇ A K 6 4
                  ♣ A 7 4

♣Q led

                  ♠ K J 10 8 5 4
                  ♡ 9 7 5
                  ◇ J 10
                  ♣ K 2

West leads the ♣Q against 6♠. What plan do you make?

D.

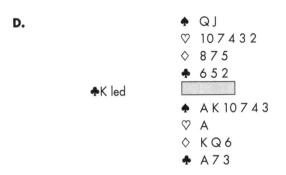

♠ Q J
♡ 10 7 4 3 2
◇ 8 7 5
♣ 6 5 2

♣K led

♠ A K 10 7 4 3
♡ A
◇ K Q 6
♣ A 7 3

What is your plan for 4♠ when West leads the ♣K?

E.

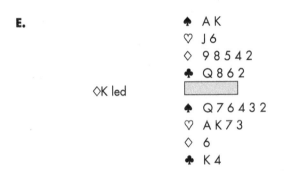

♠ A K
♡ J 6
◇ 9 8 5 4 2
♣ Q 8 6 2

◇K led

♠ Q 7 6 4 3 2
♡ A K 7 3
◇ 6
♣ K 4

How will you play 4♠ when West leads the ◇K and continues with a second round of diamonds?

F.

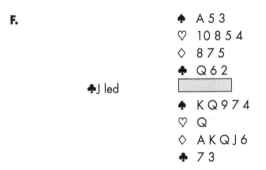

♠ A 5 3
♡ 10 8 5 4
◇ 8 7 5
♣ Q 6 2

♣J led

♠ K Q 9 7 4
♡ Q
◇ A K Q J 6
♣ 7 3

West leads the ♣J against 4♠ and the defenders play two more rounds of clubs. What plan do you make?

ANSWERS

A. You have four potential losers — one spade, two diamonds and one club. You should aim to take finesses in both spades and diamonds, hoping that at least one of these will succeed. Since there are only two entries to dummy (the ♣A and the ♡K), you must take one of the finesses at Trick 2 rather than drawing trumps. You win the club lead and play a spade to the queen. Whether or not this finesse wins, you will later draw trumps, ending in the dummy, and play a diamond toward the king. If both finesses succeed, you will score an overtrick. To make the contract, you will need one of the finesses to win.

> **PLAN: I will win the club lead and finesse the ♠Q. Later, I will draw trumps, ending in the dummy, and lead toward the ◇K. Unless both finesses fail, I will make the contract.**

B. You have a certain loser in both diamonds and spades. So, the contract depends on losing only one trick in hearts, the trump suit. Suppose you win the spade lead with the king and continue with a trump to the king. If East wins with the ace and returns a spade, you will be in dummy for the last time and will not know if you need to finesse the ♡9 (to pick up a potential ♡A10xx with East). To avoid this dilemma, you should lead the ♡Q after winning the spade lead in your hand. If one or the other defender wins with the ♡A and returns a spade, you will then be able to cash the ♡K and see from the fall of the cards whether you need to finesse the ♡9 on the third round.

> **PLAN: I will win with the ♠K and lead the ♡Q. If the defenders win and knock out the ♠A, I can cash the ♡K next to see whether a finesse is necessary in trumps.**

C. You have two potential losers — both in hearts. One possible chance of reducing this to one loser is to finesse the ♡Q. Suppose you take this finesse first and it loses. To recover, you would then need to take a successful finesse in diamonds by running the jack. There is no need to rely on luck in this way. You should draw all the trumps, ending in the South hand, and then run the ◇J. Even if East wins with the ◇Q, you will have established two surplus diamond winners on which to discard your heart losers. Once West has failed to lead a heart, you can guarantee the contract by playing in this way.

> **PLAN: I will win the club lead, draw trumps and run the ◇J. Even if the finesse loses, I will be able to throw both potential heart losers on dummy's surplus diamond winners.**

D. You have four potential losers — two diamonds and two clubs. If East holds the ◇A, you can avoid one of the diamond losers by leading twice toward your ◇KQ6. You must use the ♠Q and ♠J as the entries for these two diamond plays. Win the club lead with the ace, cross to the ♠Q and lead a diamond to the king. If this wins, return to dummy with the ♠J and lead a diamond toward the queen. You will draw the outstanding trump(s) as soon as you regain the lead. (If the defenders take their two club tricks and East then plays another club, you will ruff with the ♠A to avoid an overruff.)

PLAN: I will win the club lead and cross to the ♠Q to lead toward my diamonds. If the ◇K wins, I will cross to the ♠J to lead toward the ◇Q. I will need East to hold the ◇A.

E. You must hope that the trumps break 3-2, but this still leaves you with four losers in the side suits. You cannot ruff a heart with the ♠A or ♠K, since this would promote an extra trump trick for the defenders. What else can you try?

You can give yourself a 50% chance by leading toward the ♡J in the hope that West holds the ♡Q. You ruff the second diamond and play dummy's ♠AK. You then return to your hand with a diamond ruff and draw the last trump. Then you lead a low heart toward dummy's jack. (This is another example of leading toward the card that you are hoping to score.) When West holds the ♡Q you will score three heart tricks, whether or not West rises with the queen on the first round. You will lose only one heart, one diamond and one club.

PLAN: I will ruff the second diamond, draw trumps and lead toward the ♡J, hoping that West holds the ♡Q.

F. You have lost two clubs and there is a certain third loser in hearts. You must therefore try to avoid a loser in the trump suit. After ruffing the third club with a low trump, you should start the trump suit by cashing the ♠K. If neither the jack nor the ten appears from West on the first round, you will need to find a 3-2 trump break. Suppose instead that West follows with the ♠J or ♠10. If that card is a singleton, you can still pick up the trumps for no losers. You cross to the ♠A on the second round. If West shows out on this trick, you will finesse the ♠9 next; you can then draw East's last trump with the ♠Q. If instead West began with ♠J10, trumps are 3-2 and you will play your trumps from the top.

Suppose that you made the mistake of crossing to the ♠A on the first round, the ♠J or ♠10 appearing from West. You would be in dummy for the last time and would not know whether to finesse the ♠9 on the next round. Starting with the ♠K allows you to see two rounds before deciding whether to finesse.

PLAN: I will ruff the third club and play the ♠K followed by the ♠A. If West began with a singleton ♠J or ♠10, I will finesse the ♠9 on the third round.

3

MAKING A PLAN — TO DISCARD LOSERS

In this chapter we will look at several deals where the winning plan is to discard one or more losers. The simplest form of this play is when you draw all the trumps and then play surplus winners in dummy, throwing your losers. Let's start with an example of that:

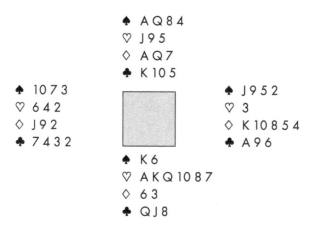

	♠ A Q 8 4	
	♡ J 9 5	
	◇ A Q 7	
	♣ K 10 5	
♠ 10 7 3		♠ J 9 5 2
♡ 6 4 2		♡ 3
◇ J 9 2		◇ K 10 8 5 4
♣ 7 4 3 2		♣ A 9 6
	♠ K 6	
	♡ A K Q 10 8 7	
	◇ 6 3	
	♣ Q J 8	

West	North	East	South
			1♡
pass	1♠	pass	3♡
pass	4NT	pass	5◇
pass	6♡	all pass	

West leads the ♡2 against 6♡ and you see these potential losers:

Losers: ♠0 ♡0 ◇1 ♣1   **Total:** 2

You are certain to lose a trick to the ♣A. How can you avoid a loser in diamonds too?

One possibility would be to finesse the ◇Q, but that would rely on luck. When East holds the ◇K, as in the diagram, you would go down. A much better idea, which does not rely on luck at all, is to discard your potential diamond loser on dummy's third spade winner.

You win the trump lead and draw trumps in two more rounds. You then play the ♠K, ♠A and ♠Q, discarding the ◇3. The only remaining task is to knock out the ♣A, establishing two winners in the suit, and the slam is yours.

> **PLAN: I will win the trump lead, draw trumps and play three top spades, throwing a diamond. Then I can set up the clubs.**

You would play in just the same way if West happened to lead a diamond: win with the ◇A, draw trumps, discard your diamond loser on the third round of spades and set up the clubs.

Establishing a discard

Sometimes you must establish a suit in dummy before you are able to take a discard. Suppose you have ◇QJ7 in the dummy and ◇K4 in your hand. Once the defenders' ◇A has been removed, you will be able to discard a loser on the third round of diamonds. Let's put that combination into a full deal:

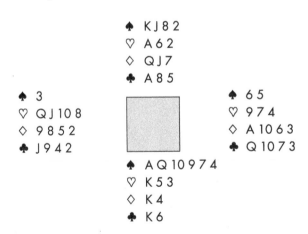

	♠ K J 8 2	
	♡ A 6 2	
	◇ Q J 7	
	♣ A 8 5	

West		East
♠ 3		♠ 6 5
♡ Q J 10 8		♡ 9 7 4
◇ 9 8 5 2		◇ A 10 6 3
♣ J 9 4 2		♣ Q 10 7 3

	♠ A Q 10 9 7 4	
	♡ K 5 3	
	◇ K 4	
	♣ K 6	

West	North	East	South
	1NT	pass	3♠
pass	4♠	pass	4NT
pass	5♡	pass	6♠
all pass			

How will you plan the small slam in spades when West leads the ♡Q? You start with these potential losers:

Losers: ♠ 0 ♡ 1 ◇ 1 ♣ 0   **Total: 2**

There is nothing you can do about the diamond loser, but you can aim to discard the heart loser on dummy's surplus diamond winner. You win the heart lead (in either hand) and draw trumps in two rounds. You then lead the ◇K to East's ◇A. You win the heart return and play the ◇Q and ◇J, throwing your heart loser. The slam is yours.

> **PLAN: I will win the heart lead, draw trumps and set up the diamonds. When I regain the lead, I will throw my heart loser on the third round of diamonds.**

The need to take a discard, or to establish a discard, is sometimes so pressing that you may have to address it before you draw trumps. We will look at this topic in Chapter 6 (Planning When to Draw Trumps).

Taking a finesse to establish a discard

Sometimes you can establish a discard only when a high card held by a defender is well placed. Here you need a bit of luck in spades to achieve your aim:

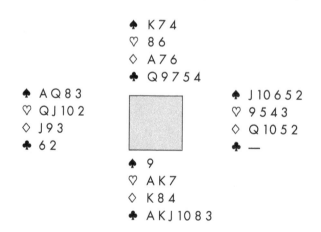

	♠ K 7 4	
	♡ 8 6	
	◇ A 7 6	
	♣ Q 9 7 5 4	
♠ A Q 8 3		♠ J 10 6 5 2
♡ Q J 10 2		♡ 9 5 4 3
◇ J 9 3		◇ Q 10 5 2
♣ 6 2		♣ —
	♠ 9	
	♡ A K 7	
	◇ K 8 4	
	♣ A K J 10 8 3	

West	North	East	South
			1♣
pass	3♣	pass	4NT
pass	5◇	pass	6♣
all pass			

What is your plan for 6♣ when West leads the ♡Q? This is the loser situation:

Losers: ♠ 1   ♡ 1   ◇ 1   ♣ 0   **Total:** 3

The heart loser presents no problem — you can ruff it in the dummy. To avoid a diamond loser, you will have to set up a discard on dummy's spade suit. This will require West to hold the ♠A.

You win the heart lead in your hand and draw trumps with the ace and king. Next you lead a spade toward dummy. Luck is with you and West does hold the ♠A. If he rises with the card on the first round, dummy's ♠K will be established for a diamond discard; you will lose just one trick, in spades. If instead West plays low on the first round of spades, dummy's ♠K will win and you will not lose any tricks in the spade suit. Your only loser will be a diamond.

> **PLAN: I will win the heart lead, draw trumps and lead a spade toward dummy. If West holds the ♠A, I can establish a discard for the diamond loser. The heart loser can be ruffed.**

Sometimes you have to risk going two down, in order to give yourself a chance of making the contract. That's what happens on the next deal:

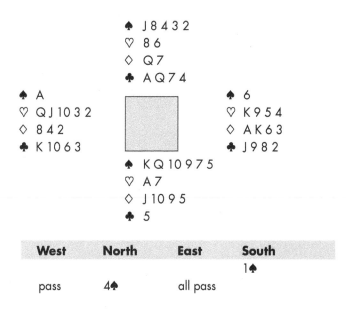

West	North	East	South
			1♠
pass	4♠	all pass	

East-West remain silent and you win the auction in 4♠. How will you plan this contract when West leads the ♡Q? These are the potential losers:

Losers: ♠ 1   ♡ 1   ◇ 2   ♣ 0   **Total:** 4

You win the heart lead and see that it would not be a good idea to play trumps straight away; the defenders would win the ♠A and cash three more tricks. To reduce the number of losers to three, you need to discard your heart loser. At Trick 2 you must steel yourself to play a club to the queen. When the cards lie as in the diagram, the finesse will win. You can then throw your heart loser on the ♣A and draw trumps. The contract is yours.

What if the club finesse had lost? You would then have gone two down, losing an unnecessary club trick, when you could have escaped for one down by not taking the finesse. Your priority is always to make the contract, of course. It is well worth risking a second undertrick (costing only an extra 50 or 100, depending on whether you are vulnerable) when the prize for making the spade game will be much larger (420 or 620).

> **PLAN: I will win the heart lead and take an immediate club finesse. If this wins, I will discard my heart loser on the ♣A.**

Establishing long cards in a suit

When dummy contains a suit of at least five cards, you may be able to ruff a round or two in your hand. By doing so, you hope to remove the defenders' cards in the suit and establish one or more 'long cards'. You can then use these to discard losers from the other hand. Here is a simple example.

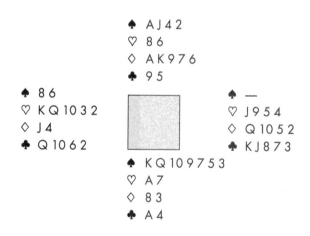

```
              ♠ A J 4 2
              ♡ 8 6
              ◇ A K 9 7 6
              ♣ 9 5
♠ 8 6                        ♠ —
♡ K Q 10 3 2                 ♡ J 9 5 4
◇ J 4                        ◇ Q 10 5 2
♣ Q 10 6 2                   ♣ K J 8 7 3
              ♠ K Q 10 9 7 5 3
              ♡ A 7
              ◇ 8 3
              ♣ A 4
```

West	North	East	South
	1◇	pass	1♠
pass	2♠	pass	4NT
pass	5♡	pass	6♠
all pass			

How will you plan 6♠ when West leads the ♡K? This is the loser position:

Losers: ♠ 0   ♡ 1   ◇ 0   ♣ 1   **Total:** 2

Whenever dummy arrives with a five-card side suit, say a special 'thank-you' to partner. You will often be able to use that suit to dispose of some of your own losers. Here you must aim to establish (set up) dummy's diamond suit. If the defenders' diamonds break 3-3, one diamond ruff in your hand will be good enough. You will then have two winning diamond spot cards in the dummy and can discard both your potential losers for an overtrick. It is more likely that the diamond suit will break 4-2. In that case you will need to take two diamond ruffs in order to set up one long card in the dummy.

You win the heart lead with the ace and draw trumps with the king and queen. (You must keep the ace and jack of trumps as later entries to the dummy.) Next you play the ace and king of diamonds and ruff a diamond. West shows out on the third round, so East still has a high diamond left. You cross to the ♠J and ruff a second diamond in your hand, establishing dummy's last diamond as a winner. You can then cross to dummy with the ♠A to discard one of your losers on the established ◇9.

> **PLAN: I will win the heart lead, draw trumps with the king and queen and set up the diamonds, to discard at least one loser.**

Establishing suits is an important topic and we will see many more examples in Chapter 5.

Discarding loser-on-loser, to set up a second discard

We will end the chapter with a valuable discarding technique known as 'loser-on-loser'. It's not so easy to describe in mere words, so we will look straight away at a deal illustrating the idea.

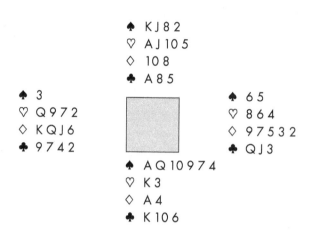

	North	South	
♠	K J 8 2		

Hand diagram:

North: ♠ K J 8 2 ♡ A J 10 5 ◇ 10 8 ♣ A 8 5

West: ♠ 3 ♡ Q 9 7 2 ◇ K Q J 6 ♣ 9 7 4 2

East: ♠ 6 5 ♡ 8 6 4 ◇ 9 7 5 3 2 ♣ Q J 3

South: ♠ A Q 10 9 7 4 ♡ K 3 ◇ A 4 ♣ K 10 6

West	North	East	South
	1♣	pass	1♠
pass	2♠	pass	4NT
pass	5♡	pass	6♠
all pass			

West leads the ◇K against your spade slam and you see this loser situation:

Losers: ♠0 ♡0 ◇1 ♣1   **Total:** 2

You win the diamond lead and draw trumps in two rounds. How can you avoid one of your losers? Perhaps dummy's heart suit will provide a discard or two. Suppose you play the ♡K and then finesse the ♡J. When the cards lie as in the diagram, the finesse will win; you will discard a loser on the ♡A and make the contract. Will your partner congratulate you afterwards? No! You would have gone down if the heart finesse had lost and there is a much better way of playing the contract.

To guarantee the contract no matter how the cards lie, you should play the ♡K and ♡A. You then lead the ♡J and discard the ◇4. West wins with the ♡Q but cannot cash a diamond because you have thrown away your loser in that suit. When you regain the lead, you will be able to throw your club loser on the established ♡10.

Notice that you do not care which opponent holds the ♡Q. If East plays the ♡Q on your jack, you will ruff and later discard a diamond or club loser on the ♡10. If East has the ♡Q and does not cover the ♡J, then you will win the trick, discarding the diamond loser.

Until now, we have been discarding a loser on winners. Here you discard a loser (the ◇4) on a loser (the ♡J). For the moment, you are merely swapping one trick for another. The benefit comes when you take a second discard on the established ♡10.

PLAN: I will win the diamond lead, draw trumps and play the two top hearts. I can then throw the diamond loser on the ♡J, a loser-on-loser play, and the club loser on the ♡10.

Remember these points

- Whenever possible, you should draw trumps before taking any discards. Otherwise a defender may ruff one of your winners.

- Sometimes you must 'set up a discard'. In other words, you must establish a surplus winner in a suit, on which you will take the discard. For example, suppose you hold ◊QJ7 in dummy opposite ◊K3 in your hand. By knocking out the ◊A, you will establish a discard on the diamond suit,

- You can also set up a discard by taking a finesse. With ♡K962 in dummy opposite a singleton ♡7 in your hand, you would lead toward dummy's ♡K. When the ace lies in front of the king, the defender must either rise with the ace, setting up a discard, or surrender his trick in the suit by allowing the king to win.

- When dummy has a long side suit, you may be able to 'establish the suit'. You ruff a round or two in your hand until the defenders have no more cards in the suit. You can then take a discard on a winner in the established suit.

Now try these...

A.

      ♠ Q 10 6
      ♡ K 6 4
      ◇ K Q 7 2
      ♣ A Q 3

♣J led   ▭

      ♠ A K J 3 2
      ♡ Q J 10 2
      ◇ A 5
      ♣ 8 5

West leads the ♣J against your contract of 6♠. What is your plan?

B.

      ♠ Q 3
      ♡ A 6 4
      ◇ Q J 7
      ♣ 10 9 7 3 2

♡K led   ▭

      ♠ A K J 7 6 4
      ♡ 7 5 2
      ◇ K 3
      ♣ A 4

How will you play 4♠ when West leads the ♡K?

C.

      ♠ 8 4 2
      ♡ K 4 2
      ◇ 10 6 4 3
      ♣ Q J 6

♠Q led   ▭

      ♠ A 7
      ♡ A Q J 10 6 5
      ◇ A 9 5
      ♣ A 5

West leads the ♠Q against 4♡. How will you plan the play?

D.

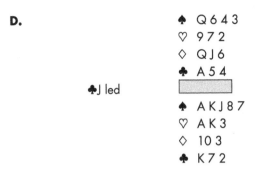

♠ Q 6 4 3
♡ 9 7 2
◇ Q J 6
♣ A 5 4

♣J led

♠ A K J 8 7
♡ A K 3
◇ 10 3
♣ K 7 2

You reach 4♠ and West leads the ♣J. What plan will you make?

E.

♠ A K 7
♡ A Q J 9
◇ 9 7 4
♣ K Q 7

◇Q led

♠ 6 5 2
♡ K 8 6 3 2
◇ A 5 3
♣ 9 2

West leads the ◇Q against your contract of 4♡. What is your plan?

F.

♠ A 9 3
♡ 10 5 2
◇ A Q J 4
♣ A 9 5

♠K led

♠ 10 5 4
♡ A
◇ 8 2
♣ K Q J 10 7 3 2

West leads the ♠K against 6♣. How will you plan the play?

ANSWERS

A. Your potential losers are: one in hearts and one in clubs. If you finesse the ♣Q at Trick 1 and it loses, the defenders will also take a heart trick and you will go down. There is no need to risk the club finesse, since the diamond suit contains an extra winner, giving you a discard of the club loser in your hand.

So, win the first trick with the ♣A. You can then draw trumps and play the three top diamond honors (◇A first, then the ◇K and ◇Q), discarding the last club from your hand. Finally, you will establish the heart suit by knocking out the ♡A.

PLAN: I will win with the ♣A, draw trumps and play the three top diamonds, discarding my club loser. I will then establish the heart suit.

B. Your potential losers are: two in hearts, one in diamonds and one in clubs. The diamond suit will provide one surplus winner, giving you a discard. You win the opening lead with the ♡A. Should you then draw trumps straight away? No, because a skilful defender could then defeat you by ducking when you subsequently lead the ◇K. He would win the second round of diamonds and you would have no entry to reach the established diamond winner in dummy.

So, play a diamond to the king at Trick 2. It will not help the defenders to hold up the ◇A now, because you would continue with a second round of diamonds. When you regain the lead, you will cross to the ♠Q and discard your club loser on the established ◇J.

PLAN: I will win with the ♡A and play a diamond to the king. If the defenders win, once I regain the lead I will draw trumps and take two discards on the ◇QJ. If instead they duck, I will play another diamond and later cross to the ♠Q to throw my club loser on the ◇J.

C. You have four potential losers in the side suits. You could use dummy's ♡K entry to take a finesse in clubs, running the queen, but this would be a poor plan. If the club finesse lost, the club suit would be blocked and you would have no way to reach the ♣J in dummy.

After winning the spade lead, you should draw two rounds of trumps with the ace and queen. Let's say that the trumps break 3-1. You then play ace and another club, setting up a surplus club winner in the dummy. When you regain the lead, you will cross to the ♡K and discard a diamond loser on the established club winner.

PLAN: I will win the spade lead and play the ace and queen of trumps. Then I will play ace and another club. Later I will cross to the ♡K to discard a diamond on the established club winner.

D. Your have four potential losers in the side suits. Your plan should be to establish a surplus diamond trick, on which you can discard a heart or a club loser. You win the club lead with the king and draw trumps with the honors in your hand, retaining the ♠Q as an entry to dummy. Next you lead the ◊10, forcing out one of the defenders' top diamonds. You win the club continuation with the ace and lead the ◊Q. The defenders will win and cash one club trick but you can cross to the ♠Q subsequently to discard your heart loser on the established ◊J.

PLAN: I will win the club lead, draw trumps with the honors in my hand and play the ◊10. I will then be able to establish a diamond as a discard for my heart loser.

E. You have a total of four losers in the side suits. The only chance of reducing this to three losers is to establish two winners in clubs, allowing you to discard your spade loser. For this to be possible, you will need to find West with the ♣A. Since you will need to lead twice toward dummy's club honors (if West holds up his ace on the first round), it is essential to make the first club play immediately. When you lead a club, West plays low and dummy's ♣K wins. You continue with the ace, queen and king of trumps, ending in your hand, and lead a second round of clubs toward dummy. West rises with the ♣A and the defenders take two diamond tricks. The remaining tricks are yours; you will throw your spade loser on the established ♣Q.

PLAN: I will win with the ◊A and play a club toward dummy. If West holds the ♣A, I can establish a discard for the spade loser. The ♡K is the entry for a second club lead toward dummy.

F. You have two potential losers in spades and one in diamonds. You will have to hope that the diamond finesse is right. Not only will that save you a diamond loser, it will allow you to discard one of your spade losers on the third round of diamonds.

So, win the spade lead and draw trumps. If a diamond to the queen wins the next trick, return to your hand with the ♡A and play a diamond to the jack. You can then discard a spade on the ◊A.

PLAN: I will win the spade lead, draw trumps and finesse the ◊Q. If this wins, I will return to my hand and finesse the ◊J, discarding a spade on the ◊A.

4

MAKING A PLAN — TO RUFF LOSERS

In this chapter we will look at several deals where the winning play is to ruff one or more losers in the dummy. One of the main decisions to make is whether you can afford to draw trumps before taking those ruffs. See what you make of the first deal:

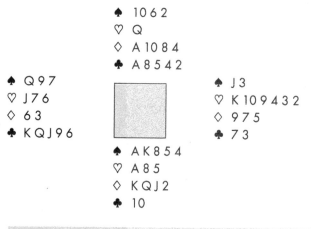

♠	1 0 6 2		
♡	Q		
◇	A 10 8 4		
♣	A 8 5 4 2		

West		East
♠ Q 9 7		♠ J 3
♡ J 7 6		♡ K 10 9 4 3 2
◇ 6 3		◇ 9 7 5
♣ K Q J 9 6		♣ 7 3

♠	A K 8 5 4
♡	A 8 5
◇	K Q J 2
♣	10

West	**North**	**East**	**South**
	pass	pass	1♠
pass	3♠	pass	4NT
pass	5♡	pass	6♠
all pass			

West leads the ♣K against your boldly-bid 6♠ and you see this loser situation:

Losers:　♠ 1　♡ 2　◇ 0　♣ 0　　　　Total:　3

If trumps broke badly, you might lose two trump tricks. Defeat would then be certain, however, so let's assume there is only one potential trump loser. You can avoid the two heart losers by ruffing them in the dummy. You win the club lead with dummy's ace. What should you do next? Draw two rounds of trumps?

Let's hope not! You need to use two of dummy's trumps for ruffing and should begin this process right away. You cross to the ♡A at Trick 2 and ruff a heart in dummy. You return to your hand with a trump to the ace and ruff your remaining heart loser with dummy's ♠10. Finally, you play a diamond to the king and draw a second round of trumps with the king. Both defenders follow and the contract is yours. All you will lose is one trump trick.

> **PLAN: I will win with the ♣A, play a heart to the ace and ruff a heart. I will return to the ♠A and ruff my last heart. Then I will cross to the ◇K and play the ♠K.**

Here is a slightly less straightforward deal on the same theme:

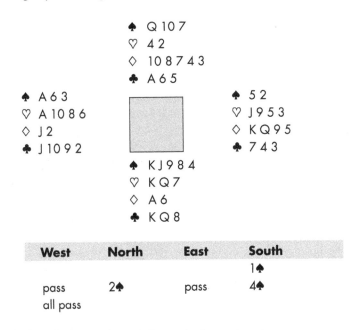

	♠ Q 10 7	
	♡ 4 2	
	◇ 10 8 7 4 3	
	♣ A 6 5	

♠ A 6 3	♠ 5 2
♡ A 10 8 6	♡ J 9 5 3
◇ J 2	◇ K Q 9 5
♣ J 10 9 2	♣ 7 4 3

	♠ K J 9 8 4
	♡ K Q 7
	◇ A 6
	♣ K Q 8

West	North	East	South
			1♠
pass	2♠	pass	4♠
all pass			

West leads the ♣J against 4♠ and this is the loser situation:

Losers: ♠ 1   ♡ 2   ◇ 1   ♣ 0   **Total:** 4

There is no chance of avoiding the losers in spades and diamonds, so you must hope to reduce your heart losers from two to one. How can this be done? If East holds the ♡A, you can lead twice toward the honors in the South hand. This is the finesse method of saving yourself a loser. It does, however, rely on luck; if West holds the ♡A, as in the diagram, you will still have two losers in the suit.

A better idea is to ruff the third round of hearts in dummy, which does not rely on a lucky lie of the cards. How can this be done? The first point to note is that you will go down if you initially play even one round of trumps. West could win and play a second round of trumps. When you won in the dummy and played a heart to the king, West would win with the ♡A and play a third round of trumps. With no trumps left in dummy, you would not be able to take a heart ruff.

So, you must head for your heart ruff immediately. You win the club lead with dummy's ace and lead a heart to the king. West wins with the ace but he cannot prevent you from scoring a heart ruff. Even if he plays ace and another trump, you would be able to win the second round, cash the ♡Q and ruff a heart. You would then return to the South hand to draw the remaining trump.

> **PLAN: I will win with the ♣A and play a heart to the king. Even if this loses to the ace with West, I will be able to ruff a heart in dummy.**

Ruffing high to avoid an overruff

When you ruff a loser, you must sometimes decide whether to ruff with a high trump or a low trump. Ruffing with dummy's highest trump will prevent (or perhaps reduce) the chance of an overruff. However, it may increase the chance that you will lose a trump trick eventually.

Let's see a couple of deals where you must make such a decision.

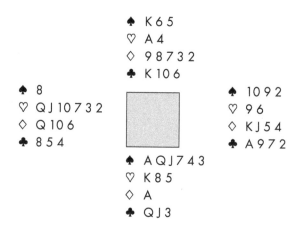

A splendid bidding sequence carries you to the excellent contract of 6♠. How will you play the slam when West leads the ♡Q? You start from this position:

Losers: ♠0 ♡1 ◇0 ♣1   **Total: 2**

The club loser is unavoidable and you must therefore avoid the potential loser in hearts. The loser can be ruffed in the dummy, but should you ruff the third round of hearts with the king or a low trump? You can see from the diagram that ruffing with the ♠6 or ♠5 will allow East to defeat you with an overruff. If you ruff with the ♠K instead, to protect yourself from an overruff, you would go down when trumps broke 4-0 and a defender subsequently scored a trick with his ♠10982.

On this particular deal, you can easily discover whether you can afford to ruff with the king of trumps. You win the heart lead with dummy's ace and play a trump to the ace. Both defenders follow, so you know that trumps are not 4-0. You draw a second round of trumps with the queen (to avoid defeat when trumps are 2-2 and East holds only one heart). You continue with the ♡K and ruff your third heart with the bare ♠K. You can then return to your hand with the ◊A to draw the last trump. Finally, you knock out the ♣A and mark up your slam.

Suppose a trump to the ace had revealed that East held ♠10982. It would then be clear that ruffing a heart with the king would promote a trump trick for him. You would have to ruff low, hoping that East held three or more hearts.

This is your plan for the contract:

> **PLAN: I will win with the ♡A and play a trump to the ace. If trumps are 4-0, I will have to ruff my heart loser low; otherwise I will ruff it high, to avoid an overruff.**

On the next deal dummy does not contain a master trump. Nevertheless, it will make a difference whether you ruff with dummy's top trump or not.

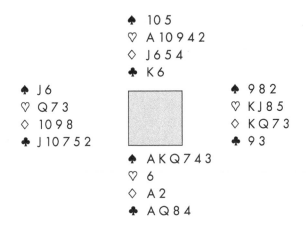

	♠ 10 5		
	♡ A 10 9 4 2		
	◊ J 6 5 4		
	♣ K 6		

West	North	East	South
			1♠
pass	1NT	pass	3♣
pass	3♠	pass	6♠
all pass			

How will you play 6♠ (yes, it was a dashing piece of bidding) when West leads the ♢10? These are your potential losers:

Losers: ♠ 1   ♡ 0   ♢ 1   ♣ 1   **Total:** 3

You must hope that there is no trump loser. You cannot avoid a loser in diamonds, so it is the potential loser in clubs that should grab your attention. The best idea is to ruff a club in dummy. You win the diamond lead, cross to the ♣K and return to the ♣A. There is no point whatsoever in trying to cash the ♣Q next; it would merely increase the chance of an adverse ruff or overruff in clubs. Instead you lead the ♣8 on the third round and West plays the ♣J. Which of dummy's trumps will you use for the ruff?

You should ruff with the ♠10. In the unlucky situation where East holds only two clubs, you may still survive. East may not hold the ♠J and in that case he will be unable to overruff. That's exactly what will happen when the cards lie as in the diagram. You can then draw trumps and make the slam.

Suppose dummy's trumps were ♠95. It would still be worthwhile to ruff with the ♠9, rather than the ♠5, just in case East held a doubleton club but West had the jack and ten of trumps.

> **PLAN: I will win with the ♢A, cash the ♣K and the ♣A and ruff a club with dummy's ♠10. By ruffing high, I will reduce the risk of an overruff.**

Creating a shortage to set up a ruff

Suppose you hold AKx in a suit and would like to ruff the losing card. You will need the opposite hand to contain fewer than three cards in the suit and sometimes you can create such a shortage by taking a discard on a superfluous winner in your hand. That's what happens here:

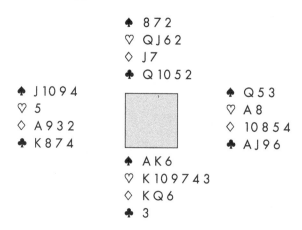

West	North	East	South
			1♡
pass	2♡	pass	4♡
all pass			

West leads the ♠J and this is the potential loser position:

Losers: ♠ 1   ♡ 1   ◇ 1   ♣ 1   Total: 4

You will surely lose tricks to the three missing aces, so you must make arrangements for your spade loser. No finesse is possible in the suit, nor is it likely that you can set up a discard on dummy's club suit. Instead, you must aim to ruff a spade in dummy and this can be done by creating a spade shortage there.

You win the spade lead and immediately lead to dummy's ◇J, continuing with a second round of diamonds if the jack wins. When you win the spade return, you will discard dummy's last spade on the third round of diamonds and ruff a spade with the queen of trumps. Only then will you start to draw trumps.

If you mistakenly start the play by drawing trumps instead, the defense will win the ♡A and lead another spade, knocking out your second high honor in the suit. Now when you lead diamonds, they can win the ◇A and cash a spade to defeat you.

PLAN: I will win the spade lead and knock out the ◇A. I can then throw one of dummy's spades on my third diamond winner and ruff a spade in dummy.

Ruff in the hand with the shorter trumps

In all the deals that we have seen so far, the ruffs have been taken in dummy — that is, in the hand with the shorter trumps (this is sometimes referred to as 'ruffing in the short hand'). There is a good reason for this. Ruffing in the hand with the shorter trumps gives you an extra trick. Ruffing in the long-trump hand may be a good idea for some tactical reason but it will not give you an extra trick. To make sure that you understand this important principle, look at the slam overleaf:

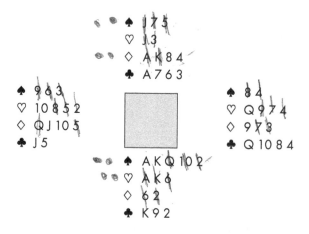

	♠ J 7 5		
	♡ J 3		
	◇ A K 8 4		
	♣ A 7 6 3		
♠ 9 6 3			♠ 8 4
♡ 10 8 5 2			♡ Q 9 7 4
◇ Q J 10 5			◇ 9 7 3
♣ J 5			♣ Q 10 8 4
	♠ A K Q 10 2		
	♡ A K 6		
	◇ 6 2		
	♣ K 9 2		

West	North	East	South
	1◇	pass	1♠
pass	2♠	pass	4NT
pass	5♡	pass	6♠
all pass			

West leads the ◇Q and you see this loser position:

Losers: ♠ 0   ♡ 1   ◇ 0   ♣ 1   Total: 2

Not difficult, is it? You can avoid the heart loser by ruffing the ♡6 in the dummy. You cannot afford to draw all the trumps first, of course, or there would be no trumps left in dummy. So, win the diamond lead, cash the ♡A and ♡K and ruff the ♡6 with the ♠J to avoid any risk of an overruff. You then draw trumps and make an easy twelve tricks.

The important point to note is that the heart ruff gave you an extra trick. You began with five trump tricks and six side-suit winners (three A-K combinations). By ruffing a heart in dummy, you scored a total of six trump tricks and brought the total to twelve. Suppose instead that you had ruffed a diamond in your hand. This would not have given you an extra trick. You began the deal with five trump tricks and you would still have only five trump tricks. You would be no nearer to making the slam because the losers in clubs and hearts would still be there.

This is one of the reasons why we plan suit contracts by counting the losers in the long-trump hand, rather than those in the short-trump hand. Ruffing a heart in dummy will reduce your total loser count; ruffing a diamond in your hand will not.

PLAN: I will win the diamond lead, play the ♡AK and ruff the ♡6 with the ♠J. I can then draw trumps.

Remember these points

- When you are planning to take a ruff or two in dummy, it may not be possible to draw trumps immediately.

- When you can afford to, without risking the subsequent loss of a trump trick, ruff with a high trump to prevent the risk of an overruff.

- Ruffing in the short-trump hand gives you an extra trick; ruffing in the long-trump hand does not.

Now try these...

A.

       ♠ A 6 2
       ♡ 9 6
       ◇ 9 8 5 4 3
       ♣ A 9 4

◇K led   [   ]

       ♠ K Q J 10 8
       ♡ J 8 3
       ◇ A 2
       ♣ K Q 5

Expressing your plan as concisely as you can, how will you play 4♠? West leads the ◇K.

B.

       ♠ K Q J 3
       ♡ 9 7 6
       ◇ K 5
       ♣ A 9 5 2

♣K led   [   ]

       ♠ A 10 9 6 4
       ♡ Q 5 3
       ◇ A 9 6 3
       ♣ 3

West leads the ♣K against your contract of 4♠. What is your plan?

C.

       ♠ 10 9 3
       ♡ A 5
       ◇ 10 8 5 2
       ♣ J 9 5 2

◇K led   [   ]

       ♠ A K Q 6 5
       ♡ K 9 7 4 2
       ◇ A
       ♣ 6 4

West leads the ◇K against 4♠. How will you plan the play?

D.

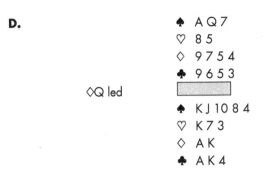

♠ A Q 7
♡ 8 5
◇ 9 7 5 4
♣ 9 6 5 3

◇Q led

♠ K J 10 8 4
♡ K 7 3
◇ A K
♣ A K 4

Expressing your plan as concisely as you can, how will you play 4♠?

E.

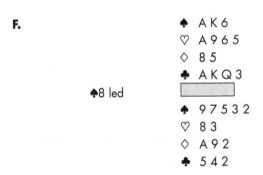

♠ K J 8 6 3
♡ 8 7 5 4
◇ A Q
♣ K 7

♡K led

♠ A Q 10 7 4
♡ A 3
◇ 8 5 2
♣ A Q 5

West leads the ♡K against 6♠. How will you plan the play?

F.

♠ A K 6
♡ A 9 6 5
◇ 8 5
♣ A K Q 3

♠8 led

♠ 9 7 5 3 2
♡ 8 3
◇ A 9 2
♣ 5 4 2

West leads the ♠8 against your spade game. How will you plan the play?

ANSWERS

A. Your potential losers are three in hearts and one in diamonds. You can save yourself one loser by ruffing a heart in dummy. You cannot afford to draw any trumps before setting up the heart ruff. Win the diamond lead and give the defenders a heart trick. If they switch to trumps now, win with the ♠K and give up another heart; win the next trump with the ♠Q and ruff a heart with the ♠A. You can then return to the ♣K to draw the outstanding trump(s).

PLAN: I will win with the ◇A and give up two rounds of hearts, intending to ruff a heart with dummy's ♠A.

B. Your potential losers are three in hearts and two in diamonds. You could avoid one of the heart losers if East held the ♡A and ♡K, by leading twice toward the ♡Q. A better idea is to ruff your two potential diamond losers. To avoid the possibility of East overruffing (if he started with a doubleton diamond), you should leave two trump honors in dummy. You can then ruff your two diamond losers with high trumps.

PLAN: I will win with the ♣A and draw two rounds of trumps with the king and ace. Whether or not there is trump still out, I will ruff my diamond losers with the ♠Q and ♠J, using a club ruff as the entry for the second ruff.

C. You have three losing cards in hearts and two in clubs, along with a possible trump loser if trumps break 4-1. You must aim to ruff a heart or two in dummy, doing your best to survive when East holds only two hearts.

Win the diamond lead and play the ♡A and ♡K immediately. When you lead a third round of hearts, let's suppose that West follows suit. What now? You should ruff with dummy's ♠10. If East has no hearts left, he may not be able to overruff. Even if he does overruff with the ♠J, you will be able to ruff the fourth round of hearts with dummy's ♠9. The fifth heart will now be a winner. You will lose just two clubs and one more trick to the heart overruff.

PLAN: I will win the diamond lead, play the ♡A and ♡K and lead a third heart, ruffing with the ♠10 if West follows suit. Even if this is overruffed, I will be able to ruff the next heart with the ♠9.

D. Your potential losers are three in hearts and one in clubs. You can avoid one of the heart losers by ruffing a heart in dummy. Suppose you make the mistake of crossing to a high trump to lead toward the ♡K. West may win with the ♡A and return a second round of trumps. When you give up another heart, the defenders will remove dummy's last trump, preventing a heart ruff. You will then go down. It is better to lead the first round of hearts from your hand, guaranteeing an eventual heart ruff.

> **PLAN: I will win with the ◇A and lead a heart from my hand. If the defenders return a trump, I will win with the ♠A and play a heart to the king. If this loses, I can ruff the third round of hearts.**

E. You have one potential loser in hearts and two in diamonds. There is no need to risk the diamond finesse! The third club winner in your hand will allow you to discard the ◇Q and you will then be able to ruff two diamonds in the dummy.

So, win the heart lead, draw trumps and play the ◇A. You then play the three top club winners, ditching the ◇Q from dummy. The way is then clear for you to ruff your two diamond losers in the dummy.

> **PLAN: I will win the heart lead, draw trumps, cash the ◇A and discard the ◇Q on the third round of clubs. I can then ruff two diamonds in the dummy.**

F. If trumps break 3-2, you have four potential losers: one trump, one heart and two diamonds. There is no need to rely on clubs breaking 3-3, which would give you a discard, because you can ruff a diamond in the dummy. After winning the trump lead with dummy's ace, you should duck a round of diamonds, preserving your ◇A as an entry on the second round. You can then win the second round of trumps with the ♠K and cross to the ◇A to take your diamond ruff.

By playing in this way, you can also make the contract when trumps break 4-1 and clubs are 3-3. After taking the diamond ruff, you will discard your heart loser on the thirteenth club. You will lose just two trumps and a diamond.

> **PLAN: I will win the trump lead and duck a diamond. When I regain the lead, I will cross to the ◇A and ruff a diamond with the ♠6.**

5

HOW TO ESTABLISH A SUIT

One of the most important techniques, when playing a hand, is that of establishing a long suit. It is easy to score tricks with aces and kings, yes, but it is just as important to score tricks with the small cards in a long suit. You can do this when the defenders no longer have any cards left in the suit.

In this chapter we will see how you can establish a suit when playing in a suit contract. Later on, in Chapter 9, we will see how this can be done in notrump.

Establishing a suit by ruffing

We will start with a fairly simple deal where you do not have to worry unduly about the entry position.

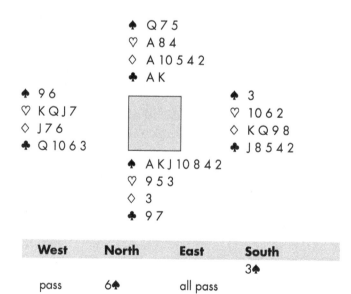

West	North	East	South
			3♠
pass	6♠	all pass	

West leads the ♡K against your spade slam and (yes!) you pause to make a plan. You can see these potential losers in the long-trump hand:

Losers: ♠ 0   ♡ 2   ◊ 0   ♣ 0   **Total:** 2

There is no possibility of ruffing a heart loser or of taking a finesse in a suit. The only chance of reducing the number of heart losers is to discard one of them. How can this be done? If the defenders' diamonds break 4-3, you can establish the diamond suit. In other words, you can play the ◊A and then ruff three diamonds in your hand. The effect of this will be that neither defender has any cards left in the suit; dummy will have one diamond left and this will be a winner. You can then discard one of your heart losers on the established long card in diamonds.

How does the play go? You win the heart lead with dummy's ace and draw trumps in two rounds with the ace and king. (You leave the ♠Q in dummy to serve as a later entry). Then you begin to establish dummy's diamond suit. You cross to the ◊A and ruff a diamond. You then cross to the ♠Q and ruff another diamond. A club to the ace allows you to take a third diamond ruff, removing the defenders' cards in the suit. Finally, you return to dummy with the ♣K to play the established ◊10, throwing one of your heart losers. The slam is yours.

> **PLAN: I will win the heart lead, play the ace and king of trumps and then attempt to establish the diamond suit for a heart discard. This will be possible if diamonds break 4-3.**

An important part of planning such a contract is to ensure that you have enough entries to the hand with the long suit. Here you needed four entries (not counting the ♡A, which had been removed at Trick 1). You needed to cross to the ◊A for the first ruff and then use two further entries to take the second and third diamond ruffs. Finally you needed a fourth entry, to reach the established card in diamonds.

On the next deal you must make full use of the entries provided by dummy's trump holding. You cannot therefore draw trumps before you start the process of setting up dummy's long suit.

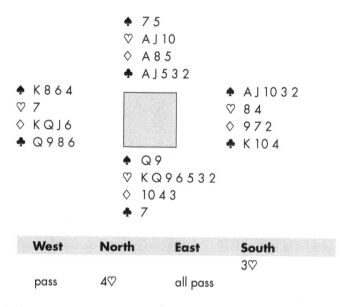

♠ 7 5
♡ A J 10
◇ A 8 5
♣ A J 5 3 2

♠ K 8 6 4
♡ 7
◇ K Q J 6
♣ Q 9 8 6

♠ A J 10 3 2
♡ 8 4
◇ 9 7 2
♣ K 10 4

♠ Q 9
♡ K Q 9 6 5 3 2
◇ 10 4 3
♣ 7

West	North	East	South
			3♡
pass	4♡	all pass	

West leads the ◇K against your heart game and you see this loser position:

Losers: ♠ 2   ♡ 0   ◇ 2   ♣ 0   **Total: 4**

As on the previous deal, you must aim to establish dummy's long suit (clubs), so that you can discard one of your losers. The ◇A has already been removed by the opening lead, so you must make full use of dummy's three entries in the trump suit.

After winning with the ◇A, you cash the ♣A and ruff a club. You then cross to the ♡10 and ruff another club, pleased to see that the suit breaks 4-3. You return to dummy with the ♡J and you take a third ruff in the club suit, establishing the ♣J as a winner. Finally, you cross to the ♡A to play the ♣J, discarding one of your losers.

Look back to Trick 2 and imagine that you had drawn even one round of trumps at that stage. You would no longer have had the entries to establish the clubs and then cross back to dummy to score the established winner in the suit.

> **PLAN: I will win the diamond lead, cash the ♣A and ruff a club. When clubs break 4-3, I can use dummy's three trump entries to establish a long club and discard a loser on it.**

Ducking an early round to preserve an entry

Suppose you want to establish a suit where you hold AK932 in the dummy and 764 in your hand. You will have to lose a round of this suit, even if the defenders' cards divide 3-2. It will often make good sense to lose the first (or second) round of the suit; you will then be able to cross to dummy on the third round, to enjoy the established long cards. Let's see an example of this technique:

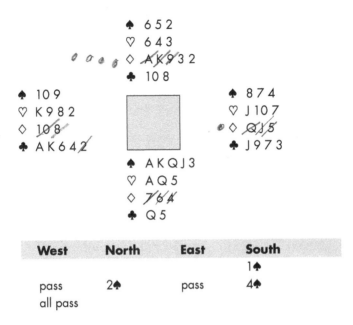

	West	North	East	South
				1♠
	pass	2♠	pass	4♠
	all pass			

West starts the defense with the ♣A and ♣K, switching to the ♠10. What plan will you make?

This is the loser position:

Losers: ♠ 0   ♡ 2   ◇ 1   ♣ 2   **Total: 5**

Two clubs have already been lost and you will surely lose a diamond trick. You must therefore aim to discard the two heart losers on dummy's diamond suit. You win the trump switch and draw trumps in two more rounds. What now?

Suppose you cash the ◇A and ◇K and play a third round of the suit, the defenders winning. That's no good! There will be no entry to dummy to enjoy the two established diamonds. Instead, you should duck the first round of diamonds (in other words, play low from both hands). Let's say that East wins and returns a heart. You rise with the ♡A and play the ◇A and ◇K, the suit breaking 3-2. That's better. Because you ducked an early diamond, you are in dummy (where you want to be) after three rounds of the suit. You cash the established ◇93 and throw two heart losers from your hand. The game is yours.

> **PLAN: I will draw trumps and duck a round of diamonds. Provided the diamonds break 3-2, I will have two discards for my heart losers.**

It's an important technique, ducking an early round of the suit to be established. Let's see another example, to fix the idea in our minds:

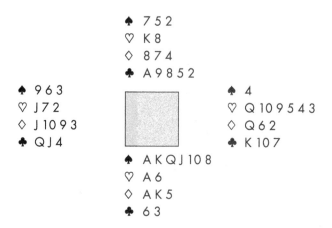

| ♠ 752
♡ K 8
◇ 8 7 4
♣ A 9 8 5 2 |
| |

♠ 9 6 3   ♠ 4
♡ J 7 2   ♡ Q 10 9 5 4 3
◇ J 10 9 3   ◇ Q 6 2
♣ Q J 4   ♣ K 10 7

♠ A K Q J 10 8
♡ A 6
◇ A K 5
♣ 6 3

West	North	East	South
			2♣
pass	2◇	pass	2♠
pass	3♠	pass	4◇
pass	5♣	pass	6♠
all pass			

Once North supports spades, both players show their first-round controls, and South bids the small slam. Owing to the unlucky mirror distribution in the red suits, it's not a particularly good contract, let's agree, but how will you plan the play when West leads the ◇J? This is the potential loser situation:

Losers: ♠ 0   ♡ 0   ◇ 1   ♣ 1   Total: 2

You must hope to establish the club suit so that you can discard your diamond loser. With so few entries to dummy, you will need the clubs to break 3-3. You win the first trick with the ◇A and draw trumps in three rounds. You lead a round of clubs and make the key play of ducking in the dummy, preserving the ♣A as a later entry. Let's say that the defenders persist with another round of diamonds, which you win with the king. You cross to the ♣A and ruff a club in your hand. Salvation! The suit breaks 3-3 and dummy's ♣98 are now established. Who says that overbidding doesn't pay? You cross to the ♡K and discard your diamond loser on the ♣9. The slam is yours.

> **PLAN: I will win the diamond lead, draw trumps and duck a round of clubs. I will win the return in hand, cross to the ♣A and ruff a club. If the suit breaks 3-3, I can cross to the ♡K to discard my diamond loser.**

Sometimes it is worth ducking an early round of the suit to be established, even when you do not have to lose a trick there. By doing so, you can overcome a bad break of the defenders' cards. Look at the heart suit on this deal:

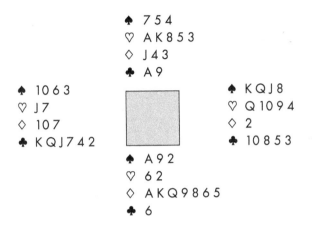

♠	7 5 4
♡	A K 8 5 3
◊	J 4 3
♣	A 9

West	North	East	South
			1◊
pass	1♡	pass	3◊
pass	4◊	pass	4NT
pass	5♡	pass	6◊
all pass			

West leads the ♣K against your diamond slam and you see this loser situation:

Losers: ♠ 2   ♡ 0   ◊ 0   ♣ 0   **Total:** 2

You will need to set up at least one discard on dummy's heart suit, to reduce the number of spade losers. With the ♣A already dislodged, you have only the ◊J as a side entry to help you set up the hearts and enjoy the established winners there. How will you play the contract?

You begin by drawing trumps with the ace and king. Suppose your next move is to play the ace and king of hearts and to ruff a heart. You will make the contract when hearts divide 3-3; indeed, you will make an overtrick. You will fail to make the slam when hearts split 4-2, which is more likely. You will have only one entry (the ◊J) remaining to dummy and the hearts will not yet be established.

Let's try something different (and perhaps surprising, if you have not seen this type of play before). After drawing trumps, you duck a round of hearts, playing a low heart from both your own hand and the dummy. You ruff the club return, cross to the ♡A and play the ♡K, throwing a spade. You see the difference? Hearts break 4-2 but you are in dummy after three rounds and can now ruff a heart, setting up the thirteenth card in the suit. You can then return to the ◊J to enjoy the established ♡8, throwing your remaining spade loser to make the slam.

Make sure you have understood why the early duck of a trick allows you to set up the suit against a 4-2 break. This play will give you many a contract, once you have it in your armory.

> **PLAN: I will win the club lead, draw trumps and duck a round of hearts. I can then set up the hearts if they break 4-2.**

Finessing to establish a suit against a bad break

Sometimes you have the chance of a finesse in the suit that you are trying to establish. You must then calculate whether taking the finesse will improve your prospects of success. Look at the club suit here:

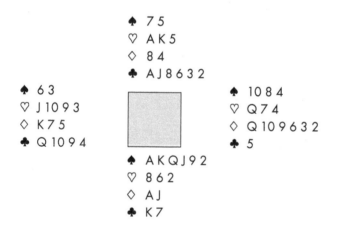

```
              ♠ 7 5
              ♡ A K 5
              ◇ 8 4
              ♣ A J 8 6 3 2
♠ 6 3                          ♠ 10 8 4
♡ J 10 9 3                     ♡ Q 7 4
◇ K 7 5                        ◇ Q 10 9 6 3 2
♣ Q 10 9 4                     ♣ 5
              ♠ A K Q J 9 2
              ♡ 8 6 2
              ◇ A J
              ♣ K 7
```

North opens 1♣ and you carry the bidding to a small slam in spades. What will your plan be when West leads the ♡J? These are the potential losers:

Losers: ♠0 ♡1 ◇1 ♣0   Total: 2

You will have to establish dummy's club suit. After winning the heart lead with the king, you draw trumps in three rounds. You then play the ♣K and lead a second round of clubs, West following with the ♣10 or ♣9. What card should you play from dummy?

If clubs are breaking 3-2, you can win with dummy's ♣A and establish the suit with just one ruff; you will score an overtrick. Suppose that you rise with the ♣A and (horror of horrors) East shows out instead. Disaster! You would then need two ruffs to establish the club suit and you have only one entry to dummy remaining. You will go down.

Once you think about it, you can see that a finesse of the ♣J will give you the slam, however the cards lie. If East shows out when you take the finesse, you can ruff a round of clubs to set up the suit. You can then return to dummy's ♡A to discard the two red-suit losers. If instead the finesse loses to East's ♣Q, the suit will have broken 3-2 and dummy's remaining clubs will be good. So, a club finesse will give you the contract whether it wins or loses — just the sort of finesse to go for!

> **PLAN: I will win the heart lead, draw trumps, cash the ♣K and finesse the ♣J. I can then set up the clubs even when West holds ♣Qxxx.**

Remember these points

- In a suit contract, you can sometimes establish a suit by taking one or more ruffs. For example, with Axxxx in dummy opposite a singleton, you can take three ruffs in your hand and establish the thirteenth card (provided the suit breaks 4-3.)

- With a suit such as Axxxx in dummy opposite xx, you will have to lose a round at some stage. It is normally right to duck the first round so that you can use the ace as an entry on the second round.

- Even with AKxxx opposite xx, it may be beneficial to duck the first round. You can then cross to the ace and establish the suit with a single ruff when it breaks 4-2.

- Since you may need to use the trump suit for entries when establishing a suit, consider carefully whether you can afford to draw trumps first.

Now try these...

A.

                ♠ J 5 4
                ♡ 7 5
                ◇ A 9 7 4 3
                ♣ K J 2

♣10 led

                ♠ A 7
                ♡ A K Q J 10 2
                ◇ K 6
                ♣ A Q 4

How will you play 7♡ when West leads the ♣10?

B.

                ♠ Q 9
                ♡ A K 4 2
                ◇ K 9
                ♣ A 9 7 6 3

♠A led

                ♠ 8 3
                ♡ 8 6 3
                ◇ A Q J 10 8 7 3
                ♣ 2

West leads the ♠A and ♠K against 5◇ and switches to the ♡J at Trick 3.
What is your plan to make the remaining tricks?

C.

                ♠ 6 5
                ♡ Q 10 2
                ◇ 9 3 2
                ♣ A 10 8 7 4

◇K led

                ♠ A 3
                ♡ A K J 9 6 3
                ◇ A 7 6
                ♣ 6 5

What is your plan to make 4♡ when West leads the ◇K?

D.

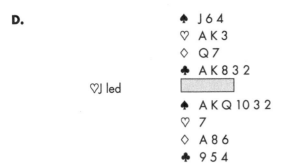

♠ J 6 4
♡ A K 3
◇ Q 7
♣ A K 8 3 2

♡J led

♠ A K Q 10 3 2
♡ 7
◇ A 8 6
♣ 9 5 4

Excelling yourself in the bidding, you reach 7♠. What is your plan when West leads the ♡J? (You will find that West has three trumps.)

E.

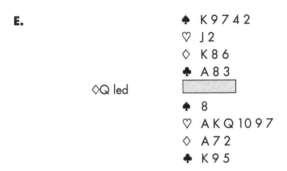

♠ K 9 7 4 2
♡ J 2
◇ K 8 6
♣ A 8 3

◇Q led

♠ 8
♡ A K Q 10 9 7
◇ A 7 2
♣ K 9 5

Both of you overbid on the same deal and you end in a dubious 6♡ contract. What is your plan when the ◇Q is led?

F.

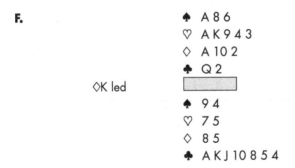

♠ A 8 6
♡ A K 9 4 3
◇ A 10 2
♣ Q 2

◇K led

♠ 9 4
♡ 7 5
◇ 8 5
♣ A K J 10 8 5 4

West leads the ◇K against 6♣. How will you plan the play?

ANSWERS

A. You must aim to set up dummy's diamonds to give you a spade discard. You win the first trick with the ♣A (so dummy's ♣K and ♣J will give you two entries later) and draw trumps. When you continue with the ◇K and ◇A, both defenders follow suit. You ruff a diamond in your hand and will still make the contract even if the suit breaks 4-2 and one of the defenders shows out on this trick. You lead the ♣4 to dummy's ♣J and ruff another diamond. You can then overtake the ♣Q with the ♣K and discard your spade loser on the established thirteenth card in diamonds.

PLAN: I will win the club lead with the ace, draw trumps and try to set up the diamonds. Since I can use the ♣J and ♣K as entries, I will make the contract even if diamonds break 4-2.

B. To avoid a heart loser, you will have to establish dummy's club suit. This can be done when the defenders' clubs split 4-3. Since dummy's two trumps will be needed as entries, you must play the ♣A at Trick 4 (after winning the heart switch) and then ruff a club. You cross to the ◇9 and ruff another club, return to dummy with the ◇K and ruff yet another club. You then draw any outstanding trump and return to dummy's remaining heart honor to discard a heart on the thirteenth club.

PLAN: I will win the switch with the ♡K, play the ♣A and ruff a club. I will use the ◇9 and ◇K as entries for two more club ruffs. Then I will cross to the ♡A to discard a heart on an established club.

C. You must aim to set up dummy's clubs for a spade discard. You win the diamond lead and, without touching the trump suit, duck a round of clubs. The defenders score two diamond tricks and West switches to a trump. What now?
  You win the trump switch in your hand, cross to the ♣A and ruff a club with a high trump, to avoid the risk of an overruff. West shows out on the third round of clubs and you return to dummy with a trump to the ten. Another club ruff with a high trump establishes the thirteenth club in dummy. You cross to the queen of trumps and discard your spade loser on the good ♣10.

PLAN: I will win the diamond lead and duck a club. I will then cross to the ♣A and set up the club suit (ruffing high twice, if necessary). I can then discard the spade loser.

D. When clubs break 3-2, you can establish the club suit and discard your two diamond losers. You win the heart lead and play the ♠A and ♠K, East showing out on the second round. Abandoning trumps for the moment, you play the two top clubs (both defenders following) and discard your last club on the ♡K. You then ruff a club with the ♠Q and return to dummy with the ♠J to discard your two diamond losers on the established ♣8 and ♣3.

> **PLAN: I will win with the ♡K and play the ♠AK. I then cash the two top clubs, throw a club on the ♡A and ruff a club high. Finally, I cross to the ♠J to discard the diamond losers on the two established clubs.**

E. You start with three potential losers and will need to set up dummy's spades and discard your minor-suit losers. For this to be possible, West will have to hold the ♠A and the suit will need to break 4-3. You win the diamond lead in your hand and lead a spade. Let's say that West goes in with the ♠A and plays the ◊J, won with the ◊K. You cash the ♠K, throwing a diamond, and ruff a spade with the ♡9. When everyone follows, you are home. You play the ace and jack of trumps, ruff another spade and draw the remaining trump(s). Finally, you return to dummy with the ♣A and play the established spot card in spades, discarding your club loser. If instead West does not rise with the ♠A, win with the ♠K and again set up a long spade to take one minor-suit discard.

> **PLAN: I will win with the ◊A and play a spade toward dummy. When West holds the ♠A and spades break 4-3, I can set up two discards.**

F. You have a potential loser in both spades and diamonds. If you can establish the heart suit, you will be able to discard at least one of these losers. Win the diamond lead and draw one round of trumps with the ace. To establish the hearts against a 4-2 break, you will need to use dummy's ♣Q as an entry. So, play the ace and king of hearts next and ruff a heart with a high trump. Let's assume that hearts break 4-2 and one of the defenders shows out on this trick. You return to dummy with the ♣Q and ruff the fourth round of hearts high. You can then draw any outstanding trump and return to the ♣A to discard your spade loser on the established winner in hearts.

> **PLAN: I will win with the ◊A and cross to the ♣A. Aiming to set up dummy's hearts, I will play the ace and king of the suit and ruff a heart high. If hearts break 4-2, I can return to the ♣Q and ruff another heart high. Eventually I will cross to the ♠A to discard a spade on the established winner in hearts.**

6

PLANNING WHEN TO DRAW TRUMPS

When you are planning a suit contract, one of the most important considerations is whether you should draw trumps immediately. The general rule is: Draw trumps immediately unless there is a good reason not to do so.

We will start the chapter by reminding ourselves why it is usually a good idea to draw trumps straight away.

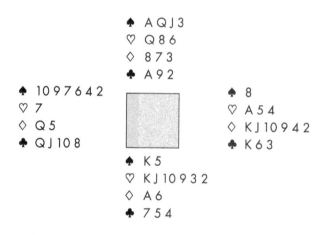

	♠ A Q J 3	
	♡ Q 8 6	
	♢ 8 7 3	
	♣ A 9 2	
♠ 10 9 7 6 4 2		♠ 8
♡ 7		♡ A 5 4
♢ Q 5		♢ K J 10 9 4 2
♣ Q J 10 8		♣ K 6 3
	♠ K 5	
	♡ K J 10 9 3 2	
	♢ A 6	
	♣ 7 5 4	

West	North	East	South
			1♡
pass	1♠	pass	2♡
pass	4♡	all pass	

West leads the ♣Q against 4♡ and you see these potential losers:

Losers: ♠ 0　♡ 1　♢ 1　♣ 2　　　**Total: 4**

Let's see what went wrong when the deal was originally played. The declarer won the club lead with dummy's ace and tried to discard one of his club losers on dummy's spade suit. He played a spade to the king and another spade back to dummy's ace. Disaster! East ruffed the second round of spades and the defenders scored two club tricks. Declarer won the diamond switch and, somewhat belatedly, played a trump. East won with the ace of trumps and cashed the ◇K to put the game two down.

Declarer was unlucky that the spades broke so badly, but there was no excuse for risking the contract in such a way. At Trick 2 he should have played a trump. The defenders were welcome to win with the ace and cash two clubs. When declarer won the return, he could draw the outstanding trumps and discard his diamond loser on the third round of spades. The contract would be his.

> **PLAN: I will win the club lead and draw trumps. Then I will throw my diamond loser on dummy's spades.**

Taking a discard before drawing trumps

On the previous deal it was safe to play trumps immediately, because the defenders did not have enough quick tricks to beat the contract when they won the first round of trumps. The situation is quite different on this deal:

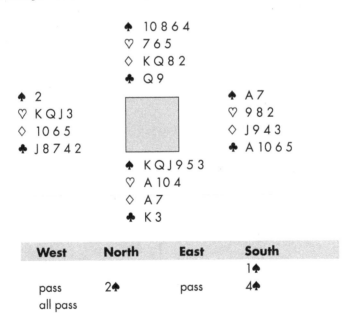

```
              ♠ 10 8 6 4
              ♡ 7 6 5
              ◇ K Q 8 2
              ♣ Q 9
♠ 2                          ♠ A 7
♡ K Q J 3                    ♡ 9 8 2
◇ 10 6 5                     ◇ J 9 4 3
♣ J 8 7 4 2                  ♣ A 10 6 5
              ♠ K Q J 9 5 3
              ♡ A 10 4
              ◇ A 7
              ♣ K 3
```

West	North	East	South
			1♠
pass	2♠	pass	4♠
all pass			

West leads the ♡K against your spade game and this is the loser position:

Losers: ♠ 1 ♡ 2 ◇ 0 ♣ 1   **Total:** 4

You win the opening lead with the ♡A. What are your prospects if your next move is to play a trump? Hopeless! The defenders will win with the ♠A and, before you can blink, cash two heart tricks and the ♣A. You will be one down.

You cannot afford to let the defenders gain the lead in trumps until you have discarded one of your heart losers. After winning the heart lead, you must play the ◇A, ◇K and ◇Q, throwing one of your heart losers. Only then can you safely play a trump. You will lose one trump, one heart and one club, making the contract.

> **PLAN: I will win the heart lead and play the three top diamonds, discarding a heart. Then I will draw trumps.**

A similar situation may arise when you have a possible finesse in the trump suit. Would you have played this spade slam correctly?

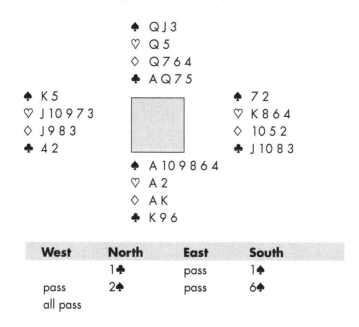

```
                    ♠ Q J 3
                    ♡ Q 5
                    ◇ Q 7 6 4
                    ♣ A Q 7 5
  ♠ K 5                              ♠ 7 2
  ♡ J 10 9 7 3                       ♡ K 8 6 4
  ◇ J 9 8 3                          ◇ 10 5 2
  ♣ 4 2                              ♣ J 10 8 3
                    ♠ A 10 9 8 6 4
                    ♡ A 2
                    ◇ A K
                    ♣ K 9 6
```

West	North	East	South
	1♣	pass	1♠
pass	2♠	pass	6♠
all pass			

West leads the ♡J and this is the loser situation:

Losers: ♠ 1 ♡ 1 ◇ 0 ♣ 0   Total: 2

You might as well try dummy's ♡Q on the first trick. As you rather expected, East covers with the king and you win with the ace. What now? Suppose you cross to dummy with a club and run the queen of trumps. All will be well if the finesse succeeds; indeed, you will be able to discard your heart loser later and score an overtrick. When the cards lie as in the diagram, the trump finesse will lose and West will gleefully cash a heart trick. Down one!

Since a trump finesse may cause you to lose the lead, you should attend to your heart loser before playing trumps. You cash the ◇A and ◇K and cross to the ♣Q to play the ◇Q, on which you discard the ♡2 from your hand. As it happens, all is well. Diamonds break 4-3 and no one ruffs the third round of diamonds. You have disposed of your heart loser and can now afford to lose a trump trick.

> **PLAN: I will play dummy's ♡Q. If East covers with the king, I will win with the ace and try to discard the heart loser on the diamonds. Then I can draw trumps.**

Establishing a discard before drawing trumps

Sometimes the need to establish a discard is so pressing that you cannot afford to draw trumps straight away. Would you have foreseen the danger on this deal?

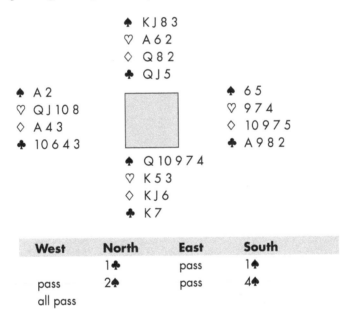

	♠ K J 8 3	
	♡ A 6 2	
	◇ Q 8 2	
	♣ Q J 5	

♠ A 2		♠ 6 5
♡ Q J 10 8		♡ 9 7 4
◇ A 4 3		◇ 10 9 7 5
♣ 10 6 4 3		♣ A 9 8 2

	♠ Q 10 9 7 4	
	♡ K 5 3	
	◇ K J 6	
	♣ K 7	

West	North	East	South
	1♣	pass	1♠
pass	2♠	pass	4♠
all pass			

How will you plan the play in 4♠ when West leads the ♡Q? This is the loser position:

Losers: ♠ 1 ♡ 1 ◇ 1 ♣ 1   **Total: 4**

The only way to reduce the loser count is to discard your heart loser on dummy's clubs. What will happen if you win the heart lead and play a trump? West will win with the ♠A and play another heart, setting up a defensive trick in the suit. It will be too late to establish the clubs then, because the defenders will cash a total of four tricks when you force out the ♣A.

You need to establish a discard on the clubs immediately, before your second heart stopper has been removed. The first essential step is to win the heart lead with the king, retaining dummy's ♡A as an entry. You then lead the ♣K. If East ducks this, you persevere with a second round of clubs to the queen and ace. Because you won the opening heart lead in your hand, you can now win the heart continuation with dummy's ace. You discard your heart loser on the ♣J and only then play trumps. After drawing trumps, you will establish the diamond suit and make your game.

> **PLAN: I will win the heart lead with the king and set up the clubs. I can then throw a heart on dummy's third club winner, draw trumps and establish the diamonds.**

Taking a ruff before drawing trumps

When you will need to take a ruff in the dummy, you must not give the defenders a chance to draw dummy's last trump.

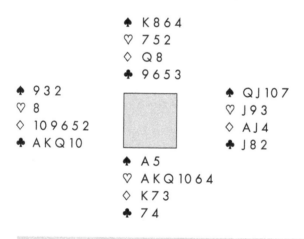

West	North	East	South
			1♡
pass	2♡	pass	4♡
all pass			

West leads the ♣A against 4♡ and continues with the ♣K and ♣Q. How will you plan the contract? This is the loser position:

Losers: ♠0 ♡0 ◇2 ♣2   **Total: 4**

You ruff the third round of clubs and see that you will need to ruff a diamond in dummy, to avoid losing two tricks in that suit. What will happen if you play the ace and king of trumps next? You will go down! West will show out on the second round of trumps. When you subsequently play a diamond to the queen, preparing for your diamond ruff, East will win with the ◇A and play a third round of trumps. A diamond ruff will no longer be possible and you will go one down.

Play one round of trumps if you wish, but you must then play a diamond to the queen. Let's say that East wins and switches to the ♠Q. You win with the ♠A and draw a second round of trumps, West showing out. You then cash the ◇K and ruff a diamond in dummy. Finally you return to your hand with a club ruff, draw East's last trump and make the remaining tricks.

PLAN: I will ruff the third club, draw just one round of trumps and then play a diamond to the queen, preparing for a diamond ruff.

Let's next see a deal where entries are difficult and it is essential to take a ruff in dummy before you play even one round of trumps.

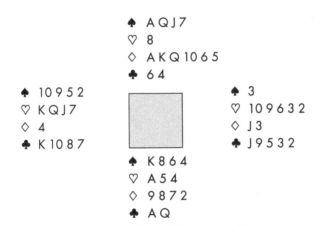

```
                    ♠ A Q J 7
                    ♡ 8
                    ◇ A K Q 10 6 5
                    ♣ 6 4
  ♠ 10 9 5 2                        ♠ 3
  ♡ K Q J 7                         ♡ 10 9 6 3 2
  ◇ 4                               ◇ J 3
  ♣ K 10 8 7                        ♣ J 9 5 3 2
                    ♠ K 8 6 4
                    ♡ A 5 4
                    ◇ 9 8 7 2
                    ♣ A Q
```

Playing with your favorite partner, you reach a splendid grand slam in spades. How will you play the contract when West leads the ♡K? This is the initial loser situation:

Losers: ♠0 ♡2 ◇0 ♣1   **Total:** 3

You can discard the ♣Q and one heart on dummy's surplus diamond winners, so you will need to ruff the other heart in dummy. You win the heart lead with the ace. Let's see what will happen if you fail to make a plan and cross to the ♠A. You will go down! When you continue with the ♠Q, East will show out. You can cross to the ♣A to ruff a heart with the ♠7. What then? You can draw a third round of trumps with dummy's jack but there is no entry to the South hand to draw West's last trump. If instead you try to recover by taking the club finesse at Trick 4, you will again go down.

The contract is easy if you take the trouble to make a plan. After winning with the ♡A, you immediately ruff a heart with the ♠7. You then play the ♠AQJ, return to your hand with the ♣A and draw West's last trump with the ♠K. You can then run the diamond suit to discard your remaining two losers.

> **PLAN: I will win the heart lead, ruff a heart with the ♠7 and draw three rounds of trumps with the ace, queen and jack. If trumps are 4-1, I can cross to the ♣A to draw the last trump, before running the diamonds.**

Remember these points

- The general rule is: Draw trumps immediately unless there is a good reason not to.

- When you are planning to ruff a loser or two in the dummy, you may have to delay drawing trumps until after taking the ruffs.

- Sometimes the need to take a discard, or to establish a suit that will provide a discard, is more pressing than the need to draw trumps.

Now try these...

A.

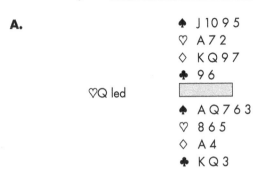

♠ J 10 9 5
♥ A 7 2
♦ K Q 9 7
♣ 9 6

♥Q led

♠ A Q 7 6 3
♥ 8 6 5
♦ A 4
♣ K Q 3

Expressing your plan as concisely as you can, how will you play 4♠?

B.

♠ A
♥ Q J 10 6
♦ Q 10 5 2
♣ 10 7 6 2

♠2 led

♠ K Q J 10 9 7 6
♥ A 9 8 4
♦ —
♣ Q 5

West leads the ♠2 against 4♠. How will you plan the play?

C.

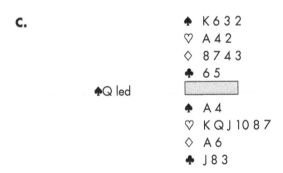

♠ K 6 3 2
♥ A 4 2
♦ 8 7 4 3
♣ 6 5

♠Q led

♠ A 4
♥ K Q J 10 8 7
♦ A 6
♣ J 8 3

West leads the ♠Q against your contract of 4♥. What is your plan?

D.

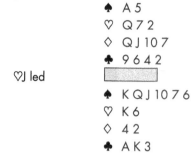

♠ A 5
♡ Q 7 2
◇ Q J 10 7
♣ 9 6 4 2

♡J led

♠ K Q J 10 7 6
♡ K 6
◇ 4 2
♣ A K 3

West leads the ♡J against 4♠. How will you plan the play?

E.

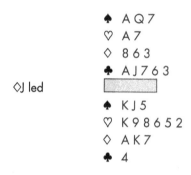

♠ A Q 7
♡ A 7
◇ 8 6 3
♣ A J 7 6 3

◇J led

♠ K J 5
♡ K 9 8 6 5 2
◇ A K 7
♣ 4

What is your plan for 6♡ when West leads the ◇J?

F.

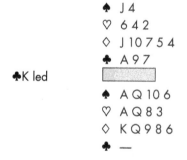

♠ J 4
♡ 6 4 2
◇ J 10 7 5 4
♣ A 9 7

♣K led

♠ A Q 10 6
♡ A Q 8 3
◇ K Q 9 8 6
♣ —

How will you play 5◇ when West leads the ♣K?

ANSWERS

A. You have five potential losers, including one in trumps. It is much too dangerous to win the heart lead and run the ♠J. If the trump finesse loses, the defenders will cash three more winners in the side suits to beat the contract. Instead, you must attempt to discard a heart loser on the diamond suit. Play the ◇A, ◇K and ◇Q, throwing a heart. If no one ruffs, you can then run the ♠J, seeking an overtrick. If someone does happen to ruff the third diamond winner, you can eventually re-enter dummy by ruffing the third round of clubs to take a trump finesse.

> **PLAN: I will win with the ♡A and play three top diamonds, discarding a heart loser.**

B. You have one possible loser in hearts and two in clubs. That is a total of only three losers — exactly what you need to make a contract of 4♠! Nevertheless, a careless player might go down on such a contract. Suppose you win with the bare ♠A and decide to take advantage of being in dummy by running the ♡Q. West may win with the ♡K and give East a heart ruff. The defenders may then take two club winners, followed by another heart ruff. Down two!

You can avoid any such disaster by drawing trumps. At Trick 2 you reach your hand by ruffing a diamond and draw the remaining trumps. There is no entry to dummy for a heart finesse, but this does not matter since you can afford a heart loser. You play ace and another heart, setting up the suit, and the contract is yours.

> **PLAN: I will win the trump lead, reach my hand with a diamond ruff and draw the remaining trumps. I will then establish the heart suit.**

C. You must aim to ruff the third round of clubs in dummy. Suppose you make the mistake of drawing a round of trumps after winning the spade lead. You are likely to go down when trumps are 3-1! When you subsequently surrender two club tricks, the defender with the three trumps will have a chance to play a second and third round of trumps. How will you score a club ruff then?

Instead you should win the spade lead and give up a round of clubs. The defenders are welcome to win and switch to trumps. You will win the first round of trumps and give up another club. If the defenders play another trump, you will still have a trump left in dummy. You can ruff your remaining club with the ♡A and then return to the South hand to draw the last trump.

> **PLAN: I will win the spade lead and give up two rounds of clubs before drawing any trumps, eventually ruffing the third club with the ♡A.**

D. You have a total of four potential side-suit losers and must aim to discard the club loser on dummy's diamonds. You will not be able to draw any trumps before setting up the discard because the ♠A is the only entry to dummy.

Play low from dummy at Trick 1. East cannot rise with the ♡A or you would have two heart winners and a club discard. You win with the ♡K and immediately lead a diamond to the queen. When East wins and plays a club, you win with the ace and play another diamond. It makes no difference which defender wins the second round of diamonds. You will win the club continuation and draw two rounds of trumps with the king and ace. You will then discard the ♣3 on an established diamond winner in dummy. Later you will draw the outstanding trump(s) and claim your contract.

PLAN: I will win with the ♡K and lead a diamond. Eventually I can set up a diamond winner in dummy and reach it with the ♠A to discard my club loser.

E. You must hope that trumps break 3-2, which will allow you to escape for one trump loser. To avoid losing a diamond trick too, you will have to set up dummy's club suit for a discard. You win the diamond lead and cannot afford to draw two rounds of trumps immediately because you need to use dummy's ♡A as an entry. Instead, you cross to the ♣A and ruff a club in your hand. You continue with the king and ace of trumps, before ruffing another club. If the clubs break 4-3, as well as the trumps breaking 3-2, you will make the contract. You cross to the ♠Q and ruff yet another club. The ♠A will serve as an entry to reach the thirteenth club, on which you will discard your diamond loser. Your only loser will be in the trump suit.

PLAN: I will win the diamond lead and try to set up the clubs, to discard a diamond. Since I need the ♡A as an entry, I must take one club ruff before playing the king and ace of trumps.

F. Suppose your first move, after winning with the ♣A, is to play a trump. East may win and switch to a heart. You will then go down when West holds both the major-suit kings. Instead, you should set up some discards from dummy by running the ♠J at Trick 2. If this loses to West's ♠K, he cannot attack hearts from his side of the table. You will ruff the next club and play a trump. If East wins with the ◇A and switches to a heart, you can rise with the ♡A, draw trumps, and discard two hearts from dummy on the third and fourth rounds of spades.

If instead East covers the ♠J with the ♠K, you will win with the ♠A and play trumps. You can then discard one heart on the third round of spades.

PLAN: I will win with the ♣A and run the ♠J, setting up two discards for dummy's heart losers if the finesse loses.

PART II

PLANNING A NOTRUMP CONTRACT

7

HOW TO PLAN A NOTRUMP CONTRACT

We have already seen that the easiest method of planning a suit contract is to count the losers from the long-trump hand. In notrump contracts it makes more sense to begin by counting the immediately available winners in each suit — in other words, the top tricks. Suppose you reach a contract of 3NT and can sèe seven immediate winners when the dummy goes down. You must then plan to establish and score two extra winners, before the defenders can cash enough tricks to defeat you.

Let's see a straightforward example of this:

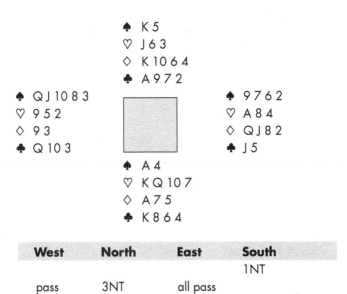

West	North	East	South
			1NT
pass	3NT	all pass	

West leads the ♠Q against 3NT. These are the immediate winners (top tricks) in each suit:

Spades: Two. You can score two tricks with the ace and king.
Hearts: None. You cannot score any tricks until the ♡A is knocked out.
Diamonds: Two.
Clubs: Two.

Using a similar format to the one that we used for expressing the losers in a suit contract, we will summarize this as:

Top Tricks: ♠ 2   ♡ 0   ◇ 2   ♣ 2   **Total: 6**

The next step is to make a plan for the contract. To make 3NT, you will need three extra tricks to bring the total to nine. Where can these come from? The heart suit will provide three extra tricks, once the ♡A has been knocked out. Is that a good plan, then, to play hearts after winning with the ♠A? Yes, because you still have a stopper remaining in the spade suit and you will easily score nine tricks before the defenders can score five.

> **PLAN: I will win the spade lead and establish three extra tricks in hearts.**

Now let's see a 3NT contract where the defenders quickly remove your only stopper in their main suit:

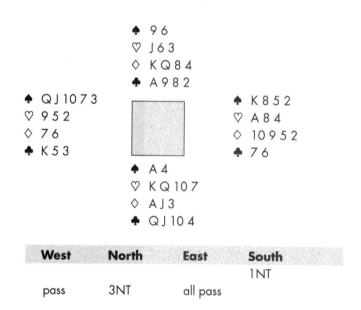

West	North	East	South
			1NT
pass	3NT	all pass	

West leads the ♠Q against 3NT and these are your immediate winners in each suit:

Spades: One with the ace.
Hearts: None. You cannot score any tricks until the ♡A is knocked out.
Diamonds: Four tricks are ready to run.
Clubs: One with the ace.

We summarize this as:

Top Tricks: ♠ 1 ♡ 0 ♢ 4 ♣ 1   **Total: 6**

As on the previous deal, the heart suit will provide three extra tricks, once the ♡A has been knocked out. Is it a good plan, then, to play hearts after winning with the ♠A? Not this time, because the defenders will score five tricks before you can score nine. They will take the ♡A immediately and defeat you by scoring four spades and one heart.

What else can you try? You must look to the club suit for the three extra tricks that you need. If West holds the ♣K, you can pick it up with a repeated finesse and score four club tricks without losing the lead. This plan gives you a 50% chance of success, which is a distinct improvement on the near certainty of failure if you play hearts instead. So, this is the plan you will choose:

> **PLAN: I will win the spade lead and run the ♣Q. If West holds the ♣K, the club suit will provide the three extra tricks that I need.**

On this particular deal, the best available plan does not guarantee the contract and you will need a bit of luck to succeed. Still, remember the wise saying: Half a loaf is better than none!

Remember these points

- When planning a notrump contract, you count your 'top tricks' (immediate winners) rather than your losers.

- You count the available top tricks in each suit, arriving at a total that will often be less than that required to make the contract.

- You must then seek a safe (or the safest available) plan to set up the extra tricks that you need.

- Your plan must give you a chance of making the contract before the defenders can score enough tricks to defeat you.

Now try these...

A.

♠ 10 6 5
♡ K Q 7 6
◇ J 6
♣ A Q J 10

♠2 led
[ ]

♠ J 9 4
♡ A J 8
◇ A Q 10
♣ 9 7 5 2

West leads the ♠2 against 3NT and the defenders score four tricks in the suit, which divides 4-3. West then switches to the ♡10.
    (a) How many top tricks do you hold in each suit?
    (b) What is the total number of top tricks?
    (c) What is your plan?

B.

♠ 8 3
♡ Q J 6
◇ Q J 9 6
♣ A Q 9 4

♠6 led
[ ]

♠ A J
♡ A 10 9 3
◇ K 10 5
♣ J 10 7 6

West leads the ♠6 against 3NT, East playing the ♠K.
    (a) How many top tricks do you hold in each suit?
    (b) What is the total number of top tricks?
    (c) What is your plan?

ANSWERS

A. (a) You have four top tricks in hearts, one in diamonds (the ace) and one in clubs (the ace).

(b) Top tricks: ♠0 ♡4 ◇1 ♣1 Total: 6.

(c) You need three extra tricks to make 3NT. The diamond suit cannot possibly yield more than two extra tricks, even if East holds the ◇K. You must therefore play for four club tricks, hoping that West holds the ♣K. Win the heart switch with the ♡J and play a club to dummy's queen. If the finesse wins, return to the ♡A and finesse dummy's ♣J. If clubs break 3-2, the ♣A will bring down West's ♣K and you will have four club tricks for the contract. If West began with ♣Kxxx, another club finesse is required. You will cross to the ◇A to finesse the ♣10.

PLAN: I will win the heart switch with the ♡J and finesse West for the ♣K, hoping to score four club tricks.

As before, you can see how abbreviated a typical plan is. It would not be so clear if it included all the details of going to and fro between the hands.

B. (a) You have one certain trick, the ace, in each of spades, hearts and clubs.

(b) Top tricks: ♠1 ♡1 ◇0 ♣1 Total: 3.

(c) Starting with only three top tricks is not a promising sign! You cannot afford to play diamonds to generate extra tricks, because the defenders would then score the ◇A and at least four spades. To make the contract, you must score four club tricks and four heart tricks. For this to be possible both the club and heart finesses will need to succeed.

You win the spade lead and run the ♣J. If this wins, as you must hope, you continue to finesse clubs until West's ♣K appears. You then run the ♡Q. If it's your lucky day and this finesse wins too, you will make the contract.

PLAN: I will win the spade lead and finesse in both clubs and hearts. If both finesses win, I will make the contract.

PLANNING A HOLD-UP PLAY IN NOTRUMP

When a defender leads a suit where you hold three cards headed by the ace, your sole stopper, it is usually right to hold up the ace until the third round (in other words you allow the defenders to win the first two rounds). What is the point of that? You hope to exhaust the holding of the other defender. You can then afford to lose the lead to him, in your search for extra tricks; he will not be able to return the suit that was led originally.

Let's see a straightforward example of a hold-up play:

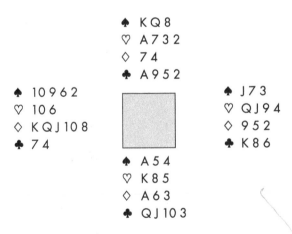

	♠ K Q 8	
	♡ A 7 3 2	
	◊ 7 4	
	♣ A 9 5 2	

♠ 10 9 6 2		♠ J 7 3
♡ 10 6		♡ Q J 9 4
◊ K Q J 10 8		◊ 9 5 2
♣ 7 4		♣ K 8 6

	♠ A 5 4	
	♡ K 8 5	
	◊ A 6 3	
	♣ Q J 10 3	

West	North	East	South
			1♣
pass	1♡	pass	1NT
pass	3NT	all pass	

West leads the ◊K against 3NT. Suppose you win with the ◊A immediately, thinking that a hold-up is something that happens only in a bank. You have these quick winners available:

Top Tricks: ♠ 3   ♡ 2   ◊ 1   ♣ 1   **Total: 7**

Only club suit offers you the chance of the two extra tricks that you need. When you run the ♣Q, East wins with the ♣K and returns a diamond. Not good, is it? West will score four diamond tricks and you will be down one.

Instead you should hold up the ◇A for two rounds, aiming to exhaust East of his cards in the suit. It is a sound general rule that you should hold up an ace for two rounds, if it is safe to do so. You win the third round of diamonds with the ace and again run the ♣Q. East wins with the ♣K and... what a difference! He has no diamonds left. Whatever other suit he returns, you will be able to win and score nine tricks for the contract.

PLAN: I will hold up the ◇A until the third round and then run the ♣Q.

On that deal only East could gain the lead in clubs, because the club finesse was into his hand; it was therefore fairly certain that a hold-up in diamonds would give you the contract. Even when you need to knock out an ace in one of the other suits, and either defender might hold that ace, it can still prove beneficial to hold up. Look at this deal:

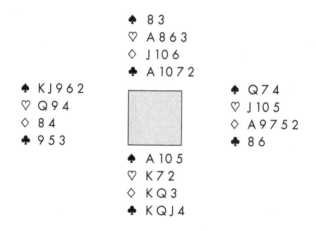

	♠ 8 3	
	♡ A 8 6 3	
	◇ J 10 6	
	♣ A 10 7 2	
♠ K J 9 6 2		♠ Q 7 4
♡ Q 9 4		♡ J 10 5
◇ 8 4		◇ A 9 7 5 2
♣ 9 5 3		♣ 8 6
	♠ A 10 5	
	♡ K 7 2	
	◇ K Q 3	
	♣ K Q J 4	

West	North	East	South
			1♣
pass	1♡	pass	2NT
pass	3NT	all pass	

West leads the ♠6 against 3NT and (having recently bought an excellent book on the subject) you pause to make a plan. You start from this position:

Top Tricks: ♠ 1   ♡ 2   ◇ 0   ♣ 4   **Total: 7**

You need two extra tricks to bring the total to nine and these can easily be established in diamonds. What will happen if you win with the ♠A at Trick 1 and play a diamond? It's not difficult to see. East will win with the ◇A and return a spade. The defenders will score four spades and one diamond, putting you down one.

To make the contract, you must hold up the ♠A for two rounds; East will then have no spades left. When you seek your extra tricks by playing on diamonds, your luck is in — East (the safe hand, with no spades) holds the ◇A. Whatever suit he chooses to return, you will win and claim your nine tricks for the contract. If East did have a spade left, the suit would be breaking 4-4 and pose no threat.

> **PLAN: I will hold up the ♠A until the third round and then play diamonds, hoping that East holds the ◇A.**

On the deal that we have just seen, you still needed a measure of luck after the hold-up play. If West had held the ◇A, along with five spades, you would have gone down. (There would have been no way to make the contract, in that case).

Holding up a king

When your right-hand opponent has won the first trick with the ace, you may have the opportunity to hold up your king on the next round. That's the case here:

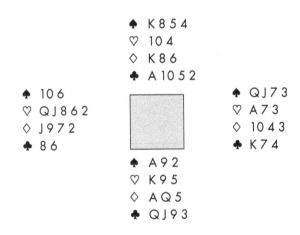

	♠ K 8 5 4		
	♡ 10 4		
	◇ K 8 6		
	♣ A 10 5 2		

♠ 10 6   ♠ Q J 7 3
♡ Q J 8 6 2   ♡ A 7 3
◇ J 9 7 2   ◇ 10 4 3
♣ 8 6   ♣ K 7 4

♠ A 9 2
♡ K 9 5
◇ A Q 5
♣ Q J 9 3

West	North	East	South
			1NT
pass	2♣	pass	2◇
pass	3NT	all pass	

Counting top tricks

When you count your top tricks in a notrump contract,
you should include any extra trick that has been
established by the opening lead. For example, ♣AQ4
in your hand would normally be only one top trick. If
West has chosen a club (into your A-Q) as his opening
lead, you will count two top tricks in clubs.

West leads the ♡6 and East wins with the ♡A. What plan will you make when East returns the ♡7? This is the top trick position (including the trick already established for the ♡K):

Top Tricks: ♠ 2   ♡ 1   ◊ 3   ♣ 1   **Total:** 7

Suppose you win the second round of hearts with the king. You will need to set up the club suit to bring your total to nine tricks. You run the ♣Q to East's ♣K and he still has a heart left! He leads the ♡3 to his partner's hand and the defenders score four hearts and a club to beat you.

To prevent this undesirable outcome, you should hold up the ♡K on the second round. West is welcome to win and clear the heart suit. When East wins with the ♣K, he will have no heart to return. Nine tricks will be yours.

> **PLAN: I will hold up the ♡K until the third round and then finesse clubs into the safe hand.**

When it is wrong to hold up

We have already seen the advantage that a hold-up play may bring — it can break communication between the defenders, after which you can establish extra tricks by allowing the safe hand to win the lead. Sometimes a hold-up play would involve a big risk, namely that the defender may make a killing switch to a different suit. In such a case, it may be best to win the opening lead and hope to cash or safely establish the tricks that you need. Look at this deal:

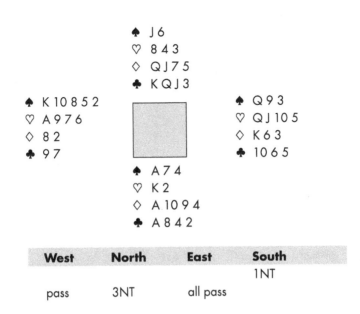

	♠ J 6	
	♡ 8 4 3	
	◇ Q J 7 5	
	♣ K Q J 3	

♠ K 10 8 5 2		♠ Q 9 3
♡ A 9 7 6		♡ Q J 10 5
◇ 8 2		◇ K 6 3
♣ 9 7		♣ 10 6 5

	♠ A 7 4	
	♡ K 2	
	◇ A 10 9 4	
	♣ A 8 4 2	

West	North	East	South
			1NT
pass	3NT	all pass	

West leads the ♠5 against 3NT. What plan will you make? This is the top trick position:

Top Tricks: ♠ 1 ♡ 0 ◇ 1 ♣ 4   **Total: 6**

It is possible that West has led from a combination headed by the ♠KQ, so you might as well try your luck with dummy's ♠J. East covers with the ♠Q and you must now decide whether to hold up your ♣A. What would your decision be?

If you hold up the ♠A, you are taking a risk that East will switch to hearts and the defenders may then cash at least five tricks against you. A hold-up in spades would not even help you very much. Suppose the defenders fail to find the heart switch; they persevere with spades and you win the third round. To bring your total to nine, you will have to score four diamond tricks and the diamond finesse is into the dangerous hand. If it wins, the contract is yours; if it loses, the spade hold-up will not have helped you at all!

So, a hold-up cannot achieve anything and it may cost a lot if East switches to hearts. You should therefore win the first round of spades, cross to dummy with a club and run the ◇Q in the hope that East holds the ◇K. You will then be able to score four clubs, four diamonds and the ♠A.

> **PLAN: I will win the spade lead, cross to dummy with a club and finesse in diamonds, hoping to score four diamond tricks.**

Let's see another deal where it would not be wise to hold up.

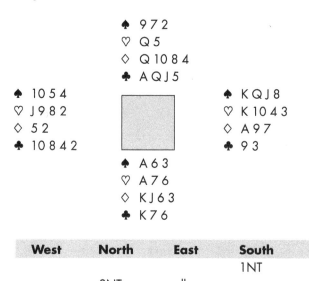

| ♠ 9 7 2 |
| ♡ Q 5 |
| ◇ Q 10 8 4 |
| ♣ A Q J 5 |

♠ 10 5 4   ♠ K Q J 8
♡ J 9 8 2   ♡ K 10 4 3
◇ 5 2   ◇ A 9 7
♣ 10 8 4 2   ♣ 9 3

          ♠ A 6 3
          ♡ A 7 6
          ◇ K J 6 3
          ♣ K 7 6

West	North	East	South
			1NT
pass	3NT	all pass	

West leads the ♡2 against 3NT. You try your luck with dummy's ♡Q but East produces the ♡K. What plan will you make? This is the top trick position:

Top Tricks: ♠ 1 ♡ 1 ◇ 0 ♣ 4   **Total: 6**

The diamond suit will produce the three extra tricks that you need, but you must do your best to prevent the defenders from scoring more than three tricks to go with the ◇A. The first decision is whether to hold up in hearts. What do you think?

Suppose you follow the general guideline of holding up an ace for two rounds. When East's ♡K wins the first trick, he will have the chance to switch to the ♠K. You would then have no way to avoid the loss of one heart, three spades and the ◇A. Down one!

Since West has led the ♡2, it is almost certain that hearts are breaking 4-4. (It is common practice to lead the fourth-best card from a suit that contains at least one honor but is not headed by an honor sequence. If West's fourth-best heart is the 2, he cannot have a fifth-best heart!) You can therefore afford to win the first round of hearts and then establish the diamonds. The defenders will be able to take no more than three hearts and one diamond.

PLAN: I will win the heart lead immediately and set up the diamonds.

Holding up with two stoppers

Sometimes it is right to hold up, even when you have two stoppers in the suit that has been led. This is likely to be the case when you will need to knock out two defensive high cards (thereby losing the lead twice) in order to arrive at your trick target. The next deal will make this idea clearer:

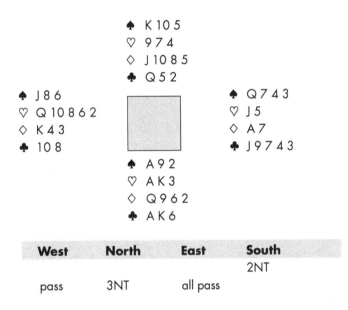

West	North	East	South
			2NT
pass	3NT	all pass	

West leads the ♡6 against 3NT, East playing the ♡J. What plan will you make? This is the top trick position:

Top Tricks: ♠ 2   ♡ 2   ◇ 0   ♣ 3   **Total: 7**

To create the two extra tricks that you need, you will have to set up the diamond suit. You have two stoppers to knock out in diamonds. In the dangerous case where hearts are 5-2, you must try to prevent the defenders from scoring three hearts to go with the two top diamonds.

Suppose you win the first round of hearts and play a diamond. East will win with the ◇A and return his remaining heart. Ducking the second round of hearts will not help at all, since West will win and then clear the heart suit. When you play another diamond West will win with the ◇K and cash two more hearts to beat the contract.

To make the contract, you need to hold up on the first trick even though you hold two heart stoppers. East's ♡J wins and he continues with a second round, which you win. The defenders cannot now beat the contract. If East wins the first round of diamonds, as before, he will have no heart to return. If instead West wins the first diamond, it will not do him much good to clear the heart suit; East will win the second round of diamonds and will have no way to reach the two established hearts in his partner's hand.

> **PLAN: I will let East's ♡J win and take the heart continuation. It will then be safe to establish the diamonds (unless West happens to hold both the ◇A and ◇K).**

The same technique, holding up with a double stopper, can save you a guess when you have two aces to knock out:

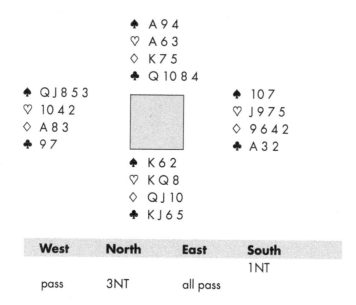

West	North	East	South
			1NT
pass	3NT	all pass	

West leads the ♠5 against 3NT and, very commendably, you pause to make a plan. You start with these immediate winners:

Top Tricks: ♠2 ♡3 ◇0 ♣0   **Total: 5**

You can set up three extra tricks from the club suit but you will still need a diamond trick to make the contract. Let's see what may happen if you win the first round of spades. You win East's ♠10 with the ♠K and lead a club to dummy's queen. East wins with the ♣A and returns his remaining spade, the defenders clearing the suit. When you play a diamond, seeking your ninth trick, West will win and cash enough spades to beat you.

As the cards lie, you could have made the contract by leading a diamond at Trick 2. That's because West happens to hold the diamond ace and not the club ace. If West were to win the first round of diamonds with the ace and clear the spade suit, East would have no spade to play when he won with the ♣A later.

So, if you win the first round of spades, you will have to make a lucky guess as to which minor-suit ace you knock out first. Good bridge players hate having to guess! Since you have two stoppers to knock out, and do not fear a switch to any other suit, you should hold up on the first round of spades. East returns his remaining spade and you win in one hand or the other. It now makes no difference which minor-suit ace you knock out first. When East takes his ace, he will have no spade to play. Indeed, you will end with an overtrick, scoring three clubs and two diamonds in addition to the five top tricks you had at the start.

> **PLAN: I will let East's ♠10 win and take the spade continuation. It will then be safe to establish winners in both minors (unless West happens to hold both the ◇A and the ♣A).**

Remember these points

- When you hold the ace of the suit that has been led, it is normally right to hold up the ace for two rounds. The intention is to leave the other defender with no cards in the suit.

- Think carefully about holding up an ace when this will give the defenders a chance to put the contract in danger with a switch to a different suit.

- When you need to knock out two of the opponents' winners to achieve the tricks you need, it may be right to hold up in a suit even if you have two stoppers.

Now try these...

A.

                    ♠ Q J 10 5
                    ♡ Q 10 4
                    ◇ J 8 5 3
                    ♣ 7 4

♣5 led

                    ♠ K 2
                    ♡ A K J 3
                    ◇ A 9 7 2
                    ♣ A 9 2

How will you play 3NT when West leads the ♣5, East playing the ♣Q?

B.

                    ♠ 8 7 4
                    ♡ A J 3
                    ◇ K J 8 7 2
                    ♣ K 4

♠2 led

                    ♠ A 10 6
                    ♡ K 10 7
                    ◇ 10 9 5
                    ♣ A Q 6 3

You bid to 3NT and West leads the ♣2, East playing the ♠J. What is your plan for the contract?

C.

                    ♠ 5 4
                    ♡ 7 5 2
                    ◇ A J 10 9 3
                    ♣ Q J 2

♠6 led

                    ♠ A 9 2
                    ♡ Q 10 3
                    ◇ K Q 6 5
                    ♣ A 10 6

West leads the ♣6 against 3NT, East playing the ♣Q. How will you plan the play?

D.

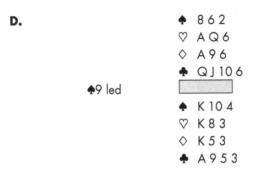

♠ 8 6 2
♡ A Q 6
◇ A 9 6
♣ Q J 10 6

♠9 led

♠ K 10 4
♡ K 8 3
◇ K 5 3
♣ A 9 5 3

North opens 1♣, East overcalls 1♠ and you end in 3NT. What is your plan when West leads the ♠9 and East plays the ♠J?

E.

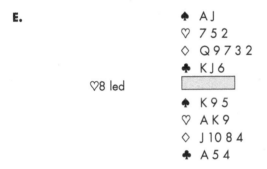

♠ A J
♡ 7 5 2
◇ Q 9 7 3 2
♣ K J 6

♡8 led

♠ K 9 5
♡ A K 9
◇ J 10 8 4
♣ A 5 4

East opens 1♡ and you overcall 1NT on the South cards, raised to 3NT by North. How will you play when West leads the ♡8, East following with the ♡10?

F.

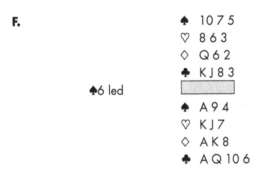

♠ 10 7 5
♡ 8 6 3
◇ Q 6 2
♣ K J 8 3

♠6 led

♠ A 9 4
♡ K J 7
◇ A K 8
♣ A Q 10 6

You reach 3NT and West leads the ♠6, East playing the ♠Q. What is your plan?

ANSWERS

A. You have six top tricks and can establish three more in the spade suit by knocking out the ace. You must take steps to reduce the chance of losing four clubs and the ♠A. This can be achieved by holding up the ♣A for two rounds. In the dangerous case where clubs are 5-3, this will remove East's club holding. After winning the third round of clubs, you will play the ♠K. When (by good fortune) it is East who holds the ♠A, you will make the contract. Either he will have no club to return, or clubs will have started 4-4 and the defenders will be able to score only three clubs and the ♠A.

PLAN: I will hold up the ♣A for two rounds and knock out the ♠A, hoping East holds that card.

B. You have six top tricks and will need to set up the diamonds to make the contract. Remember the guideline: Hold up an ace for two rounds if it is safe to do so. The defenders cannot effectively switch to clubs or hearts, so you should hold up the ♠A for two rounds. This will exhaust East's spades when the suit is divided 4-3, as indicated by the opening lead of the ♠2. You will then make the contract when East holds the ◊A and ◊Q. He will have no spade to play when he gains the lead twice in diamonds.

Suppose instead that you mistakenly hold up the ♠A only once. East would still have a spade left when he won the first diamond trick! You would lose two diamonds and three spades, going down one.

PLAN: I will hold up the ♠A for two rounds and then run the ◊10. When East holds the ◊AQ, he will have no spade to play.

C. You should not hold up in spades. One reason is that East would have a chance to switch to hearts, which could give the defenders four tricks in that suit. The main reason is that a hold-up in spades is unlikely to help you. There isn't much point in removing East's spade holding, because when you take the club finesse this will be into the dangerous West hand. Apart from anything else, you will need the club finesse to win in order to score nine tricks.

PLAN: I will win the spade lead, cross to a diamond honor and run the ♣Q.

D. You have seven top tricks, including one in spades, and the club suit will give you two more tricks even if the club finesse loses. What you cannot afford is to lose one club trick (to the ♣K) and four spade tricks. How does the spade suit lie? If West's ♠9 is a singleton and East overcalled on ♠AQJxxx, the contract is safe; if the club finesse loses, West will have no spade to return. What if West began with ♠9x and East overcalled on ♠AQJxx? In that case it is essential that you hold up the ♠K at Trick 1. East is welcome to clear the spade suit because West will then have no spade to play if a subsequent club finesse loses.

PLAN: I will hold up the ♠K for one round. If the club finesse then loses, West will have no spade to play.

E. You have six top tricks. If you can add three diamond tricks, this will bring the total to nine. Meanwhile, you must try to prevent the defenders from scoring three hearts and two diamonds. Suppose you win the first trick with the ♡K and play a diamond. If West holds the ◊A or ◊K, he will win the first round of diamonds and return his remaining heart. East will then have too many hearts to cash when he wins with the ◊A.

A better idea is to hold up at Trick 1, playing your ♡9 under East's ♡10. You win the heart continuation with the ♡K and play a diamond. When the defenders hold one diamond honor each, there is nothing they can do. West will have no heart to play when he wins a trick with his diamond stopper.

(If East holds the ◊A and ◊K, which is quite possible after his opening bid, you cannot make the contract.)

PLAN: I will duck East's ♡10 and win the next heart. When West holds one of the diamond stoppers, he will then have no heart to play.

F. You have eight top tricks and will need a trick from the heart suit to make the notrump game. Aiming to break communications between the defenders, you should hold up the ♠A for the first two rounds. West persists with a third round of spades and East discards a club. What now? You cross to dummy with a club (or a diamond) and lead toward your ♡KJ7. Which honor should you play, the king or the jack? It is not a guess, because if West holds the ♡A you cannot make the contract! When West holds the ♡A, he is certain to score that card and four winners in spades. Your only chance is therefore to rise with the ♡K in the hope that East holds the ♡A. When he does, you will have nine tricks and your contract.

PLAN: I will hold up the ♠A until the third round, cross to a club honor and play a heart to the king.

9

ESTABLISHING A SUIT IN NOTRUMP

When you have a trump suit at your disposal, establishing a suit is usually quite easy. Whether or not you have to duck a round at some stage, you can ruff a round or two until the opponents' cards are exhausted. This mechanism is not available when establishing a suit in a notrump contract, but the concept of ducking is still important. We will look at this technique first.

Ducking to preserve an entry

We will start with a fairly simple deal that illustrates the potential advantage of ducking an early round of a suit.

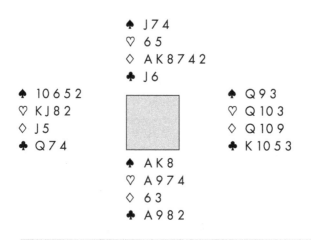

        ♠ J 7 4
        ♡ 6 5
        ♢ A K 8 7 4 2
        ♣ J 6

♠ 10 6 5 2   ♠ Q 9 3
♡ K J 8 2   ♡ Q 10 3
♢ J 5   ♢ Q 10 9
♣ Q 7 4   ♣ K 10 5 3

        ♠ A K 8
        ♡ A 9 7 4
        ♢ 6 3
        ♣ A 9 8 2

West	North	East	South
			1NT
pass	3NT	all pass	

West leads the ♡2 against 3NT, East playing the ♡Q. What is your plan? You can see these immediate winners:

Top Tricks: ♠ 2   ♡ 1   ◊ 2   ♣ 1   **Total: 6**

Three extra tricks from the diamond suit will bring your total to nine. How can you score the five diamond tricks that you need? The defenders' diamonds will need to split 3-2 and you will have to take care with your entries to the dummy.

What will happen if you cash the ace and king on the first two rounds of diamonds and then surrender the third round? The defenders' cards do indeed split 3-2 and the suit will be established. Unfortunately, you will have no entry to the three good diamonds in the dummy. To ensure that you preserve the entry to dummy, you must duck the first round of diamonds. You will then be able to cross to dummy on the second round.

How does the play go? You win the first round of hearts, since otherwise the defenders may switch to clubs and establish too many winners (West's fourth-best lead of the ♡2 tells you that the suit is breaking 4-3). You then play a low diamond from both your own hand and the dummy, allowing the defenders to win the first round of the suit. The defenders are welcome to score three heart tricks at this stage. When you regain the lead, you will cross to the ◊A, noting that the suit breaks 3-2. Four more tricks in diamonds give you the contract.

PLAN: I will win with the ♡A and duck the first round of diamonds. Provided diamonds are 3-2, I will have nine tricks.

Sometimes you need to duck the first two rounds of the suit that you wish to establish. Look at the clubs on this deal:

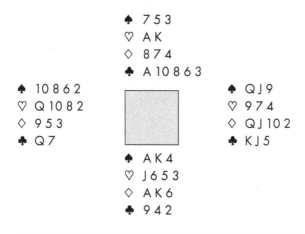

	♠ 7 5 3	
	♡ A K	
	◊ 8 7 4	
	♣ A 10 8 6 3	
♠ 10 8 6 2		♠ Q J 9
♡ Q 10 8 2		♡ 9 7 4
◊ 9 5 3		◊ Q J 10 2
♣ Q 7		♣ K J 5
	♠ A K 4	
	♡ J 6 5 3	
	◊ A K 6	
	♣ 9 4 2	

West	North	East	South
			1NT
pass	3NT	all pass	

West leads the ♡2 against 3NT. What is your plan when you count these top tricks?

Top Tricks: ♠ 2 ♡ 2 ◇ 2 ♣ 1   **Total: 7**

If you can score two extra tricks in clubs, this will bring the total to nine. The heart entries to dummy will soon be a distant memory, so you will need to preserve the ♣A as a third-round entry to the dummy.

You win the heart lead with the king and lead dummy's ♣3, ducking a round of the suit. West wins with the ♣Q and, as expected, plays another heart to dislodge dummy's ace. Continuing with your plan, you duck another round of clubs by leading the ♣6. East wins the second round of clubs and the defenders cash two heart tricks, bringing their total to four. Whichever suit they play next, you will be able to cross to dummy's ♣A and enjoy two further tricks in the club suit. The game is yours.

> **PLAN: I will duck two rounds of clubs. If the suit breaks 3-2, I will be able to cross to the ♣A on the third round and score the two extra club tricks that I need.**

Ducking to guard against a bad break

Imagine that you have a side suit of ◇AKQ762 in an otherwise entryless dummy, opposite ◇84 in you hand. If the diamonds break 3-2, you have six diamond tricks ready to run. Suppose you need only five diamond tricks to fulfill your contract. It may then be a good idea to duck the first round of diamonds. By doing so, you will score the five diamond tricks that you need, even when the defenders' diamonds break 4-1. That's the situation on this deal:

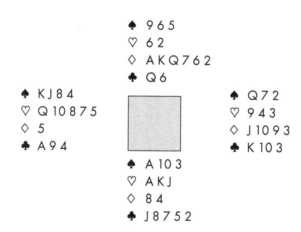

        ♠ 9 6 5
        ♡ 6 2
        ◇ A K Q 7 6 2
        ♣ Q 6

♠ K J 8 4   ♠ Q 7 2
♡ Q 10 8 7 5   ♡ 9 4 3
◇ 5   ◇ J 10 9 3
♣ A 9 4   ♣ K 10 3

        ♠ A 10 3
        ♡ A K J
        ◇ 8 4
        ♣ J 8 7 5 2

West	North	East	South
			1♣
pass	1◇	pass	1NT
pass	3NT	all pass	

Let's suppose first that West leads the ♡7 to East's ♡9 and your ♡J. What plan will you make? After the helpful heart lead, you have these top tricks:

Top Tricks: ♠ 1   ♡ 3   ◇ 3   ♣ 0   **Total: 7**

You need only five diamond tricks to bring the total to nine. Even if the defenders' diamonds split 4-1, you can score five diamond tricks provided you duck the first round of the suit. East wins the first round of diamonds and returns the ♡4. You now have nine tricks ready to go. The ◇AKQ will draw East's remaining diamonds and the ◇76 will then be good.

> **PLAN: I will win with the ♡J and duck a round of diamonds. I will then have nine tricks, even if diamonds break 4-1.**

To extract some more mileage from the deal, look back at the North-South cards in the diagram and imagine that (on some different lie of the defenders' cards) West has led the ♠2. How would you plan the contract then? The initial winner position would be different after a spade lead:

Top Tricks: ♠ 1   ♡ 2   ◇ 3   ♣ 0   **Total: 6**

With only two top tricks now available in hearts, you would need a full six tricks from the diamond suit, to bring your total to nine. You should win the third round of spades and play the diamond suit from the top, hoping to find a 3-2 break. (You could not afford to duck a diamond anyway, because the defenders would then beat the contract by scoring at least two spades and two clubs.)

> **PLAN: I will win the third round of spades and play the three top diamonds, hoping for a 3-2 break.**

This deal tells us that you cannot tell the best way to play a suit, just by looking at that suit in isolation. You must consider your plan for the whole deal.

Overtaking to establish a suit

When you are hoping to establish a long suit in dummy, remember that the defenders may make life awkward by holding up a stopper. Look at the heart suit on this deal:

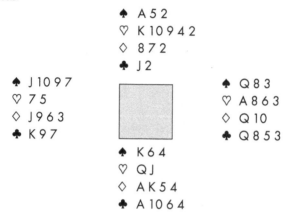

	♠ A 5 2	
	♡ K 10 9 4 2	
	◊ 8 7 2	
	♣ J 2	
♠ J 10 9 7		♠ Q 8 3
♡ 7 5		♡ A 8 6 3
◊ J 9 6 3		◊ Q 10
♣ K 9 7		♣ Q 8 5 3
	♠ K 6 4	
	♡ Q J	
	◊ A K 5 4	
	♣ A 10 6 4	

West	North	East	South
			1NT
pass	2◊	pass	2♡
pass	2NT	pass	3NT
all pass			

North shows his hearts with a transfer bid and you end in 3NT. West leads the ♠J and, to the admiration of all present, you pause to make a plan. This is the winner situation:

Top Tricks: ♠ 2   ♡ 0   ◊ 2   ♣ 1   **Total: 5**

You have five top winners and four more are easily available in the heart suit, it seems. You win the spade lead with the ♠K, preserving the ♠A as a subsequent entry to dummy. You lead the ♡Q next and this card is allowed to win. What now? Suppose you continue with the ♡J, playing a low card from dummy. East will hold up the ace again and there will be no way to make the contract! Since there is only one entry left to the dummy (the ♠A) you will score only two tricks from the heart suit.

To ensure that you score the four heart tricks that you need, you must overtake the ♡J with dummy's ♡K on the second round. It will do East no good to hold up his ace now. Since the lead would be in dummy, you would then continue with the ♡10 and (if necessary) the ♡9. Overtake on the second round and nothing can stop you from scoring four heart tricks and making the contract.

PLAN: I will win with the ♠K and lead the ♡Q. If this is allowed to win, I will overtake the ♡J with the ♡K and establish four tricks in hearts.

Suppose you have a side suit of ♣K10976 in dummy opposite ♣AQ in your hand, with one entry to dummy in a different suit. When you need only four club tricks, and can afford to lose the lead, it may pay you to overtake the ♣Q on the second round of the suit. Look at this full deal:

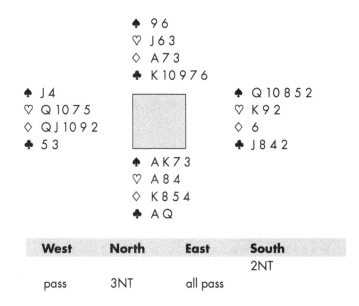

	West	North	East	South
				2NT
	pass	3NT	all pass	

How will you play 3NT when West leads the ♢Q? You start with these top tricks:

Top Tricks: ♠ 2   ♡ 1   ◊ 2   ♣ 3   **Total: 8**

You need one extra trick and it is unlikely to come from a 3-3 diamond break, after West has chosen to lead a diamond. Instead you should look for a fourth trick from the club suit.

Suppose you win the diamond lead with the king, cash the ace and queen of clubs and cross to dummy with the ◊A. All will be well if clubs break 3-3 (or if the ♣J fell on the first two rounds). When the cards lie as in the diagram, you will go down. West will show out on the ♣K and there will be no point in setting up a fourth club trick because there is no further entry to the dummy.

The best chance of scoring four club tricks is to cash the ♣A and then overtake the ♣Q with the ♣K. When both defenders follow to two rounds of clubs, the contract is secure. You lead the ♣10 from dummy, forcing out the ♣J, and dummy's ♣97 will then be good. The ◊A remains as an entry to the two established winners in clubs.

You would still make the contract, of course, if clubs broke 3-3. In that case overtaking the ♣Q would cost you an overtrick. This is a very worthwhile insurance premium to allow you to make the contract when a defender holds ♣Jxxx.

> **PLAN: I will win with the ◇K, play the ♣A and overtake the ♣Q with dummy's ♣K. I can then use dummy's ♣109 to force out the ♣J, ensuring four club tricks when the suit breaks no worse than 4-2.**

Making the best play in a single suit

An important part of planning many contracts is to determine the best play within a single suit. Suppose you are in 3NT and need three heart tricks to make the contract. What play would you choose with this holding:

♡ A 7 2
♡ Q J 6 4

An inexperienced player might lead the ♡Q, finessing through West. It's not a good idea! West will cover with the king if he holds that card; you will then score the three tricks that you need only when hearts break 3-3.

A better idea is to play the ace on the first round and then to lead twice toward the queen-jack. You will still make three tricks when hearts break 3-3; you will succeed also when East holds the ♡K.

Let's put that combination into the context of a complete deal:

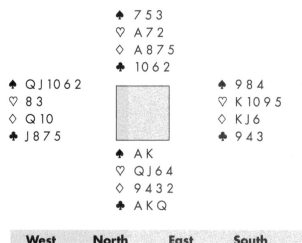

	♠ 7 5 3		
	♡ A 7 2		
	◇ A 8 7 5		
	♣ 10 6 2		

♠ Q J 10 6 2   ♠ 9 8 4
♡ 8 3   ♡ K 10 9 5
◇ Q 10   ◇ K J 6
♣ J 8 7 5   ♣ 9 4 3

♠ A K
♡ Q J 6 4
◇ 9 4 3 2
♣ A K Q

West	North	East	South
			1◇
pass	2◇	pass	3NT
all pass			

How will you play 3NT when West leads the ♠Q? You start with these top tricks:

Top Tricks: ♠ 2   ♡ 1   ◊ 1   ♣ 3   **Total: 7**

It is unlikely that you will have time to establish an extra trick from the diamond suit. You should rely on the heart suit to provide the two extra tricks that you need.

You win the spade lead and cross to the ♡A. You then lead toward the ♡Q, hoping that East holds the ♡K. The queen wins the second round of the suit and you return to the ◊A to lead a third round of hearts toward the jack. Whether or not East chooses to rise with the ♡K on the third round, you will score three tricks from the suit, bringing your total to nine.

As you see, it would have cost the contract to make the greatly inferior play of leading the ♡Q at Trick 2. East would have won with the ♡K and cleared the spade suit. You would then have looked in vain for a 3-3 heart break, going down one.

> **PLAN: I will win the spade lead and use the ♡A and ◊A to lead twice towards the ♡QJx. If East holds the ♡K or hearts split 3-3, I will make the contract.**

On the next deal, it is the diamond suit that you need to establish:

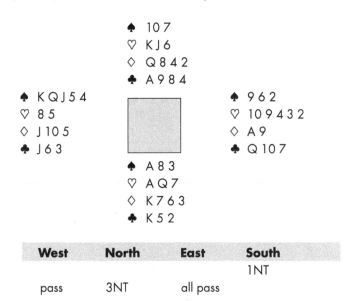

| ♠ 10 7
| ♡ K J 6
| ◊ Q 8 4 2
| ♣ A 9 8 4

♠ K Q J 5 4   ♠ 9 6 2
♡ 8 5   ♡ 10 9 4 3 2
◊ J 10 5   ◊ A 9
♣ J 6 3   ♣ Q 10 7

| ♠ A 8 3
| ♡ A Q 7
| ◊ K 7 6 3
| ♣ K 5 2

West	North	East	South
			1NT
pass	3NT	all pass	

West leads the ♠K against 3NT. What is your plan? You have this top trick position:

Top Tricks: ♠ 1   ♡ 3   ◊ 0   ♣ 2   **Total: 6**

One extra trick from the club suit would not help you very much, so you must aim to establish three tricks from the diamond suit. You hold up the ♠A until the third round and East plays his spot cards upwards (the ♠2 first, then the ♠6). This is a count signal to indicate three cards in the suit. What now?

To score three diamond tricks, you will need to find an opponent with a doubleton ace in the suit. You must lead a low card through the ace to the honor sitting behind it; you can then duck the second round, allowing the bare ace to win. Which defender should you play for the ◊A on this particular deal? It will have to be East. If West has the ◊A, he will be able to cash enough spade tricks to beat you when he gains the lead.

So at Trick 4, you cross to dummy with the ♡J. You then lead a diamond toward the king; East follows with the ◊9 and the ◊K wins. Next you play a low diamond from both hands. East has to play the ◊A and you will then have three diamond tricks. You can win East's return and claim the contract. Magic!

> **PLAN: I will win the third round of spades, cross to the ♡J and lead a diamond toward the king, hoping that East holds a doubleton ◊A.**

Remember these points

- When dummy's long suit is headed by the ace, it is often right to delay playing the ace until you lead the last card in the suit from your hand. With ◊A9732 in dummy opposite ◊854 in your hand, duck two rounds and then cross to the ◊A.

- By ducking a round of a suit such as ♣AKQ73 (in a dummy with no side entry) opposite ♣82, you will be able to score four tricks when the defenders' cards break 4-2.

- You can gain an entry to dummy by overtaking an honor in your hand. For example, with ♣A10986 in dummy opposite ♣KQ you can overtake the ♣Q on the second round and lead the ♣10 to clear the suit.

Now try these...

A.

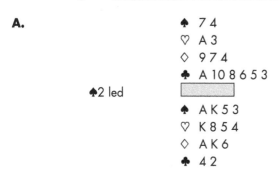

♠ 7 4
♡ A 3
◇ 9 7 4
♣ A 10 8 6 5 3

♠2 led

♠ A K 5 3
♡ K 8 5 4
◇ A K 6
♣ 4 2

Expressing your plan as concisely as you can, how will you play 3NT?

B.

♠ 9 7
♡ 8 5 4 3
◇ A K Q 4 2
♣ 7 6

♡K led

♠ A K 6 5
♡ A 7 2
◇ 9 5
♣ A K 5 4

West leads the ♡K against your contract of 3NT. What is your plan? (If you hold up the ♡A, West will play the ♡Q, East following with the ♡10.)

C.

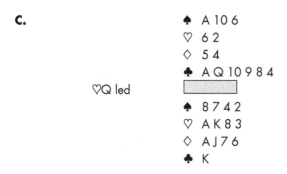

♠ A 10 6
♡ 6 2
◇ 5 4
♣ A Q 10 9 8 4

♡Q led

♠ 8 7 4 2
♡ A K 8 3
◇ A J 7 6
♣ K

How will you give yourself the best chance in 3NT when West leads the ♡Q?

D.

            ♠ 8 6 5 2
            ♡ A 8 7 4
            ◇ A
            ♣ A 7 4 3
    ♠3 led [   ]
            ♠ A Q
            ♡ K 5
            ◇ J 10 6 5 4 2
            ♣ K 9 2

West leads the ♠2 against 3NT, East playing the ♠10. What is your plan?

E.

            ♠ A Q 6 2
            ♡ 6 3 2
            ◇ A 9 2
            ♣ 10 8 6
    ♠J led [   ]
            ♠ K 5 3
            ♡ Q J 10 4
            ◇ K 7 4
            ♣ A K 2

West leads the ♠J against your contract of 3NT. What is your plan?

F.

            ♠ K 6
            ♡ 8 6 3
            ◇ 9 7 2
            ♣ Q 8 7 6 3
    ♠3 led [   ]
            ♠ A 8
            ♡ A 10 9 4
            ◇ A K Q 4
            ♣ K 4 2

East opens the bidding 1♠ and you end in 3NT. How will you plan the play when West leads the ♠3?

ANSWERS

A. You have seven top tricks and must try to set up dummy's clubs. Even if the defenders' clubs split 3-2, as you must hope, you will need to lose two rounds of the suit. One of these must be on the first round of clubs, so that you can use the ♣A as an entry on the second round. You win the spade lead and duck a round of clubs. You win the defenders' return (with the ♡K if they switch to hearts). You cross to the ♣A and concede a third round of clubs. Provided the suit breaks 3-2, the remaining clubs will be established and you can use the ♡A as an entry. The defenders will score just two spades and two clubs; you know from the ♠2 lead that spades will break 4-3 and pose no threat.

> **PLAN: I will win the spade lead and duck a round of clubs. When I win the return, I will play ace and another club. I can reach the established club tricks with the ♡A.**

B. Since you are well protected in both the black suits, nothing can be lost by holding up on the first round of hearts. West continues with the ♡Q, East following with the ♡10, and you win with the ♡A. What now? You have eight top tricks and just four diamond tricks (one extra trick, in other words) will carry you to the contract. You should therefore duck the first round of diamonds, to guard against a 4-2 break in the suit. Even if West wins the ducked round of diamonds, you can lose no more than three hearts and one diamond. When you regain the lead, you will have nine tricks to take, provided the diamonds are no worse than 4-2.

> **PLAN: I will win the second round of hearts and duck a round of diamonds. This will allow me to score four diamond tricks, even against a 4-2 break.**

C. You have four top tricks outside the club suit, so five club tricks will give you the contract. You win the heart lead and should then overtake the ♣K with the ♣A. You continue with the ♣Q and then force out the defenders' ♣J. Nothing can prevent you from winning the return, crossing to the ♠A and scoring the remainder of dummy's club suit.

> **PLAN: I will win the heart lead and overtake the ♣K with the ♣A. I can then establish five tricks in clubs, reaching them with the ♠A.**

D. After the spade lead into your ace-queen, you have seven top tricks and will need to set up the diamonds. At Trick 2 you cross to the ◇A. You return to your hand with the ♣K (this is a safer entry than the ♡K, because you hold seven clubs between the hands and only six hearts). Which diamond card should you play now? In your local club you might see some players leading the ◇J, because they are used to playing one of touching honors. It is not a good play; you will then make the contract only when diamonds are 3-3. Instead you should lead a low diamond. You will still make the contract when diamonds break 3-3 but you will succeed also when a defender started with a doubleton diamond honor and it appears on the second round. When you win the spade continuation with the ace, you can use your ◇J10 to force out the other honor.

PLAN: I will win the spade lead, cross to the ◇A, return to the ♣K and lead a low diamond. I can then establish the diamonds when they break 3-3, or 4-2 with a defender holding a doubleton honor.

E. You have seven top tricks and would like to add two more tricks from the heart suit. Suppose you win with the ♠K and lead the ♡Q from your hand. It's not a good idea. If East holds ♡Ax or ♡Kx, you will be able to score only one heart trick and will go down. Instead you should aim to lead toward your heart holding.

Win the spade lead in dummy and lead a heart to the queen. The key situation is when the two top hearts lie in different hands. If West wins the first round from ♡Ax or ♡Kx, you can make both your remaining heart honors by leading twice toward your ♡J104. If instead West wins from ♡Axxx or ♡Kxxx, your next heart lead from dummy will cause East's bare heart honor to appear. Again you will score tricks with the ♡J and ♡10.

PLAN: I will win with the ♠A and lead toward my heart holding (three times, if necessary).

F. You have six top tricks and will need to establish the club suit to make the contract. Since you will have only one spade stopper remaining, you must set up the clubs while losing the lead only once in the suit. Do you see how the defenders' clubs must lie for this to be possible? East is marked with the ♣A, after his opening bid, and you will need this card to be doubleton.

You win the first trick with dummy's ♠K and lead a low club toward your hand. When East holds ♣Ax, he is powerless. If he rises with the ace on the first round, you will have four club tricks. If instead he plays low, you will win with the ♣K and duck the next round of clubs to the bare ace. When you win the next round of spades with the ace, you can enter dummy with the ♣Q.

PLAN: I will win with the ♠K and lead a club toward my hand, hoping to find East with a doubleton ♣A.

10

PLANNING TO WIN THE NOTRUMP RACE

Most notrump contracts take the form of a race between the two sides. In 3NT, for example, the declarer must try to score nine tricks before the defenders can score five. In this chapter we will see how you, as the declarer, can plan to win the race. It is often important that you choose the right suit as your source for the extra tricks that you need and we will look at this topic first.

Choosing the right suit to play

How would you tackle this 3NT contract?

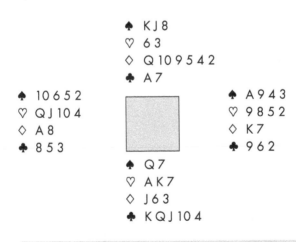

West	North	East	South
			1NT
pass	3NT	all pass	

West leads the ♡Q against 3NT and you see these immediate winners:

Top Tricks: ♠0 ♡2 ◇0 ♣5   **Total:** 7

To make 3NT, you will need two extra tricks. You would often look for these in the longest side suit that is not already established. What will happen here, though, if you turn to the diamond suit, leading a diamond after winning the heart lead? The defenders will win and clear the hearts. When you knock out the remaining diamond stopper, they will score a total of one spade, two hearts and two diamonds. Down one!

The diamond suit will provide enough tricks to make the contract, it is true, but you cannot establish these quickly enough. The defenders would score five tricks first and you would lose the race!

To make the contract, you must play spades. This suit, too, can provide the extra two tricks that you need but you will have only one stopper to knock out. You win the heart lead and play the ♠Q. Let's say that the defenders win the first (or second spade) and clear the heart suit. You will then have nine tricks — the seven original top tricks, plus the two extra tricks that you have established in spades. This is your plan for the 3NT contract:

PLAN: I will win the heart lead and knock out the ♠A, setting up the two extra tricks that I need.

Let's see another deal where you must choose which suit to rely on for the extra tricks that you need:

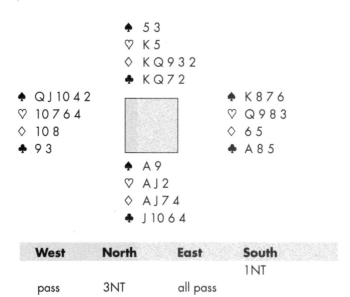

	♠ 5 3	
	♡ K 5	
	◇ K Q 9 3 2	
	♣ K Q 7 2	
♠ Q J 10 4 2		♠ K 8 7 6
♡ 10 7 6 4		♡ Q 9 8 3
◇ 10 8		◇ 6 5
♣ 9 3		♣ A 8 5
	♠ A 9	
	♡ A J 2	
	◇ A J 7 4	
	♣ J 10 6 4	

West	**North**	**East**	**South**
			1NT
pass	3NT	all pass	

How will you plan the play when West leads the ♠Q against 3NT? This is the winner position:

Top Tricks: ♠ 1 ♡ 2 ◇ 5 ♣ 0 Total: 8

You have eight tricks ready-to-go and therefore need only one more trick to bring you to the finishing tape. Should you seek it from hearts or clubs?

In clubs, you can achieve three certain extra tricks by knocking out the ace. In hearts, you can score one extra trick only if you are lucky and the finesse against the ♡Q succeeds. Usually, this would be a strong argument for playing clubs instead of hearts. Not here! What will happen if you win the first or second round of spades and play a club? You will lose the race. The defenders will win with the ♣A and score four spade tricks to beat the contract.

Even though you will need a bit of luck to succeed, you should win the spade lead (a hold-up can hardly help), cross to dummy with the ♡K and finesse the ♡J. When the cards lie as in the diagram, the heart finesse will succeed and you will make the contract. Playing this way gives you a 50% chance of making the contract; playing on clubs instead would surely result in failure.

> **PLAN: I will win the spade lead, cross to the ♡K and finesse the ♡J. If the finesse wins, I will make the contract.**

Reading the opening lead

To make the best plan, you will sometimes have to read the lie of the suit that has been led. Suppose the defenders lead a spade and you win at some stage with your only stopper. If the lead was from a four-card suit and the defenders' spades are breaking 4-4, they will have only three spade tricks to cash; you can therefore afford to lose the lead while setting up your extra tricks. If instead the lead was from a five-card suit, the situation is different. You cannot afford to lose the lead, since the defenders would then be able to cash four spades. Instead you must seek to claim eight more tricks in a hurry.

Let's look at a pair of deals that illustrate the situation.

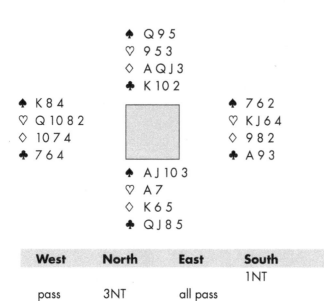

♠ Q 9 5
♥ 9 5 3
♦ A Q J 3
♣ K 10 2

♠ K 8 4
♥ Q 10 8 2
♦ 10 7 4
♣ 7 6 4

♠ 7 6 2
♥ K J 6 4
♦ 9 8 2
♣ A 9 3

♠ A J 10 3
♥ A 7
♦ K 6 5
♣ Q J 8 5

West	North	East	South
			1NT
pass	3NT	all pass	

West leads the ♥2 against 3NT and East plays the ♥K. What plan will you make? You see these immediate winners:

Top Tricks: ♠ 1 ♥ 1 ♦ 4 ♣ 0   **Total: 6**

You need three extra tricks to bring the total to nine. Should you seek them from spades, where you will need a successful finesse against the king, or from clubs?

Everything depends on how the defenders' hearts are breaking. If the hearts are 4-4, you can make your game by setting up the clubs. When the defenders take the ♣A, they will have only three heart winners to cash. If instead hearts are 5-3, you cannot afford to play clubs. The defenders would then win the race, scoring the ♣A and four winners in hearts. Your only chance in that situation would be to take the spade finesse, hoping that East holds the ♠K and you can score four spade tricks without losing the lead.

So, how are the hearts breaking? West has led the ♥2. This tells you that hearts are almost certainly 4-4. (As we mentioned before, if the ♥2 is West's fourth-best heart he cannot hold a fifth-best heart!) You might as well duck the first round of hearts. East then returns the ♥4, which is surely his own fourth-best card in the suit, confirming your reading of the cards (with two spot cards remaining, it would be correct for East to lead back the higher one). The correct play on this deal is therefore to establish the club suit.

PLAN: I will win the second round of hearts. Since hearts appear to be 4-4 after the ♥2 lead, I will establish the clubs.

Now let's see a deal where you expect the defenders' suit to break 5-3.

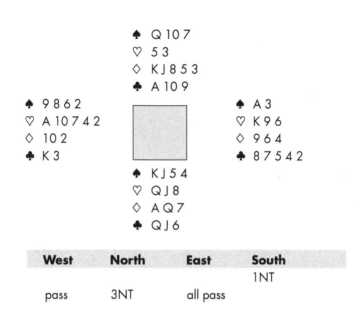

	♠ Q 10 7	
	♡ 5 3	
	◇ K J 8 5 3	
	♣ A 10 9	
♠ 9 8 6 2		♠ A 3
♡ A 10 7 4 2		♡ K 9 6
◇ 10 2		◇ 9 6 4
♣ K 3		♣ 8 7 5 4 2
	♠ K J 5 4	
	♡ Q J 8	
	◇ A Q 7	
	♣ Q J 6	

West	North	East	South
			1NT
pass	3NT	all pass	

West leads the ♡4 against 3NT. East wins with the ♡K and returns the ♡9, covered by your ♡Q. West can be certain, from the cards that his partner has played, that you also hold the ♡J. (That's because East would not return the ♡9 from ♡KJ9 or ♡KJ96.) He therefore refuses to win with the ace, following with the ♡2. Do you see the purpose of this hold-up play by West? He is maintaining communication with his partner. If East were to gain the lead subsequently, he would be able to return his last heart; West would win with the ♡A and cash his winners in the suit.

Back to your problem as declarer. This is the winner situation after the ♡Q has won the second trick:

Top Tricks: ♠ 0   ♡ 1   ◇ 5   ♣ 1   **Total: 7**

You need two extra tricks to bring the total to nine. Should you simply establish the spade suit by knocking out the ♠A? This will be safe only when hearts break 4-4. Is that likely, or even possible? No! West led the ♡4 (his fourth-best heart) and followed with the ♡2 (his fifth-best heart) on the second round. If you play a spade, you will lose one spade and four hearts.

There is an alternative potential source of two extra tricks — the club suit. If West holds the ♣K, a club finesse will give you two extra tricks. This is only a 50% chance, yes, but that is better than a 0% chance by setting up the spades.

> **PLAN: I can tell that hearts are 5-3. When the ♡Q is allowed to win, I will run the ♣Q in the hope that West holds the ♣K.**

Preventing a dangerous switch

Sometimes the risk to your contract does not come from the suit that the defenders have chosen to lead. You must then be careful not to give them a chance to switch to the danger suit in time to defeat you. Many players would go wrong on this deal:

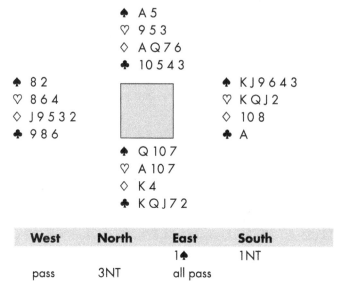

	♠ A 5
	♡ 9 5 3
	◇ A Q 7 6
	♣ 10 5 4 3

♠ 8 2		♠ K J 9 6 4 3
♡ 8 6 4		♡ K Q J 2
◇ J 9 5 3 2		◇ 10 8
♣ 9 8 6		♣ A

	♠ Q 10 7
	♡ A 10 7
	◇ K 4
	♣ K Q J 7 2

West	North	East	South
		1♠	1NT
pass	3NT	all pass	

How will you plan the play in 3NT when West leads the ♠8? As always, you begin by counting your top tricks in each suit:

Top Tricks: ♠ 1   ♡ 1   ◇ 3   ♣ 0   Total: 5

You will need four extra tricks to bring the total to nine and these can easily be established in clubs. What will happen if you play low from dummy at Trick 1, East winning with the ♠K? He will realize, from the bidding and his partner's opening lead, that you hold two stoppers in spades. It will be clear for him to switch to the ♡K. The best you can do then is to hold up the ♡A until the third round, but this will not rescue you. When you play a club, East will win with the ace and cash a heart to put you down one.

You cannot afford to give East a chance to switch to hearts. You must win the first trick with dummy's ♠A and then establish the club suit. There is no risk involved, since the bidding and the opening lead tell you that East holds the ♠K. Your ♠Q10 will therefore act as a stopper when East wins with the ♣A.

> **PLAN: I will win with the ♠A and set up the clubs.**

Yes, you're right; this is the one of the shortest plans in the book! Rest assured that many players would have gone down in 3NT, nevertheless.

Attacking the entry to the danger hand

When you need extra tricks from two different suits, it can be important to play the right suit first. You will often have to play first the suit where the danger hand (the defender who has led his longest suit) is likely to gain the lead. A couple of examples will make this clear:

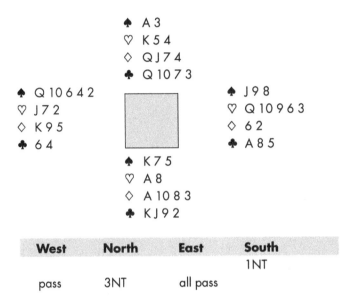

	West	North	East	South
				1NT
	pass	3NT	all pass	

How will you plan the play in 3NT when West leads the ♠4? As always, you begin by counting your top tricks in each suit:

Top Tricks: ♠2 ♡2 ◇1 ♣0 **Total: 5**

The club suit will give you three extra tricks but you will also need one extra trick from the diamond suit. Suppose you win with the ♠A and play a club. East will take his ♣A and clear the spades. When you subsequently run the ◇Q, seeking the extra trick(s) that you need from diamonds, West will win and cash enough spades to beat you.

How can you avoid this outcome? There is no advantage in holding up on the first round of spades; indeed, this would risk a damaging switch to hearts. After winning the first trick with the ♠A you must play first on diamonds, the suit where only West can gain the lead. You run the ◇Q to West's ◇K at Trick 2.

You have attacked, and removed, the entry to the West hand. When West persists with spades, you hold up the ♠K until the third round to exhaust East's spades. You then play on clubs, hoping that East, the safe hand, will hold the ♣A. He does indeed, on this occasion, and you make the contract.

Make sure you understand why it was right to play on diamonds first, rather than clubs. If West held both the ◊K and the ♣A, along with five spades, you would go down anyway. If East held the ◊K, you would make the contract whichever order you played the minor suits. The only situation where your order of play would make a difference was when the diamond finesse was wrong but East held the ♣A. In that case it was essential to attack first the potential entry to the West hand.

PLAN: I will win with the ♣A and run the ◊Q, attacking the entry to the danger hand. If the finesse loses and West clears the spades, I will make the contract when East has the ♣A.

Here is another example of the technique:

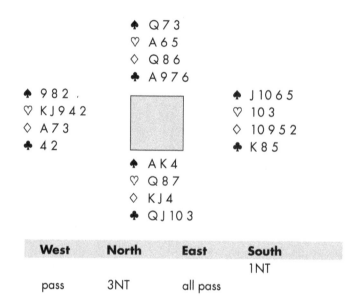

West	North	East	South
			1NT
pass	3NT	all pass	

West leads the ♡4 and you run this successfully to East's ♡10 and your ♡Q. What now? These are your top tricks, including two in hearts:

Top Tricks: ♠ 3   ♡ 2   ◊ 0   ♣ 1   **Total: 6**

A successful club finesse would produce three extra tricks and give you the contract. What if the finesse loses, though? East will win and clear the heart suit; you will then go down when the cards lie as in the diagram; you would lose three hearts, one diamond and one club.

In the dangerous case where East holds the ♣K, you will need an extra trick from the diamond suit. You can guarantee the contract by seeking this diamond trick first, before you take the club finesse! In other words, you should first attack the suit which might allow the danger hand (West) to gain the lead.

Play a diamond at Trick 2 and everything will be easy. If West chooses to play low, you will win with the ◊Q, return to your hand with a spade and run the ♣Q. You will not mind at all if the club finesse loses now, because you will have the three extra tricks (two in clubs, one in diamonds) that you need. Suppose instead that West rises with the ◊A and clears the hearts. Again you will make the contract. The club finesse will be into the safe hand and East will have no heart to return.

PLAN: After winning with the ♡Q, I will play one round of diamonds before finessing in clubs.

Note that it was right to play diamonds before clubs, even though you did not need to persist with diamonds until West's stopper in the suit was removed.

Remember these points

- When planning a notrump contract, ensure that your plan will allow you to 'win the race'. In other words, make sure it will give you the tricks that you need before the defenders can score enough tricks to beat you.

- The correct line of play will often depend on whether the opening lead is from a five-card suit or a four-card suit. By observing the opening lead, and sometimes the play to the second trick, you may be able to tell how the defenders' main suit is breaking.

- When the opening lead is a two, or the lowest spot card that is not visible in your hand and the dummy, you can assume that the leader holds only four cards in the suit.

- Be wary of allowing your right-hand opponent to win the opening lead when he may then have the chance to make a damaging switch.

- When you may have to knock out two stoppers, to set up the tricks you need, it is normally right to 'attack first the entry to the danger hand'. When you then drive out the stopper held by the other defender, he will have no cards left in the suit that was led.

Now try these...

A.

        ♠ K Q 4
        ♡ A 9 2
        ◇ Q 10 6 2
        ♣ Q 4 3

♠J led

        ♠ A 3
        ♡ Q J 10
        ◇ J 9 7 4
        ♣ A K 7 2

Expressing your plan as concisely as you can, how will you play 3NT?

B.

        ♠ A 6
        ♡ 6 3 2
        ◇ Q 9 7 3
        ♣ K Q 8 7

♠5 led

        ♠ Q 7 3 2
        ♡ A J
        ◇ A J 10 8 4
        ♣ A 2

West leads the ♠5 against 3NT. What is your plan?

C.

        ♠ 9 4 3
        ♡ Q 6
        ◇ K J 10 7 5
        ♣ Q 8 4

♠2 led

        ♠ A 10
        ♡ K 8 2
        ◇ A 6 4
        ♣ A K J 10 3

West leads the ♠2 against 3NT. How will you plan the play?

D.

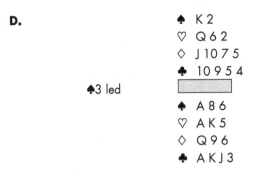

♠3 led

♠ K 2
♡ Q 6 2
◇ J 10 7 5
♣ 10 9 5 4

♠ A 8 6
♡ A K 5
◇ Q 9 6
♣ A K J 3

How will you play 3NT when West leads the ♠3?

E.

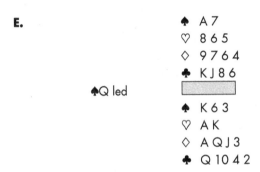

♠Q led

♠ A 7
♡ 8 6 5
◇ 9 7 6 4
♣ K J 8 6

♠ K 6 3
♡ A K
◇ A Q J 3
♣ Q 10 4 2

West leads the ♠Q against your contract of 3NT. What is your plan?

F.

♡6 led

♠ 8 6
♡ A 7 2
◇ Q J 8 6
♣ Q J 9 2

♠ Q 4
♡ Q 5 3
◇ A K 3
♣ A 10 7 4 3

West leads the ♡6 against 3NT. How will you plan the play?

ANSWERS

A. You have seven top tricks. If clubs break 3-3, you will have an eighth trick there; meanwhile, you must decide which red suit to attack first. Taking a successful finesse against the ♡K would give you the two extra tricks that you need. Suppose the finesse lost, though. East would return a spade and it could then be too late to establish the diamond suit. When the defenders took their first diamond stopper, they would clear the spades. They might then score two spades, one heart and two diamonds — winning the race.

Instead of finessing in hearts, you should establish two extra tricks in diamonds, by knocking out the ace and king of the suit. Nothing can then stop you from accumulating a total of nine tricks.

PLAN: I will win with the ♠A and play a diamond, knocking out one of the defenders' stoppers. After winning the return, I will clear the diamonds.

B. You have six top tricks and can easily establish at least three more tricks from the diamond suit. What should you do at Trick 1? Suppose you play dummy's ♠6, hoping that West holds the ♠K and you can win the first trick with your ♠Q. You may go down! East might well win with the ♠K and then switch to hearts; you would then need the diamond finesse to be right in order to win the race.

There is no need to take such a risk. Win the first trick with the ♠A and run the ◇Q into the West hand. The contract is then guaranteed, even if the finesse loses to West's ◇K. With West on lead, your remaining ♠Q73 is a secure stopper in the suit. Whatever West plays next, you will be able to score four diamonds, three clubs and the two major-suit aces.

PLAN: I will win with the ♠A and run the ◇Q. Nine tricks are then assured, even if the finesse loses.

C. You have eight top tricks. Should you seek the extra trick that you need in hearts or in diamonds? It depends on how the spades lie. If the defenders' spades break 4-4, you can play a heart and set up the ♡Q or ♡K as your ninth trick. If instead the spades are 5-3, you cannot afford to allow the defenders to gain the lead with the ♡A and must take a successful finesse (one way or the other) against the ◇Q. West's lead of the ♠2 tells you that the spades are breaking 4-4. You should therefore win the first or second round of spades and lead a heart to establish your ninth trick.

PLAN: I will win the first (or second) round of spades. Since the ♠2 lead implies spades are 4-4, I will play a heart next.

D. You have seven top tricks and the possibility of two extra tricks from either diamonds or clubs. Which minor suit should you play? Suppose you take a club finesse and it loses to the queen. The defenders will knock out your remaining spade stopper and you will have only eight tricks; it will be too late to play on diamonds, because the defenders would be able to cash two diamonds and two spades to go with the ♣Q. So, if you play on clubs first, you will need the club finesse to win. How about playing a diamond instead, planning to knock out the ace and the king? West's lead of the ♠3, when you can see the ♠2 in dummy, tells you that spades are 4-4. You can afford to lose two spades and two diamonds, so playing on diamonds to create your two extra tricks is completely safe!

PLAN: I will win with the ♠K, play a diamond, win the spade continuation and set up the diamonds. Since spades are 4-4, the defenders can score only two spades and two diamonds.

E. You have only five top tricks and will need to score extra tricks from both the diamonds and the clubs. Everything will be easy if the ◇K is onside, with East, because you will lose the lead only once (to the ♣A). When the ◇K is offside, you will need to play the minors in the correct order. You must attack first the entry to the danger hand. In other words, here, you must play diamonds before clubs.

You win the first trick with the ♠A (you cannot afford to hold up, since the defenders might switch to hearts). Then you finesse the ◇Q. Suppose that West wins with the ◇K and returns another spade. You must hold up the ♠K, aiming to exhaust East's spades. After winning the third round of spades, you set up the clubs. When East (the safe hand) holds the ♣A, you will make the contract. In the dangerous case where spades break 5-3, East will have no spade to play when he gains the lead.

PLAN: I will win with the ♠A and finesse the ◇Q, attacking the entry to the danger hand. If the finesse loses, I will hold up the ♠K until the third round and then set up the clubs.

F. You have only six top tricks and will need to work on clubs. Looking at the heart suit in isolation, it seems obvious to play low from dummy at Trick 1. By doing so, however, you are risking that East will produce the ♡K and then switch to spades, where you have no protection. A successful club finesse will bring your total to ten tricks, so you do best to rise with the ♡A and then run the ♣Q.

Suppose that you do take the risk of running the heart lead, West does hold the ♡K and you win with the ♡Q. It will not help you very much! You will have to cross to the ◇Q to take the club finesse and this will make it clear to West that you hold the ◇A and ◇K. If the club finesse is wrong, it will be obvious for him to switch to spades.

PLAN: I will win with the ♡A and run the ♣Q.

PART III

ADDING CLEVER MOVES TO YOUR PLAN

11

OTHER TYPES OF FINESSE

Way back in Chapter 4 (how good is your memory?) we looked at some basic forms of the finesse. In the main, they involved leading toward a card that you were hoping to score. For example, you might lead toward a king, or toward the queen in an ace-queen combination. We looked also at situations where you held several adjacent cards and could then afford to lead a high card to perform a finesse: for example when you held ◊QJ10 opposite dummy's ◊A42, you would lead the ◊Q, hoping to trap the king on your left. In this chapter we will see that there are many other types of finesse, any of which can help you to make the best possible plan for your contract.

The double finesse

Sometimes you have the chance to finesse twice in a suit. Look at the clubs here:

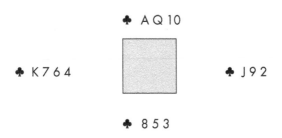

On the first round you play a low club to dummy's ten. This is your first finesse in the suit and, as it happens, the ten loses to the jack. When you regain the lead, you lead a low club to dummy's queen. This second finesse wins and you score two tricks from the suit.

Do you see why it was right to finesse the ♣10 first, rather than the ♣Q? By playing the suit in this way, you would score three club tricks when West held both the ♣K and the ♣J:

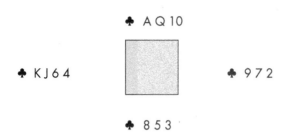

♣ A Q 10

♣ K J 6 4   ♣ 9 7 2

♣ 8 5 3

A finesse of the ♣10 wins and you return to your hand in some different suit to finesse the ♣Q next. Both finesses win and three club tricks are yours.

Suppose instead that you were to finesse the ♣Q on the first round. It would win, yes, but when you subsequently led a club toward the remaining ♣A10, West would insert one of his honors to prevent you from scoring a third club trick. So, remember that you should generally finesse the lower card first when you are taking a double finesse.

Here is a similar suit combination:

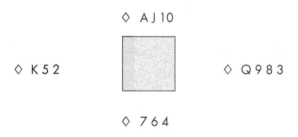

◇ A J 10

◇ K 5 2   ◇ Q 9 8 3

◇ 7 6 4

You finesse the ◇10 (or ◇J) on the first round and this loses to the ◇Q. When you regain the lead, you take a second finesse in the suit. This time you are in luck and you score two diamond tricks, the maximum possible with this combination. You will fail to score two diamond tricks only when East holds both the king and queen of diamonds.

Let's look at a complete deal that involves a double finesse:

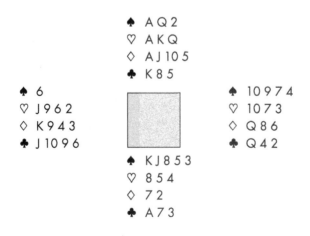

♠ A Q 2
♡ A K Q
◇ A J 10 5
♣ K 8 5

♠ 6   ♠ 10 9 7 4
♡ J 9 6 2   ♡ 10 7 3
◇ K 9 4 3   ◇ Q 8 6
♣ J 10 9 6   ♣ Q 4 2

♠ K J 8 5 3
♡ 8 5 4
◇ 7 2
♣ A 7 3

North opens 2♣ and you arrive in 6♠ on the South cards. What is your plan when West leads the ♣J? This is the loser position:

Losers: ♠ 0   ♡ 0   ◇ 1   ♣ 1   Total: 2

You are certain to lose a diamond trick and must therefore find some way to dispose of the club loser. The best chance of this is to establish a discard on dummy's diamond suit, by taking a double finesse.

Since there are plenty of entries to dummy, it is natural to win the opening club lead with the ♣K, retaining the ♣A as a potential entry to your hand later in the play.

You draw trumps in four rounds and play a diamond to the ten, losing to the queen. East returns a club and you win with the ace. Conveniently in your hand (after your thoughtful play at Trick 1, winning the club lead in the dummy), you play a diamond to the jack. This is the second half of your planned double finesse and you are pleased to see the ◇J win. You discard your club loser on the ◇A and the slam is yours.

> **PLAN: I will win the club lead in dummy, draw trumps and take a double finesse in diamonds, hoping to set up a discard for my club loser.**

The plan will fail only when East holds the ◇K and the ◇Q.

The deep finesse

Even when you are missing three honors in a suit, you may have the chance to save a trick by finessing. Look at this very common holding:

$$♡ \text{ A Q 9}$$

$$♡ \text{ J 10 6 5} \qquad\qquad ♡ \text{ K 8 3}$$

$$♡ \text{ 7 4 2}$$

Let's say that you require two tricks from the suit. This will be easy when West holds the ♡K (a simple finesse of the ♡Q will do the job). To give yourself an extra chance, you should lead a low card from your hand and finesse dummy's ♡9 on the first round. When the cards lie as in the diagram, with West holding the ♡J and ♡10, dummy's ♡9 will force East's ♡K and dummy's ♡Q will then be good for a second trick.

As you see, it would do West no good to play the ♡J or ♡10 on the first round. You would cover with dummy's ♡Q, losing to East's ♡K, and then finesse the ♡9 successfully on the second round.

Here is a similar situation:

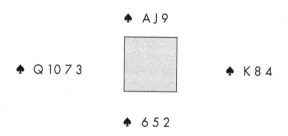

♠ AJ9

♠ Q10 7 3   ♠ K 8 4

♠ 6 5 2

Seeking two tricks from the suit, you lead a low card from your hand, West also playing a low card. Your best play from the dummy on the first round is the ♠9. With the cards lying as in the diagram, this will force East's king. When you regain the lead, you will lead toward the dummy again, this time finessing the ♠J. Success! You will have the two tricks that you wanted.

Why was it right to finesse the ♠9 on the first round, rather than the ♠J? The reason is that you would succeed when West's spades were headed by the Q10 or the K10. Finessing the ♠J on the first round would be only half as good a prospect, winning only when West's spades were headed by the KQ.

In both the cases we have seen, finessing the nine on the first round is called a 'deep finesse', because the defenders hold three cards higher than the one that you finesse on the first round.

Let's see a whole deal, where you would employ a deep finesse.

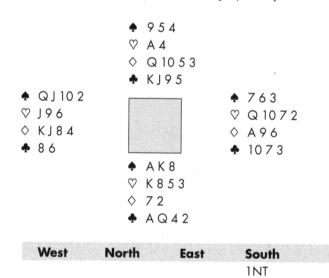

♠ 9 5 4
♡ A 4
◇ Q 10 5 3
♣ K J 9 5

♠ Q J 10 2   ♠ 7 6 3
♡ J 9 6   ♡ Q 10 7 2
◇ K J 8 4   ◇ A 9 6
♣ 8 6   ♣ 10 7 3

♠ A K 8
♡ K 8 5 3
◇ 7 2
♣ A Q 4 2

West	North	East	South
			1NT
pass	3NT	all pass	

What plan would you make when West leads the ♠Q against 3NT? This is the winner situation:

Top Tricks: ♠ 2   ♡ 2   ◊ 0   ♣ 4   **Total: 8**

Diamonds is the only suit that offers a real prospect of generating an extra trick. You win the spade lead and lead a low diamond toward dummy, West playing the ◊4. Which card should you play from dummy, would you say, the ◊Q or the ◊10?

Playing the ◊Q will be successful only when West holds the ◊AK. A better idea is to finesse the ◊10 on the first round, which will eventually create an extra trick when West's diamonds are headed by either the AJ or the KJ. On the lie of the cards shown in the diagram, the ◊10 will force East's ◊A. You win his spade return and lead a second round of diamonds toward dummy's queen. Whether or not West chooses to rise with the ◊K, you will score your ninth trick with the ◊Q. Meanwhile, the defenders will collect just two spades and two diamonds.

> **PLAN: I will win the spade lead and play a diamond to the ten. When West's diamonds are headed by the AJ or KJ, I can set up a diamond as my ninth trick.**

The two-way finesse

When you are missing the queen of a suit, you can sometimes choose to finesse either defender for the card. Suppose you have this club position:

♣ A J 5

♣ K 10 2

If you think that West holds the ♣Q, you can cash the ♣K first and then finesse dummy's ♣J. If instead you think that East has the ♣Q, you begin with the ♣A and then finesse the ♣10.

Skillful declarers will guess the position of the ♣Q correctly much more often than 50%. Sometimes the bidding will offer a big clue, as on this deal:

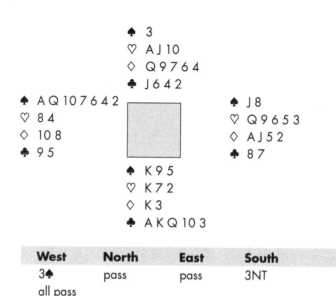

| ♠ 3 |
| ♡ A J 10 |
| ◇ Q 9 7 6 4 |
| ♣ J 6 4 2 |

West	North	East	South
3♠	pass	pass	3NT
all pass			

West leads the ♠7 against 3NT, East playing the ♠J. What plan will you make?

You can expect spades to be 7-2 and will therefore have to win the first round of spades, with the king. (Otherwise East can return a spade and you will lose seven spade tricks!) That leaves you with these top winners:

Top Tricks: ♠1   ♡2   ◇0   ♣5   **Total: 8**

You need one extra trick for the contract. You cannot hope to score a diamond trick, because the defenders would grab the ◇A immediately and cash a bundle of spade tricks. You need to score three heart tricks and will therefore have to guess which defender holds the missing ♡Q.

Nothing can be lost by cashing five rounds of clubs first. Both defenders follow to two rounds. Whatever cards they choose to throw on the remaining clubs, you should think like this: West holds nine cards in the black suits and therefore only four cards in the red suits; East began with four cards in the black suits and nine cards in the red suits. So East is much more likely than West to hold the missing ♡Q (by a factor of nine to four). You should therefore cross to the ♡A and run the ♡J through East. Justice will be done on this occasion and you will make the contract.

> **PLAN: I will win with the ♠K and play all the clubs. Since West has more black cards than East, East will have more red cards than West. I will therefore finesse East for the ♡Q.**

It is an important topic — guessing correctly which defender holds a missing queen. We will return to it in Chapter 17.

The ruffing finesse

To perform a ruffing finesse, you need a sequence of honors opposite a void. You lead one of the honors, planning to run the card if it is not covered but to ruff in the void hand if the defender does cover. Here is a typical position:

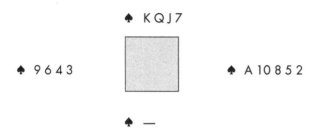

♠ K Q J 7

♠ 9 6 4 3   ♠ A 10 8 5 2

♠ —

You lead the ♠K from dummy, hoping that East holds the missing ♠A. If he plays the ♠A you will ruff in the South hand, thereby establishing the ♠Q and ♠J. If instead East follows with a low spade, you will discard a loser in some other suit. You can then repeat the ruffing finesse by leading the ♠Q.

Let's see a slam contract where such a technique is necessary.

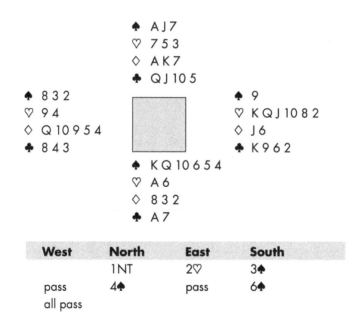

```
              ♠ A J 7
              ♡ 7 5 3
              ◇ A K 7
              ♣ Q J 10 5
♠ 8 3 2                      ♠ 9
♡ 9 4                        ♡ K Q J 10 8 2
◇ Q 10 9 5 4                 ◇ J 6
♣ 8 4 3                      ♣ K 9 6 2
              ♠ K Q 10 6 5 4
              ♡ A 6
              ◇ 8 3 2
              ♣ A 7
```

West	North	East	South
	1NT	2♡	3♠
pass	4♣	pass	6♠
all pass			

How will you play this boldly bid small slam in spades when West leads the ♡9? You start with this loser situation:

Losers: ♠ 0   ♡ 1   ◇ 1   ♣ 1   **Total: 3**

If East holds the ♣K, which is likely on the bidding, a straightforward finesse in clubs (running the ♣Q) will allow you to avoid a club loser. You will still be left with two losers in the red suits, though, and must aim to avoid one of these by taking a later ruffing finesse in clubs.

You win the heart lead with the ace and draw trumps in three rounds, ending in the dummy. When you lead the ♣Q, East does not cover and the queen wins the trick. You cross to the ♣A and then return to dummy with the ◊A. These cards remain:

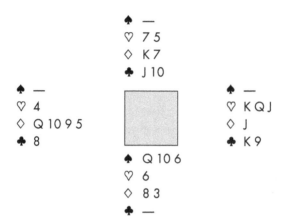

The time has come for the ruffing finesse. You lead dummy's ♣J and await East's card. If he plays the ♣9, you will discard one of your red-suit losers. If instead he covers with the ♣K, you will ruff in your hand. You can then return to dummy with the ◊K to discard a loser on the established ♣10.

> **PLAN: I will win the heart lead, draw trumps and run the ♣Q. If it wins, I will cash the ♣A and return to dummy with a top diamond to take a ruffing finesse with the ♣J10.**

Remember these points

- When you plan to finesse twice against two missing cards, this is called a 'double finesse'. For example, with ♠AQ10 in dummy opposite ♠763 in your hand, you would finesse the ♠10 first. Whether or not this lost to the ♠J, you would finesse the ♠Q next.

- When taking a double finesse, it is normally right to finesse the lower card first.

- With ♣AJ9 opposite ♣652, you would finesse the ♣9 on the first round, hoping that West held the K10 or Q10 and that the ♣9 would force the queen or king from East. You would subsequently finesse the ♣J, to score two tricks from the suit. Because you are missing three high cards, this is known as a 'deep finesse'.

- When you have no cards left in one hand, you can lead one of touching honors from the opposite hand for a 'ruffing finesse'. For example, you might lead the ♡K from ♡KQ82. If the next player covers with the ♡A, you will ruff. The ♡Q will then be established. If the next player does not cover, you will discard a loser instead of ruffing. Even if the king loses to the ace, at least the queen is now high.

Now try these...

A.

                    ♠ 8 5
                    ♡ A Q 9 3
                    ◇ K 7 5
                    ♣ A 6 5 2

♣Q led

                    ♠ A K Q J 9 3
                    ♡ 7 5 2
                    ◇ A Q 6
                    ♣ 8

West leads the ♣Q against 6♠. What is your plan for the slam?

B.

                    ♠ K J 2
                    ♡ K Q 10 3
                    ◇ 10 9 5
                    ♣ A 8 5

♣J led

                    ♠ 8 5
                    ♡ A J 8 5 4
                    ◇ A 7 2
                    ♣ K 4 2

What will your plan be when West leads the ♣J against 4♡?

C.

                    ♠ Q J 6
                    ♡ Q 9 4 2
                    ◇ A 5 3
                    ♣ Q J 8

◇Q led

                    ♠ A K 10 8 7 2
                    ♡ J 10 5
                    ◇ 9 4 2
                    ♣ A

West leads the ◇Q against 4♠. What plan will you make?

D.

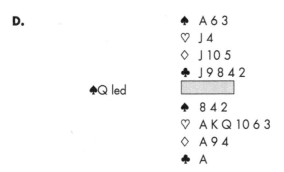

♠ A 6 3
♡ J 4
◇ J 10 5
♣ J 9 8 4 2

♠Q led

♠ 8 4 2
♡ A K Q 10 6 3
◇ A 9 4
♣ A

West leads the ♠Q against 4♡. What is your plan for the contract?

E.

♠ A 6
♡ K 10 6
◇ 10 6 5 3 2
♣ 8 7 4

♣Q led

♠ K Q J 8 4 3 2
♡ 7 4 3
◇ 9
♣ A K

What will your plan be when West leads the ♣Q against 4♠?

F.

♠ Q J 2
♡ A K 10
◇ 9 7 6 2
♣ 8 5 3

♣9 led

♠ A K 10 9 7 6
♡ 6 3
◇ A 8 3
♣ Q 7

After East opens 1♣, you play in 4♠. West leads the ♣9 to East's ♣K; East then continues with the ♣A and ♣J. What is your plan?

ANSWERS

A. You must hope to reduce the number of heart losers from two to one and this can be done only by finessing. To give yourself two possible chances in hearts, you should play a heart to the nine on the first round. When West holds the ♡J and ♡10, dummy's ♡9 will force the ♡K from East and you will lose only one trick in the suit. If instead the ♡9 loses to the ♡J or ♡10 with East, nothing has been lost. You can take your second chance in hearts — a finesse of the queen — on the next round.

   When you play a heart to the nine on the first round, this is known as a 'deep finesse'. You will make the contract in two situations: When West holds the ♡K, and when West holds the ♡J and ♡10.

> **PLAN: I will win the club lead, draw trumps and finesse the ♡9. If this loses to the ♡J or ♡10, I will finesse the ♡Q next.**

B. You have five potential losers — two spades, two diamonds and one club. You can make the contract, with a double finesse in spades, only if West holds both the ♠A and ♠Q. You win the club lead in dummy and draw trumps, ending in the South hand. You then lead a spade, playing the ♠J from dummy when West plays low. If you are in luck and the ♠J wins, you will return to your hand with the ♣K and lead a spade toward the king. If West rises with the ♠A, you will be able to discard a diamond loser on the ♠K.

> **PLAN: I will win with the ♣A, draw trumps and take a double finesse in spades (leading low to the ♠J). When West holds the ♠A and ♠Q, as I must hope, I will lose only one spade and set up a discard for one of my diamond losers.**

C. You have two potential losers in each red suit and must plan to set up a discard on dummy's clubs, using a ruffing finesse. You win the diamond lead and play the ♠6 to the ♠A (retaining the ♠Q and ♠J as entries). You cash the ♣A and return to dummy with the ♠Q. Even if there is still one trump out, you lead the ♣Q next. If East plays low, you will discard a diamond. If instead East covers with the ♣K, you will ruff and return to dummy with the ♠J to discard a diamond loser on the established ♣J. You will make the contract when East holds the ♣K.

> **PLAN: I will win with the ◇A, draw one round of trumps with the ♠A and cash the ♣A. I will then cross to the ♠Q and take a ruffing finesse in clubs. When East holds the ♣K, I can set up a discard for a diamond loser.**

D. You start with two potential losers in spades and two in diamonds. You do not have the entries to attempt to set up the club suit for a discard and must therefore rely on a double finesse in diamonds. You win the spade lead with the ace and, since you have only one entry remaining to dummy (the ♡J), you must take the first diamond finesse immediately. Let's say that you run ♢J to West's ♢Q; the defenders cash two spade tricks and switch to a club. You win with the ace, play the ace and jack of trumps and lead a diamond to your nine. Unless both the missing diamond honors are with West, this second finesse will succeed. You can then draw the last trump and claim the contract.

> **PLAN: I will win with the ♠A and take a double finesse in diamonds. The first finesse must be taken immediately, since there is only one further entry to the dummy.**

E. You have three potential losers in hearts and one in diamonds. To restrict the number of heart losers to two, you must take a deep finesse in the suit. Win the club lead and draw trumps. Next you play a heart to dummy's ten. If West happens to hold both the ♡Q and the ♡J, the ♡10 will force East's ♡A and the contract will be yours. If instead the finesse of the ♡10 loses to East's ♡Q or ♡J, you will lead toward the ♡K on the second round of the suit, hoping that West holds the ♡A.

> **PLAN: I will win the club lead, draw trumps and take a deep finesse of the ♡10. If this loses to the ♡Q or ♡J, I will lead toward the ♡K on the second round.**

F. You have two club losers (already lost) and two potential diamond losers. The only way to dispose of one of these is to take a discard on dummy's hearts. For this to be possible, you must find West with the ♡Q and ♡J and take a successful finesse of the ten. You ruff the third round of clubs high, to prevent an overruff, draw trumps and lead a heart toward dummy. If West plays low you will (cross your fingers and) finesse the ♡10. When both the missing heart honors are onside the ♡10 will win. You can then continue with the ♡A and ♡K, discarding one of your diamond losers to make the game.

    It would do West no good to rise with the ♡Q or ♡J. You would then win with the ace and re-enter your hand with the ♢A to finesse the ♡10 on the second round.

> **PLAN: I will ruff the club continuation high, draw trumps and attempt a finesse of the ♡10. If this succeeds, I can discard one of my diamond losers.**

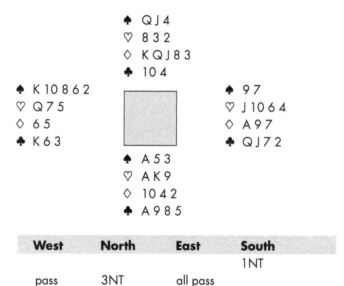

12

PLANNING YOUR ENTRIES

Much of the time, you will have no difficulty in moving backward and forward between your own hand and the dummy. In this chapter we will look at some contracts where handling the entries will form an intrinsic part of your plan.

Let's start with a deal where the key play comes as early as the first trick. Unless you are the sort of player who makes a plan right at the start, you will find that the contract very quickly waves goodbye to you.

	♠ Q J 4	
	♡ 8 3 2	
	◇ K Q J 8 3	
	♣ 10 4	
♠ K 10 8 6 2		♠ 9 7
♡ Q 7 5		♡ J 10 6 4
◇ 6 5		◇ A 9 7
♣ K 6 3		♣ Q J 7 2
	♠ A 5 3	
	♡ A K 9	
	◇ 10 4 2	
	♣ A 9 8 5	

West	North	East	South
			1NT
pass	3NT	all pass	

West leads the ♠6 and this is the quick trick position:

Top Tricks: ♠ 1   ♡ 2   ◇ 0   ♣ 1   **Total: 4**

To score another five tricks you will need to score four tricks in diamonds and a second trick in spades. It doesn't look too difficult. What can go wrong? The answer is that the defenders may hold up the ◇A until the third round and you will then need an entry to dummy, to reach the last two diamonds.

What will happen if you 'do what comes naturally' and play the ♠J from dummy, winning the first trick there? When you play diamonds, East will hold up his ace until the third round. Whatever suit he returns, you will then go down. With ♠A5 opposite dummy's ♠Q4, you will have no way of reaching the two diamond winners in the dummy. (If at any stage you played the ♠5, West would win with the ♠K.)

The solution to your entry problem is the strange-looking play of winning the first trick with the ace of spades. You clear the diamonds and it will then make no difference if East holds up the ◇A until the third round. When you regain the lead, you will lead one of your two low spades toward dummy's ♠QJ, establishing an entry to the dummy. (If East switches to a low club when he takes the ◇A, you must duck the first round to avoid the loss of three club tricks.)

> **PLAN: I will win the spade lead with the ace and clear the diamonds. Dummy's ♠QJ will then provide an entry.**

You would make a similar play with ♠Q43 in the dummy and ♠AJ5 in your hand. When West led the ♠6 you would win in hand with the ace, rather than the jack. Once the diamonds were established, you could set up an entry to dummy by leading toward the ♠Q.

Unblocking to permit a finesse

Another reason to win with a higher card than is necessary, when considering that particular trick on its own, is to free the way for a finesse. Look at the diamond suit on this deal:

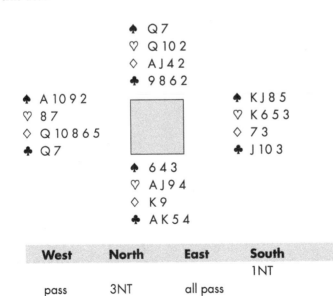

West	North	East	South
			1NT
pass	3NT	all pass	

How will you plan your 3NT contract when West leads the ◇6 (East will play the ◇7)? You can count these immediate winners:

Top Tricks: ♠ 0   ♡ 1   ◇ 2   ♣ 2   **Total: 5**

If clubs break 3-2 you could set up an extra trick in that suit, but the defenders would be able to score four spade tricks when they gained the lead in clubs. It therefore seems that you will need four heart tricks (with the finesse being right) and three diamond tricks.

Suppose that you win the first trick with the ◇9. The only way to reach dummy, to take a heart finesse, would be to overtake the ◇K with the ◇A. That's no good. You would score only two diamond tricks — not enough for the contract.

Since West's ◇6 lead is almost certainly from a suit headed by the queen, you should win the first trick with the king of diamonds instead of the nine. Everything will then go smoothly. You lead the nine of diamonds to dummy's jack, the finesse winning, and run the ♡Q. You then cash the ◇A, while you are in dummy, and continue with the ♡10 (playing the ♡9 from your hand). Finally, a finesse of the ♡J brings your total to nine tricks.

> **PLAN: I will win the diamond lead with the king, finesse the ◇J to gain entry to dummy, and hope to pick up four heart tricks with a repeated finesse against the ♡K.**

Ruffing high to maintain entries in the trump suit

We saw in an earlier chapter how important the entries in the trump suit can be. In order to use spot-card trumps as entries, you may need to retain a lower spot card in the opposite hand. Would you have made the following contract?

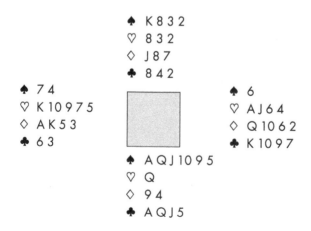

```
              ♠ K 8 3 2
              ♡ 8 3 2
              ◇ J 8 7
              ♣ 8 4 2
♠ 7 4                        ♠ 6
♡ K 10 9 7 5                 ♡ A J 6 4
◇ A K 5 3                    ◇ Q 10 6 2
♣ 6 3                        ♣ K 10 9 7
              ♠ A Q J 10 9 5
              ♡ Q
              ◇ 9 4
              ♣ A Q J 5
```

West	North	East	South
			1♠
pass	2♠	pass	4♠
all pass			

West leads the ◇A against your spade game and the defenders continue with two more rounds of the suit. What is your plan? This is the loser position:

Losers: ♠0 ♡1 ◇2 ♣2   **Total: 5**

You have three certain losers in the red suits, so you must avoid any losers in clubs. To achieve this, you will need to finesse successfully in clubs and repeat the finesse; you can then ruff the fourth round of clubs if necessary. To take two club finesses, you will need two entries to the dummy. How can you plan this?

The two entries must be the ♠K and the ♠8. What will happen if you ruff the third round of diamonds with the ♠5? You will go down! All the remaining trumps in your hand will be higher than dummy's ♠8, so that card will no longer be an entry. Instead, you should ruff the diamond with the ♠9. You can then play the ♠A and cross to the ♠8 to finesse in clubs. The finesse wins and you return to dummy with the ♠K to take another club finesse. When you continue with the ♣A, West shows out. That's no problem; you can ruff your last club in the dummy, making the contract.

> **PLAN: I will ruff the third diamond with the ♠9, preserving dummy's ♠8 as an entry. I can then enter dummy twice in trumps to take club finesses, ruffing the last club if necessary.**

Establishing an honor entry to dummy

Another way to establish an extra entry to dummy is to force out a higher card held by the defenders. On the following deal, you would like to use dummy's ♡Q as an entry:

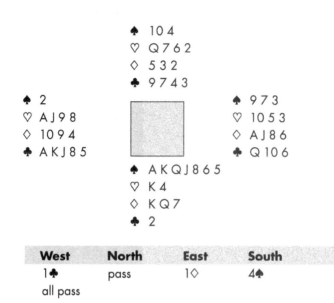

	♠ 10 4	
	♡ Q 7 6 2	
	◇ 5 3 2	
	♣ 9 7 4 3	

♠ 2		♠ 9 7 3
♡ A J 9 8		♡ 10 5 3
◇ 10 9 4		◇ A J 8 6
♣ A K J 8 5		♣ Q 10 6

	♠ A K Q J 8 6 5
	♡ K 4
	◇ K Q 7
	♣ 2

West	North	East	South
1♣	pass	1◇	4♠
all pass			

West leads the ♣A against your boldly bid spade game and continues with the ♣K. What is your plan? This is the loser position:

Losers: ♠ 0   ♡ 1   ◇ 2   ♣ 1   **Total:** 4

You are certain to lose tricks to the three missing aces. To reduce the diamond losers from two to one, you must lead twice from dummy toward your ◇KQ7, hoping to find East with the ◇A. This will require two entries to the dummy. What is your plan?

You ruff the second round of clubs and draw one round of trumps with the ace. You must now lead the ♡K from your hand, aiming to set up the ♡Q as a second entry to dummy (the ♠10 is the other entry). West has no answer to this move. If he wins with the ♡A, you will have two entries to dummy and can lead twice toward your diamonds, making the contract. If instead West holds up the ♡A, you will lead a second round of hearts. This will set up the ♡Q as an extra winner, on which you can discard the ◇7.

Suppose East had held the ♡A (in addition to the ◇A). He could then have defeated you by refusing to capture the ♡K on the first round. Many defenders would make the mistake of winning, however, and you would still make the contract against them.

> **PLAN: I will ruff the second club, draw one round of trumps with the ace and lead the ♡K. If West wins, the ♡Q will be a second entry for diamond leads toward my honors. If instead he holds up, I can establish the ♡Q as an extra winner.**

Taking an 'unnecessary finesse' to create an entry

Sometimes the only way to create an extra entry is to take a finesse that would otherwise be unnecessary. It's hard to visualize, so let's look at an example of the play.

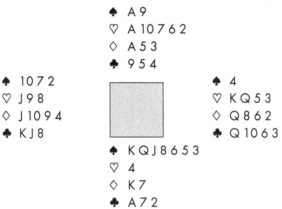

♠ A 9
♡ A 10 7 6 2
◇ A 5 3
♣ 9 5 4

♠ 10 7 2
♡ J 9 8
◇ J 10 9 4
♣ K J 8

♠ 4
♡ K Q 5 3
◇ Q 8 6 2
♣ Q 10 6 3

♠ K Q J 8 6 5 3
♡ 4
◇ K 7
♣ A 7 2

How will you play 6♠ when West leads the ◇J? This is the loser position:

Losers: ♠ 0   ♡ 0   ◇ 0   ♣ 2   **Total:** 2

The only way to reduce your club losers from two to one is to discard a club on dummy's heart suit. A surplus heart trick can be established by ruffing three hearts in the South hand, provided the defenders' hearts divide 4-3. You will need a total of four entries to the dummy — three to take heart ruffs and one to reach the established long card in the suit. The three aces are certain entries. To conjure a fourth entry, you will need to take a successful finesse of the ♠9!

You can see why this is called an 'unnecessary finesse'. You began with no losers in spades and may now create a loser by finessing the ♠9. Nevertheless, it is the only way to attempt to make the slam.

You win the diamond lead in your hand, preserving dummy's ◇A as an entry. Next you cross to the ♡A and ruff a heart. Now comes the big moment. You play a spade to the nine and — yes! — the finesse wins. Taking advantage of this extra entry, you ruff another heart and both defenders follow suit. You cross to the ♠A and ruff a fourth round of hearts with a high trump. You can then draw the last trump, cross to the ◇A and discard one of your club losers on the thirteenth card in hearts. Slam made.

> **PLAN: If hearts break 4-3, I can establish the thirteenth heart for a club discard. Since I will need four entries to dummy, I must take an 'unnecessary finesse' of the ♠9.**

Overtaking an honor to create an extra entry

Suppose you have a suit of ♣KQJ5 in your hand opposite ♣A863 in the dummy. Four easy tricks, yes, but how many entries to dummy would this suit provide? When the defenders' clubs break 3-2, you can start with the ♣K and ♣Q and then overtake the ♣J with the ♣A on the third round. You will then be able to lead the ♣5 to dummy's ♣8 on the fourth round, giving you two entries to dummy.

Let's see a deal where such fancy footwork is necessary:

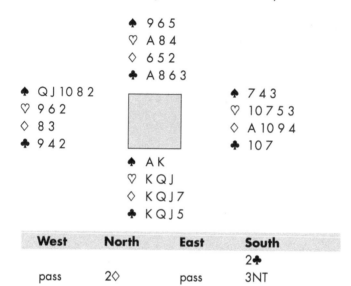

West	North	East	South
			2♣
pass	2◊	pass	3NT
pass	6NT	all pass	

West leads the ♠Q against your small slam and you count these top tricks:

Top Tricks: ♠ 2   ♡ 3   ◊ 0   ♣ 4   **Total: 9**

So, you will need three diamond tricks to make the slam. This can be done when diamonds split 3-3 or East holds the ◊A. When East holds four or more diamonds to the ace, you will need to lead the suit three times from the dummy.

You win the spade lead and play the ♣K and ♣Q, everyone following. Since there is only one club out, you can afford to overtake the ♣J with the ♣A on the third round. When you make your first diamond lead from dummy, East plays low and your ◊K wins. You re-enter dummy by leading the ♣5 to the ♣8 and play a second diamond to your queen, both defenders following with spot cards. You then return to dummy for a third time, with the ♡A, and lead yet another diamond toward your hand. Whether or not East chooses to rise with the ◊A, your ◊J will give you a third diamond trick and the slam.

What would have happened if, say, East had shown out the second round of clubs? You could not then have overtaken the ♣J on the third round, because this would set up a club trick for West. Restricted to only one club entry, you could lead diamonds only twice from the dummy. You would have had to hope that diamonds were 3-3 or that East held ◇Ax.

> **PLAN: If clubs are 3-2, I can overtake the ♣J with the ♣A on the third round, creating an extra entry to dummy. I can then lead three times toward my diamond holding.**

Discovering in time whether a finesse is necessary

Sometimes a finesse will become necessary only if there is a bad break in a suit. In such a case you may need to test the suit before you use the entry that will be needed to take such a finesse. This is the sort of deal that we have in mind:

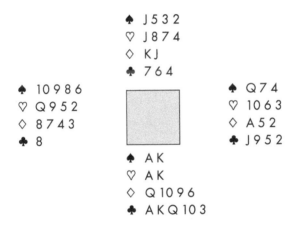

                ♠ J 5 3 2
                ♡ J 8 7 4
                ◇ K J
                ♣ 7 6 4
    ♠ 10 9 8 6   ♠ Q 7 4
    ♡ Q 9 5 2   ♡ 10 6 3
    ◇ 8 7 4 3   ◇ A 5 2
    ♣ 8   ♣ J 9 5 2
                ♠ A K
                ♡ A K
                ◇ Q 10 9 6
                ♣ A K Q 10 3

You reach the excellent contract of 6NT and West leads the ♠10. What is your plan for the slam?

Top Tricks: ♠2 ♡2 ◇0 ♣3   **Total: 7**

If the club suit provides five tricks, this will bring the total to nine and three additional diamond tricks will give you the slam. Suppose you win the spade lead and play a diamond to the king. East may win and return a diamond. You can win this in the dummy, with the ◇J, but you will then have no idea that a finesse of the ♣10 is necessary. When you eventually play clubs from the top, you will go down.

A better idea is to test the club suit, by playing two top clubs before you tackle the diamond suit. West will show out on the second round of clubs and only then do you play a diamond to the king. Whether East ducks this, or wins and returns a diamond, you will know when you reach dummy that a finesse of the ♣10 is needed.

PLAN: I will win the spade lead and play the ♣AK. I can then set up the diamonds, using the diamond entry to dummy for a club finesse if East shows up with ♣Jxxx.

Preventing a suit from becoming blocked

When you are running a suit, it is a familiar technique to play the high card or cards from the shorter holding first. For example, with K4 opposite AQJ6 you would play the king first and then cross to the ace. If you made the mistake of cashing the ace first, you would have to win the second round with the king and would then be in the wrong hand.

Sometimes it is more difficult to see that there is a risk of a suit becoming blocked. Would you have played the club suit correctly on this contract?

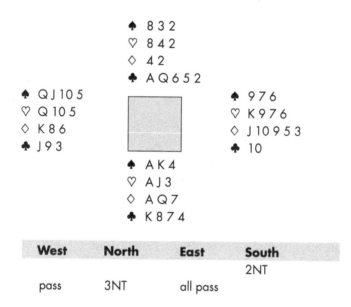

```
              ♠ 8 3 2
              ♡ 8 4 2
              ◇ 4 2
              ♣ A Q 6 5 2
♠ Q J 10 5                      ♠ 9 7 6
♡ Q 10 5                        ♡ K 9 7 6
◇ K 8 6                         ◇ J 10 9 5 3
♣ J 9 3                         ♣ 10
              ♠ A K 4
              ♡ A J 3
              ◇ A Q 7
              ♣ K 8 7 4
```

West	North	East	South
			2NT
pass	3NT	all pass	

West leads the ♠Q and you observe this top trick position:

Top Tricks: ♠2 ♡1 ◇1 ♣3   **Total: 7**

It may seem that only a 4-0 club break can prevent you from scoring five club tricks to bring your total to nine. Look what will happen if you play the club suit carelessly, though. Suppose you play the ♣K on the first round and continue with the ♣4 to dummy's ace. You will have to play the ♣Q on the third round, to pick up West's ♣J, and now your ♣8 will win the fourth round! Dummy's ♣6 is good but you will not be able to reach it. The outcome will be the same if your first move in the club suit is to play the ♣4 to dummy's ace.

You need to be in dummy after playing the fourth round of clubs and to achieve this you must unblock the ♣8 and the ♣7. You begin with the ♣K and then lead the ♣8 to dummy's ♣A. When you continue with the ♣Q, you must follow with the ♣7 from your hand. Now the fourth round of clubs will be a delight to the eye. You will lead dummy's ♣6 and drop the ♣4 from your hand. With the lead still in dummy, you can score the ♣5 and make the contract.

> **PLAN: I will win the spade lead, cash the ♣K and lead the ♣8 to dummy's ♣A. I will then play the ♣Q, unblocking the ♣7 from my hand. I can then play the ♣6 and ♣5.**

Sometimes you may have to give the defenders a seemingly unnecessary trick to prevent a suit from becoming blocked. That's what happens on this deal:

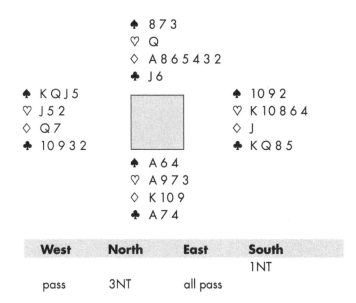

	♠ 873	
	♡ Q	
	◊ A 8 6 5 4 3 2	
	♣ J 6	

♠ K Q J 5		♠ 10 9 2
♡ J 5 2		♡ K 10 8 6 4
◊ Q 7		◊ J
♣ 10 9 3 2		♣ K Q 8 5

	♠ A 6 4	
	♡ A 9 7 3	
	◊ K 10 9	
	♣ A 7 4	

West	North	East	South
			1NT
pass	3NT	all pass	

North correctly judges that nine tricks in 3NT may be easier than eleven in 5◊. What is your plan when West leads the ♠K? You have these top tricks:

Top Tricks: ♠ 1 ♡ 1 ◊ 2 ♣ 1   **Total: 5**

So, you need six diamond tricks to make the game. You cannot afford to hold up the ♠A, since the defenders might switch to clubs (or hearts), giving them too many tricks. You win immediately with the ♠A and play the ◊K, dropping the ◊7 and ◊J from the defenders. What next? If you lead the ◊10 and this is covered by West's ◊Q and dummy's ◊A, the diamond suit will be blocked. Your ◊9 will win the third round and you will score only three diamond tricks; you will go three down!

To make the contract, you must allow West's ◊Q to win the second round. West can score three spades (you must hope it is not more than three). You will then win West's switch, cross to the ◊A on the third round of the suit and make six diamond tricks for your contract.

> **PLAN: I will win the spade lead, cash the ◊K and duck the next round of diamonds (even if they break 2-1). I can then score six diamond tricks.**

Remember these points

- By winning the first trick with an unnecessarily high card in your hand, you may ensure a later entry to dummy in that suit. For example with ♣Q73 in the dummy opposite ♣AJ5 in your hand, you win with the ♣A, rather than the ♣J, to preserve the ♣Q as an entry.

- By overtaking one honor with another, you may be able to set up an extra entry to dummy. For example, with ◊A764 in dummy opposite ◊KQJ2 in your hand, you cash the king and queen (both defenders following) and then overtake the jack with the ace. You can then overtake the ◊2 with the ◊7 on the fourth round.

- Beware of spot cards that can block a suit, causing you to end up in the wrong hand. Sometimes you can unblock these on the early rounds.

- By testing a suit before you use up dummy's last entry, you can discover in time whether a finesse will be necessary.

Now try these...

A.

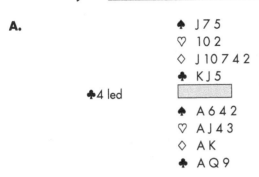

♠ J 7 5
♡ 10 2
◇ J 10 7 4 2
♣ K J 5

♣4 led

♠ A 6 4 2
♡ A J 4 3
◇ A K
♣ A Q 9

West leads the ♣4 against 3NT. What is your plan?

B.

♠ A 8 2
♡ 6
◇ 10 8 5 4
♣ A K Q J 4

♠J led

♠ K Q 7 5 4
♡ A 4 3
◇ K 6
♣ 9 5 3

West leads the jack of trumps against your contract of 6♠. What is your plan?

C.

♠ A Q 4
♡ J 6
◇ Q 10 9 7 6 2
♣ 10 7

♡10 led

♠ K 5
♡ K 7 2
◇ A J 5
♣ K J 6 5 2

You reach 3NT and West leads the ♡10. You play dummy's ♡J and East covers with the ♡Q. How will you play?

D.

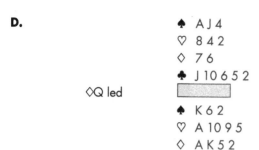

♠ A J 4
♥ 8 4 2
♦ 7 6
♣ J 10 6 5 2

♦Q led

♠ K 6 2
♥ A 10 9 5
♦ A K 5 2
♣ A Q

West leads the ♦Q against 3NT. What is your plan?

E.

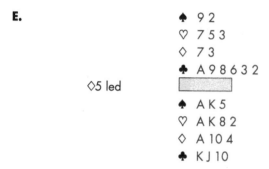

♠ 9 2
♥ 7 5 3
♦ 7 3
♣ A 9 8 6 3 2

♦5 led

♠ A K 5
♥ A K 8 2
♦ A 10 4
♣ K J 10

West leads the ♦5 against 3NT, East playing the ♦Q. What is your plan?

F.

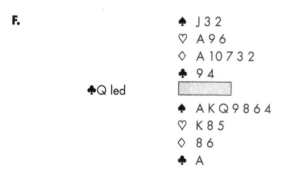

♠ J 3 2
♥ A 9 6
♦ A 10 7 3 2
♣ 9 4

♣Q led

♠ A K Q 9 8 6 4
♥ K 8 5
♦ 8 6
♣ A

Some learned bidding sequence carries you to 6♠ and West leads the ♣Q. How will you play the contract? (Trumps break 2-1.)

ANSWERS

A. You have seven top tricks and must look to the diamond suit for the two extra tricks that you need. Unless the ◇Q falls under the ace and king, you will need two entries to dummy (one to set up the diamonds, another to reach the established winners in the suit). You must therefore win the opening lead with the ♣A, whatever card East happens to play. You play the ◇A and ◇K, lead the ♣9 to dummy's ♣J and play the ◇J, to set up the suit. You will then win the defender's return, cross to the ♣K and score two extra diamond tricks with the ◇10 and the ◇7.

> **PLAN: I will win the club lead with the ♣A, an unnecessarily high card. I will unblock the ◇A and ◇K, cross to the ♣J and set up the diamonds. The ♣K will be an entry to cash the established tricks in diamonds.**

B. You must hope that trumps are 3-2 and you have no trump loser. Five trumps, five clubs, the ♡A and one heart ruff will bring the total to twelve. The only remaining problem is to plan your entries. Suppose you win the trump lead with the ♠Q. You continue with the ♡A and another heart, ruffing with the ♠8. You then play dummy's last trump, the ace. That's unfortunate! You are stuck in the dummy with no way to return to your hand to draw the last trump with the ♠K. You have to try a diamond to the ◇K and will go down when West holds the ◇A.

Stop to make a plan before you play to Trick 1 and everything is easy. You win with the ♠A, take your heart ruff and lead dummy's remaining small trump to the ♠KQ in your hand. When the defenders' trumps have been drawn, you can play five rounds of clubs and discard two of your three remaining red-suit losers.

> **PLAN: I will win with the ♠A, ruff a heart and draw trumps.**

C. You win with the ♡K and see that you must set up the diamonds without losing the lead. To make the contract when East holds ◇Kxx, you will need two spade entries to dummy. You can then finesse in diamonds and return to dummy to enjoy the established diamond winners. At Trick 2 you should cross to the ♠Q and run the ◇10. East does not cover and West follows with a low card. You continue with a low diamond, East again playing low. You finesse the ◇J successfully, cash the ◇A and return to dummy by overtaking the ♠K with the ♠A to score the remaining diamonds. You make six diamonds, the ♡K and (only) two spades — a total of nine tricks.

> **PLAN: I will try the ♡J from dummy. When I win a heart trick, I will cross to the ♠Q and run the ◇10. Assuming the finesse wins, I can repeat the diamond finesse and cash the ◇A. I will then overtake the ♠K to score six diamond tricks.**

D. You have six top tricks and must seek some extra club tricks. You win the diamond lead and play the ♣A and ♣Q. If the defenders win with the ♣K, you can cross to the ♠A to score three more club tricks. Let's suppose that the defenders allow your ♣Q to win. What now? You still need to set up the clubs. To do this, you will need two entries to dummy, one to knock out the ♣K and another to reach the established cards in the suit. You must take an 'unnecessary finesse' of the ♠J, hoping to set up an extra entry. If the finesse wins, you will play the ♣J to set up the clubs. You can then win the defenders' return, cross to the ♠A and score a total of four club tricks, ending with an overtrick.

> **PLAN: I will win the diamond lead and play the ♣A and ♣Q. If the defenders duck the second club, I will finesse the ♠J in the hope that I can set up a second entry to establish the clubs.**

E. You will not be able to play the ♣K and ♣A on the first two rounds of the suit; even if the defenders' clubs break 2-2, the remaining club in your hand will then block the suit. You will have to allow the defenders to win a trick with the ♣Q, unless it happens to fall on the first round under the ♣K. You must therefore hold up the ◇A until the third round, aiming to exhaust East's diamonds.

The ♣K draws two spot cards from the defenders, we will say, and you continue with the ♣J. If West follows with the last club spot card, or shows out, you will run the ♣J; when East wins with the ♣Q he will have no diamond to play (unless diamonds are 4-4 and pose no threat). If instead West produces the ♣Q on the second round, you will have to duck and hope that diamonds are 4-4.

> **PLAN: I will hold up the ◇A until the third round, cash the ♣K and lead the ♣J. If the ♣Q comes from West, I will have to duck. Otherwise I will run the ♣J to East.**

F. You win the club lead and draw trumps with the ace and king. You must now try to set up dummy's diamonds, to discard your heart loser. The first step is to duck a round of diamonds, preserving dummy's ◇A as an entry on the second round. You ruff the club return, cross to the ◇A and ruff a diamond, West showing out. Then you can cross to dummy with the ♠J. Another diamond ruff establishes the suit and you can return to dummy with the ♡A to discard your heart loser on the established ◇10.

> **PLAN: I will draw trumps in two rounds, duck a diamond and ruff the club return. After a diamond to the ace and a diamond ruff, I will cross to the ♠J and ruff another diamond. Provided diamonds break no worse than 4-2, I can set up the diamonds and discard my heart loser.**

13

PLANNING TO DRAW SOME TRUMPS BUT NOT ALL

In Chapter 6, we considered one of the important decisions that you have to make in a suit contract — whether to draw trumps immediately. Here we will look at something a bit different, the idea of drawing some of the defenders' trumps but not all. As you will see, there are various good reasons why you might choose to follow such a path.

Leaving a defender with the master trump

Suppose you have a trump holding of ♡AKQ82 opposite ♡973. You draw three rounds and the suit breaks 4-1, leaving a defender with the ♡J. Usually there will be no point in playing a fourth round of trumps; the purpose of drawing trumps is to prevent the defenders from taking a ruff and you would not mind that happening when the trump was a master. Look at this deal:

```
                    ♠ A K 3
                    ♡ 9 7 3
                    ◇ K Q 8 6
                    ♣ K 9 3
    ♠ 10 9 7 4                         ♠ Q J 8
    ♡ J 10 6 4                         ♡ 5
    ◇ 5                                ◇ 10 9 7 4 3
    ♣ Q J 10 8                         ♣ A 7 4 2
                    ♠ 6 5 2
                    ♡ A K Q 8 2
                    ◇ A J 2
                    ♣ 6 5
```

West	North	East	South
			1♡
pass	2◇	pass	2♡
pass	4♡	all pass	

West leads the ♣Q against 4♡ and you see these potential losers:

Losers: ♠ 1   ♡ 1   ◇ 0   ♣ 2   **Total:** 4

On many occasions with this heart holding you would have no losers in the suit — the opposing trumps would split 3-2. At the other extreme, West might hold all five trumps and there would be two trump losers. Since this would leave the contract with no chance at all, we will assume only one potential loser in the trump suit. The opening lead implies that East holds the ♣A, so you cannot avoid two club losers unless West happens to hold seven clubs and East's ♣A is singleton. You play low from dummy on the first trick, and again when West continues with the ♣J. The ♣A does not appear from East and you have to ruff the third round of clubs in your hand.

When you play the ace and king of trumps, East discards a diamond on the second round — your potential heart loser has become a certainty. You continue with the queen of trumps; West now has the master jack of trumps, while your last trump is the eight. Should you play a fourth round of trumps? No! West would win with the jack and could then cash a club to defeat the contract; you would have no trump left with which to ruff. Instead, you simply play your winners in the diamond suit. West is welcome to ruff at any stage with his ♡J. He cannot then cash a club winner because you will still have the ♡8 in your hand. Eventually, you will discard your spade loser on the fourth round of diamonds. The guideline here is: *do not draw a master trump unless there is a good reason for doing so.*

> **PLAN: I will ruff the third club, draw three rounds of trumps and play diamonds. Even if trumps split 4-1, I can discard my spade loser on the fourth diamond.**

The time has come to see a deal where there is a pressing need to draw a defender's master trump. That's because you have some winners to cash in an otherwise entry-less dummy and you do not want the defender to ruff, thereby stemming the flow of these winners:

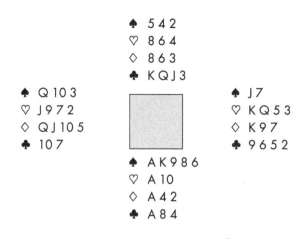

	♠ 5 4 2		
	♡ 8 6 4		
	◇ 8 6 3		
	♣ K Q J 3		

♠ Q 10 3   ♠ J 7
♡ J 9 7 2   ♡ K Q 5 3
◇ Q J 10 5   ◇ K 9 7
♣ 10 7   ♣ 9 6 5 2

♠ A K 9 8 6
♡ A 10
◇ A 4 2
♣ A 8 4

West	North	East	South
			1♠
pass	2♠	pass	4♠
all pass			

West leads the ◇Q against 4♠ and you see these potential losers:

Losers: ♠ 2   ♡ 1   ◇ 2   ♣ 0   **Total:** 5

The contract would have little chance if trumps broke 4-1 and there were two trump losers, so you should assume that the division is 3-2, leaving you with only one loser in the suit. To reduce the loser total to the required three, you will have to discard the heart loser on dummy's surplus club winner.

You win the diamond lead and play the ace and king of trumps, pleased to see both defenders follow. What now? Suppose you leave West with the master trump, the ♠Q, and turn to the club suit with the aim of discarding your heart loser. That's no good! West will ruff the third round of clubs with his master trump. Dummy's last trump, the ♠5, is not large enough to provide an entry. You will not be able to reach the ♣J, for a discard, and you will go one down.

It is not difficult to prevent such an outcome. After drawing two rounds of trumps with the ace and king, you should continue with a third round of the suit. West will win with the ♠Q and the defenders will score two diamond tricks. You can afford that. When you regain the lead, you will play four rounds of clubs, throwing your heart loser. What could be easier than that?

> **PLAN: I will win the diamond lead and play ace, king and another trump. With the defenders' master trump out of the way, I can cash four rounds of clubs to throw the heart loser.**

Reducing the risk of a ruff or overruff

On some deals it is not practical to draw all the trumps but you can still reduce the chance of an adverse ruff by drawing some of the trumps. Look at this spade game:

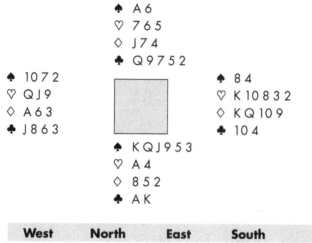

♠ A 6
♡ 7 6 5
◇ J 7 4
♣ Q 9 7 5 2

♠ 10 7 2   ♠ 8 4
♡ Q J 9   ♡ K 10 8 3 2
◇ A 6 3   ◇ K Q 10 9
♣ J 8 6 3   ♣ 10 4

♠ K Q J 9 5 3
♡ A 4
◇ 8 5 2
♣ A K

West	North	East	South
			1♠
pass	1NT	pass	4♠
all pass			

West leads the ♡Q against 4♠ and these are your possible losers:

Losers: ♠ 0   ♡ 1   ◇ 3   ♣ 0   **Total:**   4

You win the heart lead with the ♡A and see that you need to discard a loser on the ♣Q. How can this be done? You cannot draw all the trumps first, because the club suit is blocked and the ♠A is the only entry to dummy.

    Suppose you play the two top clubs in your hand, cross to the ♠A and lead the ♣Q. East will ruff with his remaining trump and you will go down (whether you overruff or discard a loser). To reduce the chance of a ruff you must draw as many round of trumps as possible before playing the ♣Q. After playing the top clubs in your hand, you should play the king and then the ace of trumps, drawing two rounds. When the cards lie as in the diagram, with East holding only two trumps, you will be rewarded. East will not be able to ruff the ♣Q and you will be able to discard a red-suit loser.

> **PLAN: I will win the heart lead, play the ♣AK and draw two rounds of trumps with the king and ace. I will then hope to discard a loser on the ♣Q.**

The same technique can work well when you have three low trumps in dummy and need to take a ruff there. By drawing two rounds of trumps, leaving one in the dummy, you can reduce the risk of an overruff:

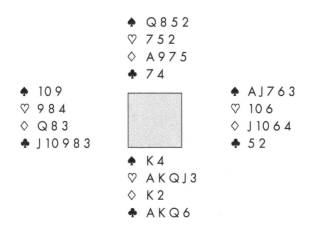

♠ Q 8 5 2
♡ 7 5 2
◇ A 9 7 5
♣ 7 4

♠ 10 9
♡ 9 8 4
◇ Q 8 3
♣ J 10 9 8 3

♠ A J 7 6 3
♡ 10 6
◇ J 10 6 4
♣ 5 2

♠ K 4
♡ A K Q J 3
◇ K 2
♣ A K Q 6

West	North	East	South
			2♣
pass	2◇	pass	2♡
pass	3♡	pass	4NT
pass	5◇	pass	6♡
all pass			

West leads the ♣J against your small slam. What plan will you make? These are your possible losers:

Losers: ♠ 1   ♡ 0   ◇ 0   ♣ 1   **Total:** 2

There is nothing you can do about the spade loser, so you must avoid losing a trick in clubs. It looks simple enough; you can ruff the third round of clubs in the dummy. The opening lead is somewhat ominous, however. West's ♣J lead suggests a sequence and therefore possible length in the suit; if he holds five clubs, East may be able to overruff the dummy.

Suppose you win the club lead, cash a second high club immediately and then attempt to ruff the ♣6. East will indeed overruff and you be one down. To give yourself a better chance, you should draw two rounds of trumps at the start. When you then use dummy's last trump to ruff the third round of clubs, East will show out of clubs but will have no trump left with which to ruff. You will return to the ◇K, draw trumps and give up a spade trick.

> **PLAN: I need to ruff a club in dummy. To reduce the risk of an overruff, I will draw two rounds of trumps first.**

Exactly the same idea can work well when you have a side suit of three cards in the dummy and four cards in your hand. It can allow you to ruff the fourth round in dummy when the defenders' cards divide 4-2. Would you have spotted the winning line on this spade game?

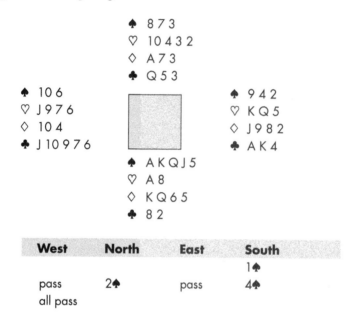

	♠ 873	
	♡ 10 4 3 2	
	◇ A 7 3	
	♣ Q 5 3	

♠ 10 6		♠ 9 4 2
♡ J 9 7 6		♡ K Q 5
◇ 10 4		◇ J 9 8 2
♣ J 10 9 7 6		♣ A K 4

	♠ A K Q J 5	
	♡ A 8	
	◇ K Q 6 5	
	♣ 8 2	

West	North	East	South
			1♠
pass	2♠	pass	4♠
all pass			

West leads the ♣J against 4♠ and the defenders play two more rounds of the suit, forcing you to ruff. How will you continue? These are your possible losers:

Losers: ♠0 ♡1 ◇1 ♣2   **Total: 4**

You cannot do anything about the heart loser, so you must consider how you can avoid losing a trick on the fourth round of diamonds. If diamonds split 3-3, even your neighbor's dog would make the contract. What can be done when diamonds are 4-2?

You can still make the contract when the defender with four diamonds also holds three trumps. After ruffing the third club, you draw just two rounds of trumps with the ace and king. You then play the three top diamonds. If diamonds break 3-3, you will simply draw the last trump and score the thirteenth diamond. When instead the cards lie as in the diagram, West will show out on the third round of diamonds but will be unable to ruff. You will then ruff your last diamond in the dummy, East following suit helplessly, and the contract is yours.

> **PLAN: I will ruff the third club and draw two rounds of trumps. Then I will play the three top diamonds. If a defender holds four diamonds and three or four trumps, I will be able to ruff my diamond loser in dummy.**

Ducking a round of trumps

In the previous section we saw a couple of deals where it suited declarer to play precisely two rounds of trumps. When your trumps are headed by the ace, but missing the king and queen, it will often assist you to duck the first round of trumps. You can then draw a second round with the ace and remain in control of the hand. It's not easy to visualize, perhaps, so let's see a couple of deals where ducking a trump will pay dividends.

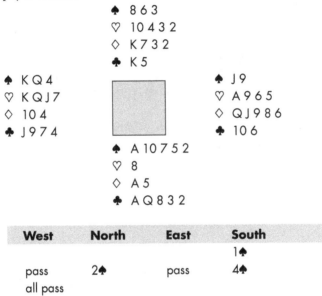

West	North	East	South
			1♠
pass	2♠	pass	4♠
all pass			

West leads the ♡K against 4♠ and continues with a second round of hearts. You see these potential losers:

Losers: ♠ 2   ♡ 1   ◇ 0   ♣ 1   **Total: 4**

If trumps break badly, you might of course lose three trump tricks. Since you would then have no hope of making the contract, you must assume that the trumps are 3-2 and that you have only two trump losers.

The heart trick has already been lost, so everything hinges on not losing a club trick. A 3-3 club break would solve the problem. If instead clubs break 4-2, you will need to ruff a club in dummy. How can you arrange this with maximum safety? Suppose you ruff the second heart, continue with the ♣K and ♣A and ruff a club. It will not be good enough when the cards lie as in the diagram. East will overruff (with the doubleton trump holding) and you will still have to lose two trump tricks to West. Your fate will be the same if you cash the ace of trumps before following that line; again you would lose three trump tricks.

You need to draw precisely two rounds of trumps before taking your club ruff and you can achieve this only by ducking the first round of trumps. Let's say that the defenders win and return another heart, forcing you to ruff again. You draw a second round of trumps with the ace, leaving the defenders with only the king of trumps. Everyone follows to the ♣K and ♣A and you can now play the queen of clubs. You won't mind if a defender ruffs a club honor with the master ♠K because you can then use dummy's last trump to ruff a club yourself. Since West holds four clubs here, alongside the last trump, no one will ruff a club honor. You can then ruff the fourth round of clubs in dummy, holding your losers to just two trumps and a heart.

> **PLAN: I will ruff the second heart and duck a round of trumps. When I regain the lead, I will play the ace of trumps followed by the three top clubs, ruffing a fourth round if necessary.**

Suppose next that you have a trump suit of AK865 opposite 974. Even if the defenders' trumps break 3-2, you will have to lose a trump trick at some stage. On many deals it will be important to choose carefully when you lose that trick. You must do so when the defenders cannot do you any damage. Look at this deal:

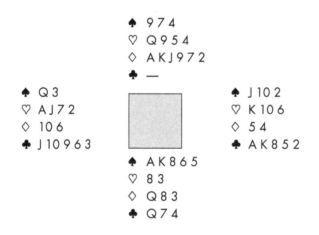

```
              ♠ 9 7 4
              ♡ Q 9 5 4
              ◇ A K J 9 7 2
              ♣ —
♠ Q 3                        ♠ J 10 2
♡ A J 7 2                    ♡ K 10 6
◇ 10 6                       ◇ 5 4
♣ J 10 9 6 3                 ♣ A K 8 5 2
              ♠ A K 8 6 5
              ♡ 8 3
              ◇ Q 8 3
              ♣ Q 7 4
```

West	North	East	South
	1◇	pass	1♠
pass	2◇	pass	3◇
pass	3♠	pass	4♠
all pass			

How will you play the spade game when West leads the ♣J? You start with these potential losers:

Losers: ♠ 1   ♡ 2   ◇ 0   ♣ 3   Total: 6

As on the previous deal, you will have to assume that trumps break 3-2, to give you a chance. You ruff the club lead in dummy, which disposes of one club loser; the other two clubs can be discarded eventually on dummy's diamonds. (You cannot ruff both of them because you do not have the necessary entries to the South hand.) How will you play the trump suit?

Suppose your first move is to play the ace and king of trumps. With no trumps left in dummy you will have no protection in the club suit. It will make no difference whether you play a third round of trumps next, or turn to the diamond suit allowing East to ruff the third round; the defenders will score two clubs and two hearts, putting you two down. Since you will have to lose a trump trick at some time or other, you should do so when the defenders cannot damage you. In other words, strange as it may seem, you should duck a round of trumps at Trick 2. Since there will still be a trump left in the dummy, a club return will cause no embarrassment; you can ruff it in the dummy, cross to the ◇Q and draw trumps. Then you can run the diamond suit, discarding your remaining clubs.

> **PLAN: I will ruff the club and duck a round of trumps. When I regain the lead, I will draw trumps and run the diamonds.**

Remember these points

- When there is only one trump out and it is a master, there is usually no point in drawing it. The defender's trump is going to make a trick anyway and you will waste two of your lower trumps drawing it. The exception is when you are planning to run a long suit in dummy and do not want the defender to ruff in.

- When you need to ruff a loser in a dummy containing three low trumps, you can reduce the risk of an overruff by drawing two rounds of trumps before taking the ruff.

- When your only high trump is the ace, it may work well to duck the first round of trumps. When you regain the lead, you will draw one more round with the ace, remaining in control of the hand.

Now try these...

A.

         ♠ J 4
         ♡ 8 5
         ◇ A 10 6 3 2
         ♣ Q J 5 4

◇K led

         ♠ 10 6 5
         ♡ A K Q 7 6 3
         ◇ 8
         ♣ A K 7

How will you play 4♡ when West leads the ◇K? You have eleven easy tricks if trumps break 3-2, so consider the case when trumps are 4-1.

B.

         ♠ 6 5 2
         ♡ A 9
         ◇ 10 7 6 4 3
         ♣ 8 5 2

♣A led

         ♠ A K Q J 7
         ♡ K Q 6 5
         ◇ A
         ♣ J 9 4

Against your contract of 4♠ West cashes the ♣A and ♣K, continuing with a low club to East's queen. What is your plan when East switches to the ♠4?

C.

         ♠ 7 5
         ♡ 9 5
         ◇ K 8 6 3 2
         ♣ A 7 4 2

♣Q led

         ♠ A K 8 6 2
         ♡ K Q J 10 4
         ◇ A 7
         ♣ 9

West leads the ♣Q against 4♠. How will you plan the play?

D.

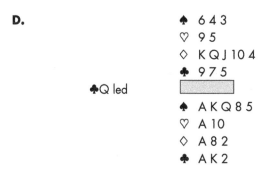

```
        ♠ 6 4 3
        ♥ 9 5
        ◊ K Q J 10 4
        ♣ 9 7 5
♣Q led  ┌──────────┐
        └──────────┘
        ♠ A K Q 8 5
        ♥ A 10
        ◊ A 8 2
        ♣ A K 2
```

How will you play 6♠ when West leads the ♣Q? (Consider the case when trumps break 4-1.)

E.

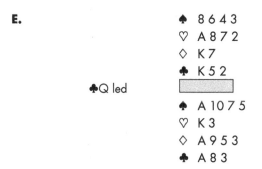

```
        ♠ 8 6 4 3
        ♥ A 8 7 2
        ◊ K 7
        ♣ K 5 2
♣Q led  ┌──────────┐
        └──────────┘
        ♠ A 10 7 5
        ♥ K 3
        ◊ A 9 5 3
        ♣ A 8 3
```

West leads the ♣Q against your contract of 4♠. What is your plan?

F.

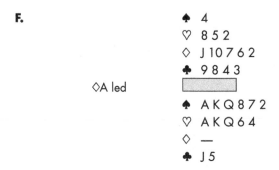

```
        ♠ 4
        ♥ 8 5 2
        ◊ J 10 7 6 2
        ♣ 9 8 4 3
◊A led  ┌──────────┐
        └──────────┘
        ♠ A K Q 8 7 2
        ♥ A K Q 6 4
        ◊ —
        ♣ J 5
```

West leads the ◊A against 4♥. How will you plan the play?

ANSWERS

A. Everything will be easy if trumps break 3-2, so you should concentrate on the case where trumps are 4-1. Suppose you win the diamond lead and draw two rounds of trumps with the ace and king, East showing out on the second round. With no trumps left in dummy, you are exposed to the possible loss of three spade tricks. Perhaps you draw a third round of trumps and turn to the clubs; you will then go down when a defender can ruff the second or third club and switch to spades.

Since you can afford to lose a trump trick, you should do this at a moment when the defenders can do you no damage. You should duck a round of trumps at Trick 2. The defenders cannot then take three spade tricks because you still have a trump in dummy and could ruff the third round. Whatever the defenders do next, you will be able to draw trumps and score four club tricks for the contract.

PLAN: To guard against a 4-1 trump break, I will duck a round of trumps at Trick 2. When I regain the lead, I will draw trumps and score my ten top tricks.

B. You have lost three club tricks already and must now avoid a heart loser to make the contract. If you continue immediately with ace, king and another heart, planning to ruff in the dummy, you will go down when the hearts split 5-2. The defender with the doubleton heart will be able to ruff with a higher trump than dummy's ♣6. To give yourself a better chance, you should draw a second round of trumps before trying to ruff a heart in dummy. You will then survive when a defender started with two hearts but has only two trumps.

PLAN: I will win the trump switch, draw a second round of trumps and then ruff my heart loser in dummy.

C. You have one loser in hearts and none in the minor suits, so you can afford to lose two trump tricks. After winning with the ♣A, you play the ace and king of trumps, everyone following. What next? There are two trumps still out and you can afford to lose tricks to them. You should turn to the heart suit, knocking out the ♡A. If a defender wins and plays another club, you will ruff and play good hearts. The defenders are welcome to ruff twice with their remaining trumps and to play further clubs. You will stay in control and lose just two trumps and a heart.

Suppose instead that you play a third round of trumps, after the ace and king, and find them breaking 4-2. The defender with the trumps will win, draw a fourth round of trumps and lead a club. You will have to ruff with your last trump and the hearts will not yet be established. When the defenders take the ♡A, they will defeat you by cashing some club tricks.

PLAN: I will win the club lead and play the ace and king of trumps. I will then establish the heart suit.

D. You have a potential loser in both hearts and clubs, but these can be discarded on dummy's diamonds. If trumps break 3-2, you will have an easy 13 tricks (five spades, five diamonds, the ♣AK and the ♡A). Let's see what may happen if trumps break 4-1. You win the club lead and play two rounds of trumps, East showing out on the second round. If you simply draw a third round of trumps and start playing on diamonds, you are likely to go down. West will ruff the third round of diamonds (or the fourth round if he started with three diamonds). Cut off from dummy, you will not then be able to discard your two losers. To make the slam you must continue with queen and another trump, giving West his trump trick. You can then win his return and play five rounds of diamonds to discard your two losers.

PLAN: I will win the club lead and draw trumps. When trumps are 4-1, I will concede a trump trick before playing diamonds to discard my two losers.

E. You can see two possible losers in trumps (you must assume that it is not more), two losers in diamonds and one in clubs. You must aim to ruff two diamonds in the dummy and you would like to draw precisely two rounds of trumps before attempting this. Otherwise, you would run the risk of a defender overruffing with a doubleton trump; you would then lose three trump tricks.

You should win the club lead and duck a round of trumps. Win the next trick and cash the ace of trumps. All will be well when trumps break 3-2 because you can then go about your business, ruffing two diamonds in dummy. You do not mind in the least when the defenders choose to take their last trump.

PLAN: I will win the club lead and duck a round of trumps. I can then play the ace of trumps and ruff two diamonds in dummy, losing only two trumps and a club.

F. You have two obvious club losers. If spades break 4-2 and hearts 4-1, you have two more potential losers in those suits. You ruff the diamond lead, cash the ♠A and ruff a spade (to establish the suit when it breaks 4-2). You then draw three rounds of trumps with the ace, king and queen. If trumps do break 4-1, one of the defenders will hold a master trump, while you hold a lower trump. No matter! You will simply play your winning spades, remaining in full control.

PLAN: I will ruff the diamond lead, cash the ♠A and ruff a spade. I will then draw three rounds of trumps and play winning spades.

14

PLANNING TO KEEP THE DANGER HAND OFF LEAD

After a hold-up play, one of the defenders may be 'safe' from declarer's point of view (for example, in notrump he has no card to play in the suit that was led). The other defender may be 'dangerous' (he has some winners to cash, or can lead through an honor in your hand or dummy). The defenders are then referred to as the 'safe hand' and the 'danger hand'. You will often have to develop extra tricks without allowing the danger hand to gain the lead and in this chapter we will see how that can be done.

Finessing into the safe hand

When you have a choice of finesses to take, in your search for extra tricks, it is usually a good idea to 'finesse into the safe hand'. What does that mean? It means that if the finesse happens to lose, it will be the safe defender who wins the trick. Look at this deal:

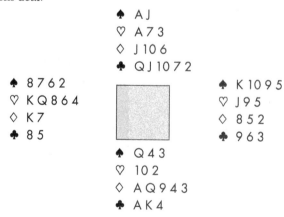

```
                  ♠ A J
                  ♡ A 7 3
                  ◇ J 10 6
                  ♣ Q J 10 7 2
  ♠ 8 7 6 2                        ♠ K 10 9 5
  ♡ K Q 8 6 4                      ♡ J 9 5
  ◇ K 7                            ◇ 8 5 2
  ♣ 8 5                            ♣ 9 6 3
                  ♠ Q 4 3
                  ♡ 10 2
                  ◇ A Q 9 4 3
                  ♣ A K 4
```

West	North	East	South
			1NT
pass	3NT	all pass	

West leads the ♡6 against 3NT and you see these winners:

Top Tricks: ♠ 1   ♡ 1   ◇ 1   ♣ 5   **Total: 8**

There is a potential for extra tricks in both spades and diamonds. In either of those suits, a successful finesse would give you at least the one extra trick that you need. What plan should you make?

Since you are well protected in the three other suits, it is clearly right to hold up the ♡A for two rounds. What is the effect of this? In the dangerous case where West began with five hearts, he is now a 'danger hand'; East has become a 'safe hand'.

How should you seek the one extra trick that you need? You are in dummy, after winning with the ♡A, and it may seem natural to run the ◇J. Natural, perhaps, but extremely risky! The diamond finesse is 'into the danger hand'. If it loses, West will cash two heart tricks and the contract will go down. So, finessing in diamonds will give you the contract only when East happens to hold the ◇K.

Even though you have fewer cards in spades than in diamonds (and can develop fewer tricks from the suit), it is the spade suit that gives you a much better chance of making the contract. Suppose you cross to your hand with a club at Trick 4 and play a spade to dummy's jack. This finesse is 'into the safe hand'. It loses to East's king, as it happens, but you will still make the contract. East has no heart to return. When you win whatever he does choose to return, you will have nine tricks. The ♠Q will be set up as your ninth trick. By playing in this way, you will make the contract whether the spade finesse wins or not.

> **PLAN: I will hold up the ♡A until the third round, cross to the ♣A and finesse the ♠J into the safe (East) hand.**

Sometimes finessing into the safe hand will give you two chances to make the contract, rather than just one chance. That's the case on this next deal:

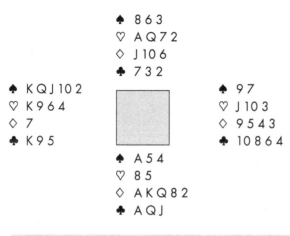

	♠ 8 6 3	
	♡ A Q 7 2	
	◇ J 10 6	
	♣ 7 3 2	

♠ K Q J 10 2   ♠ 9 7
♡ K 9 6 4   ♡ J 10 3
◇ 7   ◇ 9 5 4 3
♣ K 9 5   ♣ 10 8 6 4

            ♠ A 5 4
            ♡ 8 5
            ◇ A K Q 8 2
            ♣ A Q J

West	North	East	South
			2NT
pass	3NT	all pass	

West leads the ♠K against 3NT and you see these winners:

Top Tricks: ♠ 1   ♡ 1   ◇ 5   ♣ 1   **Total: 8**

A successful finesse in either hearts or clubs will give you a ninth trick. How should you play the contract?

The first step is to hold up the ♠A for two rounds. When West persists with a third round of spades, East discards a diamond and you win with the ace. West is now the 'danger hand', because he has two spades to cash; East is the 'safe hand'.

Suppose you cross to the ◇J and take a club finesse. This is 'into the danger hand'. If the finesse loses, as it will when the cards lie as in the diagram, West will cash two more spades and you will go down.

The right way to play the contract is to finesse the ♡Q first. This finesse is into the safe (East) hand. If the heart finesse loses, you will not yet be dead; you will still be able to finesse the ♣Q. You will have two chances to make the contract instead of one.

Make sure you have understood why it was right to finesse in hearts first. It was not because that finesse happened to be winning in our diagram, of course; it was because finessing into the safe hand would give you two separate chances to make the contract.

> **PLAN: I will hold up the ♠A until the third round and then finesse the ♡Q into the safe hand. If this loses, I will later finesse the ♣Q.**

Taking a two-way finesse into the safe hand

Suppose you have a suit of ◊A1062 opposite ◊KJ74 and need to score three diamond tricks to make the contract. You can finesse either defender for the missing ◊Q. By finessing into the safe hand you will make your contract whether the finesse wins or not! The following deal illustrates this 'win when you lose' idea:

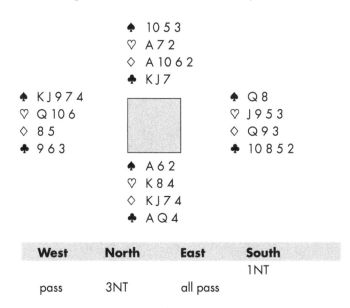

	♠ 10 5 3		
	♡ A 7 2		
	◊ A 10 6 2		
	♣ K J 7		

♠ K J 9 7 4   ♠ Q 8
♡ Q 10 6   ♡ J 9 5 3
◊ 8 5   ◊ Q 9 3
♣ 9 6 3   ♣ 10 8 5 2

♠ A 6 2
♡ K 8 4
◊ K J 7 4
♣ A Q 4

West	North	East	South
			1NT
pass	3NT	all pass	

West leads the ♠7 against 3NT and you see these winners:

Top Tricks: ♠ 1 ♡ 2 ◊ 2 ♣ 3   **Total: 8**

To bump the total to nine tricks, you need to score one extra trick from the diamond suit. Which way should you take the diamond finesse — should you finesse the ◊J (hoping that East holds the ◊Q) or the ◊10 (hoping that West holds the ◊Q)? The answer is that you should arrange the play so that it does not matter if you take a losing diamond finesse.

The first step is to hold up the ♠A for two rounds. East wins the first round with the ♠Q and returns the ♠8 to West's ♠J. When West plays a third round of spades, East discards a club and you win with the ♠A. You can now guarantee the contract by finessing diamonds into the safe (East) hand. You play the ◊K and then lead a low diamond to dummy's ◊10. As it happens, the finesse loses to East's queen. No matter! You have three diamond tricks — all that you need for the contract — and the game is yours.

If you had made the alternative play of cashing the ◊A and finessing the ◊J, you would have put the contract at risk. You would have gone down when West held the ◊Q and could cash two spade winners when the diamond finesse lost.

PLAN: I will hold up the ♠A until the third round and then take the two-way diamond finesse into the safe (East) hand.

The same idea can be put to good use when you are drawing trumps in a suit contract. You may choose to finesse into the safe hand, to give the defenders no chance to beat you. How would you have played the trump suit on this deal?

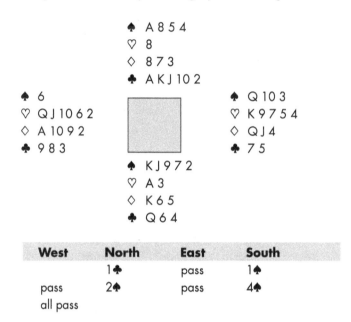

	♠ A 8 5 4	
	♡ 8	
	◇ 8 7 3	
	♣ A K J 10 2	

♠ 6		♠ Q 10 3
♡ Q J 10 6 2		♡ K 9 7 5 4
◇ A 10 9 2		◇ Q J 4
♣ 9 8 3		♣ 7 5

	♠ K J 9 7 2	
	♡ A 3	
	◇ K 6 5	
	♣ Q 6 4	

West	North	East	South
	1♣	pass	1♠
pass	2♠	pass	4♠
all pass			

West leads the ♡Q against 4♠ and you see these potential losers:

Losers: ♠ 1   ♡ 1   ◇ 3   ♣ 0   Total: 5

There is no problem with the heart loser because you can ruff it in dummy. So, you must try to avoid losing one trump and three diamonds. You note that dummy's club suit will provide two diamond discards, once you have drawn trumps.

Normally with a nine-card trump holding, and no other considerations, you would bang down the ace and king rather than take any finesses ('eight ever, nine never'). However, here there are other considerations. Before you decide how to play the trump suit, ask yourself: which defender is the 'danger hand'? You cannot afford East to gain the lead because he will then be able to lead a diamond through your king. You should therefore play the trump suit so that only West (the safe hand) has a chance to gain the lead. You play the ♠A, everyone following, and then lead a low spade from dummy, the ♠10 showing from East. If you rise with your ♠K now, you run the risk that East will subsequently win a trick with the ♠Q and kill you with a diamond return. Instead you should play the ♠J, finessing into the safe hand. You don't mind at all if the finesse loses to a doubleton ♠Q with West, because with West on lead the defenders will be able to take only one diamond trick. By finessing into the safe hand, you will guarantee yourself at least eleven tricks.

Let's see what happened to the original declarer on this hand. He won the heart lead with the ace and played for the drop in trumps, cashing the ace and king. When West showed out on the second round of trumps, he turned to the club suit, hoping to discard at least one diamond loser. Both defenders followed to the queen and ace of clubs, but East ruffed the ♣K and switched to the ◊Q. The defenders scored three diamond tricks and the contract was one down.

> **PLAN: I will win with the ♡A, cross to the ♠A and finesse the ♠J into the safe West hand. Whether or not the finesse wins, I will later throw my diamond losers on dummy's clubs.**

Ducking into the safe hand

You often need to duck a trick in order to establish a suit and it will not surprise you to hear that you should attempt to do this into the safe defender's hand. On the next deal, you need to set up an extra trick in clubs.

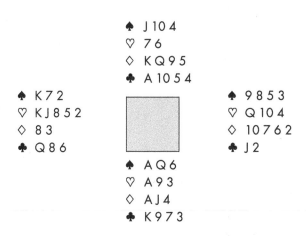

	♠ J 10 4
	♡ 7 6
	◊ K Q 9 5
	♣ A 10 5 4

♠ K 7 2		♠ 9 8 5 3
♡ K J 8 5 2		♡ Q 10 4
◊ 8 3		◊ 10 7 6 2
♣ Q 8 6		♣ J 2

	♠ A Q 6
	♡ A 9 3
	◊ A J 4
	♣ K 9 7 3

West	North	East	South
			1♣
pass	1♡	pass	2NT
pass	3NT	all pass	

West leads the ♡5 against 3NT, East playing the ♡Q. This is the top trick position:

Top Tricks: ♠ 1   ♡ 1   ◊ 4   ♣ 2   Total: 8

You need an extra trick from somewhere. A successful spade finesse would give you the contract but there is also a chance to establish the club suit. What plan would you make?

The first move is to hold up the ♡A for two rounds. In the dangerous case where hearts are 5-3, West will then become the 'danger hand'. A finesse in spades will be 'into the danger hand'; if it loses, West will cash two more hearts and beat the contract. A better idea is to establish the clubs, but this must be done without allowing West to gain the lead.

To set up the clubs, you will have to give up a trick in the suit; it makes good sense to allow the safe hand to win this trick. At Trick 4, you should lead the ♣3 from your hand. When West follows with the ♣6, you play the ♣10 from dummy. You are 'ducking into the safe hand'. East wins with the ♣J but has no heart to return, thanks to your hold-up of the ♡A. When he switches to spades, you rise with the ace and score three club tricks to bring your total to nine. Note that this line of play will succeed too when clubs break 4-1 and East began with ♣QJ82. You will play the ♣A next and can then finesse the ♣9 on the third round of the suit.

> **PLAN: I will hold up the ♡A until the third round and then lead a low club to the 10, ducking a club into the safe hand.**

Sometimes you can protect yourself against a bad break in a suit by ducking a trick into the safe hand. Look at the diamond suit on this deal:

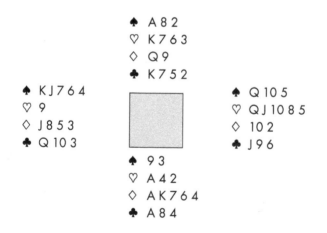

	♠ A 8 2	
	♡ K 7 6 3	
	◇ Q 9	
	♣ K 7 5 2	

♠ K J 7 6 4   ♠ Q 10 5
♡ 9   ♡ Q J 10 8 5
◇ J 8 5 3   ◇ 10 2
♣ Q 10 3   ♣ J 9 6

♠ 9 3
♡ A 4 2
◇ A K 7 6 4
♣ A 8 4

West	North	East	South
			1NT
pass	2♣	pass	2◇
pass	3NT	all pass	

West leads the ♠6 against 3NT and this is the top trick position:

Top Tricks: ♠ 1   ♡ 2   ◇ 3   ♣ 2   **Total:** 8

You need just one extra trick. You might be able to set up an extra trick in hearts or clubs, if you found a 3-3 break in the suit that you chose. It's not an attractive option because West might win the trick that you ducked and there would then be a risk that he could cash enough spades to defeat you.

It is clearly better to rely on the diamond suit. If diamonds break 3-3, you will have five tricks ready to take. That's only a 36% chance, though. How can you give yourself the best chance in the more frequent situation when diamonds break 4-2?

The first step is to break the defenders' communications by holding up the ♠A until the third round. Unless spades are 4-4 and pose no threat, East will then be a 'safe hand'. Suppose you continue by cashing the three top diamonds. You will make the contract, with an overtrick, when diamonds break 3-3. You will succeed also when East holds four diamonds; you will be able to concede the fourth round to East and he will have no spade to play. You will go down, however, when West holds four diamonds. How can you guard again this case too?

The answer is to duck an early round of diamonds into the safe (East) hand. You win the third round of spades and cross to your hand with the ♡A (or the ♣A). You then lead a diamond toward dummy; when West follows with a low spot card, you play dummy's ◇9. East wins with the ◇10. You can then win his return and score four diamond tricks for the contract. If you had not ducked a diamond into the safe hand, you would have gone down. West would have gained the lead with his ◇J and cashed two more spades to beat you.

> **PLAN: I will hold up the ♠A until the third round, cross to the ♡A or ♣A and play a diamond to the nine. By ducking into the safe hand, I will make the contract when diamonds break 4-2.**

Remember these points

- During the play of a hand, it often happens that one of the defenders becomes 'dangerous'. He may have some winners to cash; he may be able to lead through an honor in your hand or the dummy.

- Whenever possible, you should aim to keep the danger hand off lead as you develop your extra tricks.

- When you have a choice of finesses to take, it is usually a good idea to take a finesse that is 'into the safe hand'. Even if it loses, the defender will not then be able to damage you.

- When establishing a suit, it may work well to duck a trick 'into the safe hand'.

Now try these...

A.

          ♠ K Q 8
          ♥ 7 2
          ◇ K 7 3
          ♣ K Q 9 5 2
♠J led   ▢▢▢▢▢▢
          ♠ A 5 4
          ♥ K 8 5 3
          ◇ A 6 4 2
          ♣ A 10

Expressing your plan as concisely as you can, how will you play 3NT when West leads the ♠J?

B.

          ♠ 7 5 3
          ♥ K J 7 6
          ◇ 6
          ♣ A Q 10 8 3
♠6 led   ▢▢▢▢▢▢
          ♠ J 9 4
          ♥ A 10 8 3 2
          ◇ A 8
          ♣ K J 7

You reach 4♥ and West leads the ♣6 to East's ♣K. When East continues with the ♣A, West follows with the ♣2. What is your plan when East switches to the ◇K?

C.

          ♠ K Q 8
          ♥ K 7 6 4
          ◇ Q 7
          ♣ K 7 5 2
◇6 led   ▢▢▢▢▢▢
          ♠ A 10 4
          ♥ A 8 2
          ◇ K 8 5
          ♣ A 10 6 4

How will you give yourself the best chance in 3NT when West leads the ◇6?

D.

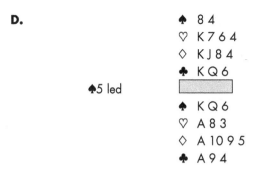

♠ 8 4
♡ K 7 6 4
◇ K J 8 4
♣ K Q 6

♠5 led

♠ K Q 6
♡ A 8 3
◇ A 10 9 5
♣ A 9 4

You reach 3NT and West leads the ♠5 to East's ♠9. What is your plan?

E.

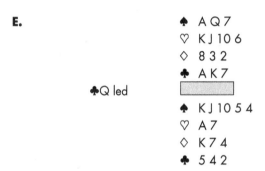

♠ A Q 7
♡ K J 10 6
◇ 8 3 2
♣ A K 7

♣Q led

♠ K J 10 5 4
♡ A 7
◇ K 7 4
♣ 5 4 2

West leads the ♣Q against your contract of 4♠. What is your plan?

F.

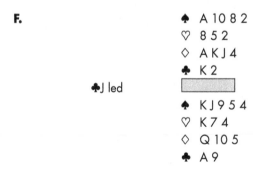

♠ A 10 8 2
♡ 8 5 2
◇ A K J 4
♣ K 2

♣J led

♠ K J 9 5 4
♡ K 7 4
◇ Q 10 5
♣ A 9

West leads the ♣J against 4♠. How will you plan the play?

ANSWERS

A. You have eight tricks on top. Even if clubs break 4-1 or 5-0, it will be easy to create a ninth trick from that source. However, it will be dangerous to allow East on lead because a heart switch through the king might then give the defenders four heart tricks (for example if West holds ♡A109x and East has ♡QJx). To make sure that East does not gain the lead in clubs, you should win the spade lead with dummy's ♠K and lead a low club to your ♣10 (finessing into the safe hand). If West wins with the ♣J, he cannot attack hearts successfully from his side of the table. Whether or not the club finesse wins, you are assured of an extra club trick and the contract.

PLAN: I will win the spade lead in dummy and play a club to the ten, establishing my ninth trick safely.

B. You have lost two spade tricks already and must seek to avoid losing a trump trick and another spade. How do you think the spade suit lies? West led a fourth-best ♠6 and followed with the ♠2 on the next round. He surely began with ♠Q10862. (That's why East did not play a third round of the suit after scoring the king and ace.) You can afford to lose a trump trick to the queen, so long as you do not also lose a spade trick. After winning the diamond switch with the ace, you should cash the ♡A and finesse dummy's ♡J. Even if this loses to a doubleton ♡Q with East, you will still make the contract; East has no spade to play and you can discard your remaining spade on the fourth round of clubs. This line will pay off when West began with ♡Qxx. If instead you play for trumps to be 2-2, West will ruff an early club and cash the ♠Q to beat you.

PLAN: I will win the diamond switch, cash the ♡A and finesse the ♡J into the safe East hand. Later I can discard my spade loser on the clubs.

C. You must try the ◇Q from dummy and this holds the trick. You now have eight top tricks and excellent prospects of an extra trick from the club suit. However, you must develop this suit without allowing East (the danger hand, who can lead through your ◇K) from gaining the lead. Cash the ♣K and lead a second round of clubs from dummy, intending to finesse the ♣10 into the safe hand. If East follows with the ♣Q or ♣J on the second round, win with the ♣A and give up a third round of clubs in the hope that West will win the trick.

PLAN: I will play the ◇Q from dummy. When this wins, I will cash the ♣K and lead a club toward the ♣10, hoping to duck into the safe hand.

D. If you include one spade trick in your total, you have eight top tricks. Just one extra trick from the diamond suit will give you the nine tricks that you seek. You should therefore win the first round of spades, cross to dummy's ◇K and run the ◇J into the safe West hand. Whether the diamond finesse wins or not, you will make the contract.

(Note that it is not a safe plan to hold up in spades, aiming to exhaust East's spades and then to finesse diamonds into the East hand. When spades break 5-3, West can hold up his ♠A on the second round of spades to preserve communications. If a diamond finesse subsequently loses, to either hand, the defenders will take a total of four spade tricks to beat the contract.)

PLAN: I will win the spade lead, cross to the ◇K and finesse diamonds into the safe West hand.

E. You have a total of four potential losers in the minor suits. Suppose you win the club lead, draw trumps, cash the ♡A and finesse the ♡J. This will be into the danger hand; if the heart finesse loses to East, he will be able to switch through the ◇K and you may go down. Instead you should take a ruffing heart finesse into the safe West hand. After drawing trumps, you play the ♡A and ♡K and then lead the ♡J. If East covers with the ♡Q, you will ruff and discard one of your losers on the established ♡10. If instead East plays a low heart or discards, you will throw a loser. Even if the finesse loses to the ♡Q with West, you will still make the contract. You can discard another loser on dummy's ♡10.

PLAN: I will win the club lead, draw trumps, play the ♡A and ♡K and then take a ruffing heart finesse into the safe West hand.

F. You have one potential loser in trumps and three more in hearts. Suppose you win the club lead and play the ace and king of trumps. If East began with ♠Qxx, your contract will be in danger. When you turn to the diamond suit, hoping to discard a heart, East may ruff the third round and switch to a heart through the ♡K.

East is the 'danger hand', because only he can lead through your ♡K. So, when you play the trump suit, you should 'finesse into the safe hand'. You should cash the ♠A and then finesse the ♠J (despite the fact that there are only four trumps missing and you would normally play for the drop). Even if the finesse loses to the ♠Q with West, your contract is safe. When you have drawn trumps, you will be able to discard a heart on the fourth round of diamonds.

PLAN: I will win the club lead, cross to the ♠A and finesse the ♠J (into the safe hand). After drawing trumps, I will discard a heart loser on dummy's diamonds.

15

PLANNING TO COMBINE TWO CHANCES

Whenever possible, you should aim to combine more than one chance rather than relying on a single fortunate lie of the cards. Sometimes you will need to decide which chance to play for first. In such a case you must ask yourself: if I try for Chance A first and it fails, will I still be able to fall back on Chance B? Look at this deal:

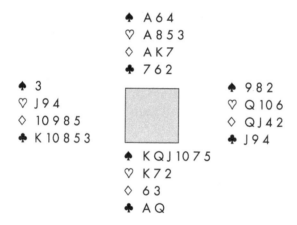

```
            ♠ A 6 4
            ♡ A 8 5 3
            ◇ A K 7
            ♣ 7 6 2
  ♠ 3                      ♠ 9 8 2
  ♡ J 9 4                  ♡ Q 10 6
  ◇ 10 9 8 5               ◇ Q J 4 2
  ♣ K 10 8 5 3            ♣ J 9 4
            ♠ K Q J 10 7 5
            ♡ K 7 2
            ◇ 6 3
            ♣ A Q
```

You bid to a small slam in spades and West leads the ◇10. What plan will you make? This is the loser situation:

Losers: ♠ 0   ♡ 1   ◇ 0   ♣ 1   Total: 2

You must hope to avoid a club loser and one possibility is a successful finesse of ♣Q. Relying on a 50% chance is not very satisfactory. Can you see a second chance? If the heart suit breaks 3-3, you will be able to establish a surplus winner in the suit; this will then provide a discard for the ♣Q.

You would like to combine these two chances and taking an early club finesse would clearly be wrong. If this chance failed, it would be too late to play for the other chance in hearts.

It is better to try for a 3-3 heart break first and this will involve ducking a round of hearts at some stage. Suppose you draw trumps in three rounds and duck the first or second round of hearts. That's no good! East will win and return a club through the ace-queen. You will then need to guess whether to finesse before you know if the hearts are breaking 3-3. In other words, you will have to choose one of the two chances, rather than combining them.

After drawing trumps, you should play king, ace and another heart. Here, East will win the third round but a club switch will no longer cause you a problem. Since you know that the hearts are 3-3, you will rise with the ♣A and cross to a diamond to discard the ♣Q on the thirteenth heart. If hearts had not broken 3-3, you would know that you had to finesse in clubs.

> **PLAN: I will draw trumps and play king, ace and another heart, hoping for a 3-3 break. If this chance fails, I will finesse the ♣Q.**

You get the idea, then. You must plan the play all the way through, making sure that you can combine the two chances. Take a look at the next deal. You must look for the two chances of making the contract and then plan how to combine them.

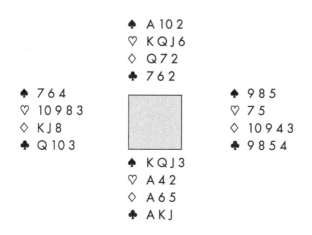

```
              ♠ A 10 2
              ♡ K Q J 6
              ◇ Q 7 2
              ♣ 7 6 2
♠ 7 6 4                      ♠ 9 8 5
♡ 10 9 8 3                   ♡ 7 5
◇ K J 8                      ◇ 10 9 4 3
♣ Q 10 3                     ♣ 9 8 5 4
              ♠ K Q J 3
              ♡ A 4 2
              ◇ A 6 5
              ♣ A K J
```

West	North	East	South
			2NT
pass	4NT	pass	6NT
all pass			

North raises your 2NT opening to 4NT, inviting a slam. Since you hold an upper-range hand within the 20–22 point range, you advance to 6NT. West leads the ♡10 and you have these immediate winners:

Top Tricks: ♠4 ♡4 ◇1 ♣2   **Total:** 11

Not for the first time in this book, you need one more trick. This could be achieved by leading toward the ◇Q and finding West with the ◇K; alternatively, you might score an extra trick with a successful finesse of the ♣J. How can you combine these two chances?

The key here is to realize that the diamond play involves giving up a trick irrespective of which defender holds the king. Suppose you win the heart lead in dummy and finesse the ♣J. This will lose to the ♣Q, as it happens, and it will be too late to try the second chance in diamonds; if you won West's return and led a diamond toward dummy, West would rise with the king to put you one down.

To make the contract when either the ◇K or the ♣Q is well-placed, you must play a diamond toward the queen first. When the cards lie as in the diagram, this will be an immediate success. Whether or not West decides to rise with the ◇K, dummy's ◇Q will give you the extra trick that you need. Suppose instead that East held the ◇K and dummy's ◇Q did not therefore give you an extra trick. You would still be alive! After winning East's return, you would be able to take your second chance, a finesse of the ♣J. Playing this way, you would make the slam when either of the finesses proved successful.

> **PLAN: I will lead toward the ◇Q. If East wins with the ◇K, I will win the return and finesse the ♣J, combining two chances.**

Playing for the drop in one suit before finessing in another

Sometimes you have two possible finesses to take and will go down if the first finesse loses. (The defenders will be able to cash enough tricks to beat you.) You may still be able to combine two chances, to some extent. This 3NT deal illustrates the situation:

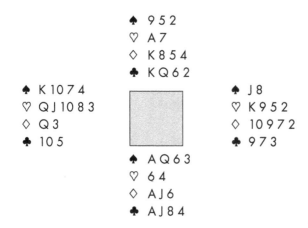

West	North	East	South
			1NT
pass	3NT	all pass	

West leads the ♡Q against 3NT and this is the winner position:

Top Tricks: ♠ 1   ♡ 1   ◇ 2   ♣ 4   **Total: 8**

You win the second round of hearts and see that you cannot afford to lose the lead; if you did, the defenders would cash the remaining hearts and defeat you. There are two possible finesses that might give you a ninth trick — you could finesse the ♠Q or the ◇J. You cannot combine these chances, however. Suppose you take one of the finesses immediately. If it happens to lose, the defenders will cash their hearts; the contract will be down before you have the chance to take the other finesse.

Taking one or other finesse will give you only a 50% chance of making the contract. How can you do better? The answer is that you should play the ace and king of diamonds first. This gives you the extra chance that the ◇Q will drop in two rounds. This will happen 16% of the time, making it a very worthwhile bonus. When the cards lie as in the diagram, the extra chance will pay off and you will have your nine tricks. If the ◇Q does not appear in two rounds, little has been lost. You will take your second, more substantial, chance — that the spade finesse will win.

> **PLAN: I will try to drop the ◇Q in two rounds. If this fails, I will finesse the ♠Q, combining two chances.**

Adding the extra chance of ruffing out an honor

Sometimes a side suit offers you an extra chance of ruffing out a defender's honor, to establish an extra trick. For example with ♣J752 opposite ♣AK, the defenders' ♣Q may fall when you ruff the third round. Such extra chances are well worthwhile and may be the difference between making a contract and going down. See if you can spot an extra chance on this spade slam:

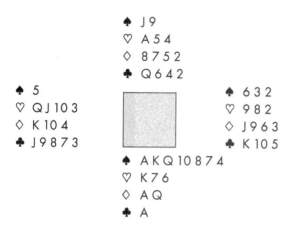

```
              ♠ J 9
              ♡ A 5 4
              ◇ 8 7 5 2
              ♣ Q 6 4 2
♠ 5                         ♠ 6 3 2
♡ Q J 10 3                  ♡ 9 8 2
◇ K 10 4                    ◇ J 9 6 3
♣ J 9 8 7 3                 ♣ K 10 5
              ♠ A K Q 10 8 7 4
              ♡ K 7 6
              ◇ A Q
              ♣ A
```

You open 2♣ on the South cards and soon arrive in 6♠. How will you give yourself the best chance when West leads the ♡Q? You start with these losers:

Losers: ♠ 0 ♡ 1 ◇ 1 ♣ 0   **Total:** 2

A successful diamond finesse would save you a loser. Can you see a second chance to combine with this? If the defender with the ♣K holds three or fewer cards in the suit, you will be able to establish the ♣Q and discard one of your losers.

You win the opening heart lead with the ♡K, preserving the entry to dummy. You then cash the ♣A, cross to dummy with the ♠9 and ruff a club in your hand. The ♣K does not appear, but East follows with the ♣10; perhaps this is a hopeful sign. You return to dummy with the ♠J and lead another round of clubs. Yes! The ♣K appears from East. You ruff in your hand, draw the last trump and cross to the ♡A to discard your heart loser on the established ♣Q. If the ♣K had not fallen, you would have used this last entry to dummy to take the diamond finesse.

> **PLAN: I will win with the ♡K and try to ruff out the ♣K. If this chance fails, I will rely on a finesse of the ◇Q.**

Playing for a good break in one suit, finessing in another

When you are playing in a suit contract, a good break in a side suit may allow you to establish it by ruffing in the opposite hand. If the suit does not break favorably, you can fall back on a finesse in a different suit. Let's see an example of this style of play.

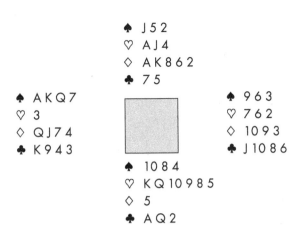

	♠ J 5 2	
	♡ A J 4	
	◇ A K 8 6 2	
	♣ 7 5	
♠ A K Q 7		♠ 9 6 3
♡ 3		♡ 7 6 2
◇ Q J 7 4		◇ 10 9 3
♣ K 9 4 3		♣ J 10 8 6
	♠ 10 8 4	
	♡ K Q 10 9 8 5	
	◇ 5	
	♣ A Q 2	

West	North	East	South
			1♡
dbl	rdbl	pass	2♡
pass	4♡	all pass	

West starts the defense against 4♡ by cashing his three top spades. How will you plan the contract when he then switches to a trump?

This was the original loser position:

Losers: ♠ 3   ♡ 0   ◇ 0   ♣ 2   **Total:** 5

The defenders have already taken their three spade tricks, so now you must attempt to avoid any club losers. What chances are there?

You can discard one club on dummy's second top diamond winner. To discard another club, you will need to establish the diamond suit. This can be done if the defenders' diamonds split 4-3, but you will need to make full use of the entries provided by dummy's trump holding.

You win the trump switch in your hand and seek to establish the diamond suit immediately. You cross to the ◇A and ruff a diamond. You then cross to the ♡J and ruff another diamond. When both defenders follow all the way, you know that the suit is breaking 4-3. You return to dummy with the ♡A and discard the ♣2 and ♣Q on dummy's ◇K8. The contract is yours.

Suppose West had started with 4-1-5-3 shape and you could not establish the diamonds with two ruffs. You would use your final entry to dummy (the ♡A), throw the ♣2 on the ◇K and then take a finesse of the ♣Q. In this way you would combine two chances: a 4-3 diamond break and a successful finesse of the ♣Q.

> **PLAN: I will try to establish the diamonds, using dummy's trumps as entries. If diamonds are not 4-3, I will rely on finessing the ♣Q.**

Testing one suit before switching to another

When you plan to establish a suit, it is often good technique to duck an early round. We saw several examples of this in earlier chapters. On some contracts, though, it is necessary to determine at an early stage whether a suit is breaking favorably. If it is not, you may have time to try your luck elsewhere. In other words, you do better to play the top cards in the suit. This will allow you to see in good time whether the break will help you.

This 3NT deal illustrates the idea:

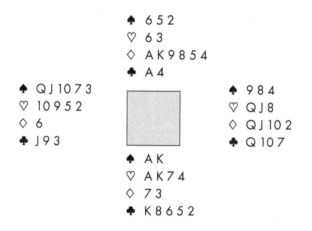

West	North	East	South
	1◊	pass	2♣
pass	2◊	pass	2♡
pass	3◊	pass	3NT
all pass			

How will you plan the contract when West leads the ♠Q? You start with these winners:

Top Tricks: ♠ 2 ♡ 2 ◊ 2 ♣ 2   **Total: 8**

You win the spade lead in your hand and see that you need to establish only one extra trick to land 3NT. The diamond suit offers you the best chance because a 3-2 break is an odds-on prospect, in fact a 68% chance. To create extra tricks in clubs, you would need a 3-3 break, which is only a 36% chance.

Suppose your first move, after winning the spade lead, is to duck a round of diamonds. The defenders will clear the spades and when you play a second round of diamonds you will find that they break 4-1. With no protection left in the spade suit, it will be too late to turn to the club suit (or to give up a second round of diamonds). You will go down.

A better way to play the contract is to cash the ◇A and ◇K. If the suit does break 3-2, you can give up the third round of diamonds, using the ♣A to reach the established winners. When the cards lie as in the diagram, you will discover in good time (before your second spade stopper has been removed) that the diamonds are breaking 4-1. You will then quit playing diamonds and try your luck in clubs. Ace, king and another club will indeed reveal a 3-3 break and you will make the contract.

By testing diamonds in this way, you can combine the chance of a 3-2 diamond break with that of a 3-3 club break.

> **PLAN: I will test the diamonds by playing the ace and king. If they break 3-2, I will establish the diamonds. Otherwise I will play clubs, hoping for a 3-3 break.**

Combining chances within a single suit

So far we have been looking at combining chances from two different suits. Even within the play of a single suit, you may find that you have two chances of generating an extra trick. Look at the club suit on this deal:

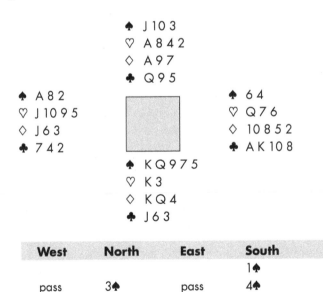

West	North	East	South
			1♠
pass	3♠	pass	4♠
all pass			

What is your plan when West leads the ♡J? This is the loser situation:

Losers: ♠1 ♡0 ◇0 ♣3   Total: 4

You win the heart lead with the king and play a trump. West ducks the first round, wins the next round with the ace and returns his last trump. What now?

You will have to play the club suit yourself and must look for the best chance of losing only two club tricks. One possibility is to lead a low card from the South hand and to finesse dummy's ♣9. If West holds the ♣10, East will be forced to win with the ace or king. Your remaining queen and jack of clubs will then be worth a trick. This will give you a 50% chance of making the contract. Can you see an additional chance?

You can also score a club trick when East holds the ♣AK. You must lead the first round of clubs from dummy. To prevent you from scoring a trick with the ♣J, East will have to rise with the ace or king. Again you will be able to establish a club trick with your remaining queen and jack.

It is easy enough to combine these two chances. You lead the ♣5 from dummy on the first round. If East follows low, you play the ♣J from your hand, hoping that East began with the ♣AK. If the ♣J loses to a big honor with West, you will finesse the ♣9 on the next round (your second chance in the suit).

> **PLAN: I will draw trumps and lead a low club toward the jack. If East holds the ♣AK, I will score a club trick. If not, I will finesse the ♣9 on the second round.**

Remember these points

- It is nearly always better to combine two different chances of making the contract, rather than relying on just one.

- For example, suppose dummy has ◇AKQ4 opposite ◇873 in your hand. A 3-3 diamond break would allow you to discard a loser from your hand. If diamonds did not break 3-3, you might be able to take a finesse in a different suit as your second chance.

- When you can see two chances to make the contract, think carefully which chance to try first. Ask yourself: if the first chance fails, will I still be able to take the second chance?

- It frequently happens that you can 'play for the drop' in one suit (your first chance) before taking a finesse in another suit (your second chance).

Now try these...

A.

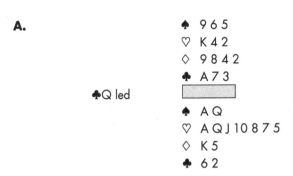

♠ 9 6 5
♡ K 4 2
◇ 9 8 4 2
♣ A 7 3

♣Q led

♠ A Q
♡ A Q J 10 8 7 5
◇ K 5
♣ 6 2

Expressing your plan as concisely as you can, how will you play 4♡ when West leads the ♣Q?

B.

♠ K 2
♡ 8 6 4 2
◇ 8 7 5
♣ Q 7 6 4

♡K led

♠ A J 5
♡ —
◇ K 6 2
♣ A K J 10 5 3 2

West, who overcalled in hearts, leads the ♡K against 5♣. What is your plan?

C.

♠ A Q 7 6
♡ Q 8 6 2
◇ A 3 2
♣ J 4

◇K led

♠ K 8 3
♡ A K J 10 7 5
◇ J 6
♣ A Q

Against your contract of 6♡, West leads the ◇K. How do you play?

D.

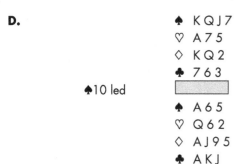

♠ K Q J 7
♡ A 7 5
♢ K Q 2
♣ 7 6 3

♠10 led

♠ A 6 5
♡ Q 6 2
♢ A J 9 5
♣ A K J

How will you play 6NT when West leads the ♠10?

E.

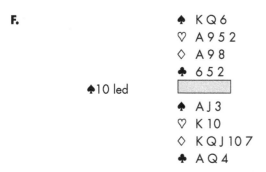

♠ Q J 6 4
♡ A Q 4 2
♢ 7 4
♣ 9 7 5

♠2 led

♠ A K 10 9 5 3
♡ 10
♢ A 10 8 5
♣ A Q

West leads a low trump against 6♠. What is your plan? (East will follow to the first round of trumps.)

F.

♠ K Q 6
♡ A 9 5 2
♢ A 9 8
♣ 6 5 2

♠10 led

♠ A J 3
♡ K 10
♢ K Q J 10 7
♣ A Q 4

You reach 6NT and West leads the ♠10. How will you play the slam?

ANSWERS

A. You have four potential losers — one spade, two diamonds and one club. You should aim to take finesses in both spades and diamonds, hoping that at least one will succeed. It does not matter which finesse you take first, but since there are only two entries to dummy (the ♣A and the ♡K), you must take one at Trick 2 rather than drawing trumps. Suppose you play a spade to the queen. Whether or not this finesse wins, you will later draw trumps, ending in the dummy and play a diamond toward the king. If one of the finesses wins, you will make the contract. If both finesses win, you will score an overtrick.

> **PLAN: I will win the club lead and finesse the ♠Q. Later, I will draw trumps, ending in the dummy and lead toward the ◇K. Unless both finesses fail, I will make the contract.**

B. You have four potential losers — one spade and three diamonds. If East holds the ◇A, you could lead successfully toward your ◇K and ruff the potential spade loser. If instead East holds the ♠Q, you could finesse the ♠J successfully and discard a diamond from dummy on your third spade; you would then lose only two diamond tricks, even if the ◇A lay over the ◇K. What you would like to do is to combine the chances in spades and diamonds, making the contract when either the ♠Q or the ◇A is onside.

Playing a diamond to the ◇K first is not a good idea; you might then lose three diamond tricks and go down even when the ♠Q was with East. You should ruff the heart lead, draw trumps, cross to the ♠K and finesse the ♠J. If the finesse wins, you have eleven tricks, as discussed already. If it loses, you will lead toward the ◇K later and still make the contract when that chance succeeds. You can discard dummy's third diamond on the ♠A.

> **PLAN: I will ruff the heart lead, draw trumps, cross to the ♠K and finesse the ♠J. If this loses, I will lead toward the ◇K later and still make the contract when East holds the ◇A.**

C. You start with one potential loser in each minor suit. There are two chances of avoiding a loser. If spades break 3-3, you will have a discard for the diamond loser. If East holds the ♣K, a club finesse will succeed. How can you combine these two chances? You must test the spades first. If they break, you discard the diamond loser on the thirteenth spade and take a club finesse for the overtrick. If they fail to break, you take the club finesse for the contract. It would be no good taking the club finesse first, because West would cash a diamond winner if it lost.

> **PLAN: I will win the diamond lead, draw trumps and test the spades. If they break 3-3, I can discard the diamond loser; if not, I will make the contract when a finesse of the ♣Q wins.**

D. You have eleven top tricks and a successful finesse of the ♣J would give you a twelfth. East may hold the ♡K, also. How can you combine these two chances?

Suppose you win the spade lead in dummy and finesse the ♣J. That's no good! If the finesse loses, you will not be able to take your second chance in hearts. East would rise with the ♡K, if he held it, and you would be one down.

You must take your chance in hearts first. Win the spade lead in dummy and lead a heart toward the ♡Q. If the ♡Q wins, or East rises with the ♡K, the slam is yours. If you are unlucky and the ♡Q loses to West's ♡K, you are still alive. You will win West's return and finesse the ♣J, combining your two chances.

Note that it would be a big mistake to cash the ♡A before leading toward the ♡Q. If West held the ♡K, the defenders would then be able to score several heart tricks before you could take the club finesse.

PLAN: I will win with the ♠K and lead a low heart toward the queen. If this chance fails, I will win the return and fall back on a finesse of the ♣J.

E. You can dismiss the diamond suit from your calculations. There is a certain loser on the second round and the other two losers can be ruffed in the dummy. How can you avoid the potential club loser? One possibility is to finesse the ♣Q. Another is a finesse of the ♡Q; if it wins you can throw the ♣Q on the ♡A.

Rather than relying on one of these 50% chances (only one, because if the first finesse loses, you will lose a diamond trick too), it is better to combine two different chances. The secondary chance here is to ruff out the ♡K in three rounds; you will combine this with the club finesse.

You win the trump lead, cash the ♡A and ruff a heart high. You then cross to the ♠Q (drawing the last trump) and ruff another heart. Next you give up a diamond, preparing for two diamond ruffs in the dummy. If the ♡K fell from either defender, you will discard the ♣Q on the established ♡Q after taking a diamond ruff. Otherwise you will finesse the ♣Q, taking your second chance.

PLAN: I will combine the chance of ruffing out the ♡K in three rounds with that of the club finesse.

F. You have eleven top tricks and a successful finesse of the ♣Q will give you the slam. The heart suit offers a second chance to combine with the first. Win the spade lead in dummy and play a heart to the ten. This will be an immediate success when East holds the ♡QJ, whether or not he chooses to play one of his honors. Suppose that the ♡10 loses to West's ♡Q (or ♡J). You will still score three heart tricks when East began with a doubleton or tripleton honor; his honor will then fall, setting up dummy's ♡9. Otherwise you will rely on the club finesse.

PLAN: I will win the spade lead and play a heart to the ten. If the hearts do not produce an extra trick, I will finesse the ♣Q.

16

PLANNING FURTHER HOLD-UP PLAYS

Back in Chapter 8, we saw the basic hold-up play, where you delayed the play of an ace (sometimes a king) in the suit that had been led against notrump. Holding up high cards is such an important part of cardplay, in both suit and notrump contracts, that we will look at some variations here.

Holding up from KQx

Suppose West leads a low spade against 3NT and you have three low cards in the dummy and ♠KQx in your hand. East plays the ♠J. Should you win the trick or hold up? The answer will often depend on your plan for the deal as a whole. Let's take a look at two different 3NT contracts. On one, it will be correct to hold up; on the other it will be better to win the first trick.

```
                  ♠ 8 6 2
                  ♡ 9 7 3
                  ◊ A 9 8 3
                  ♣ A K 5
   ♠ A 10 7 4 3                   ♠ J 9
   ♡ J 5 4                        ♡ Q 10 6 2
   ◊ 5 2                          ◊ K 6 4
   ♣ 8 7 3                        ♣ J 10 9 4
                  ♠ K Q 5
                  ♡ A K 8
                  ◊ Q J 10 7
                  ♣ Q 6 2
```

West	North	East	South
			1NT
pass	3NT	all pass	

You reach 3NT and West leads the ♠4, East playing the ♠J. You see these quick winners:

Top Tricks: ♠ 0 ♡ 2 ◇ 1 ♣ 3 **Total: 6**

What is your plan? If you win the first round of spades, you will have seven top tricks, and a successful diamond finesse would increase your total to ten. What if the diamond finesse loses, though? When the cards lie as in the diagram, East will return his ♠9 and West will score four spade tricks to beat the contract.

The only defender who can gain the lead in diamonds, when you are seeking your extra tricks, is East. You must therefore aim to remove East's cards in spades, the defenders' main suit. The correct play is to allow East's ♠J to win the first trick. The defenders cannot then beat the contract. Suppose East returns the ♠9 and you cover with the ♠K. It makes no difference whether West holds up his ace, or wins with the ace and clears the spades. When you run the ◇Q to the ◇K, East will have no spade to return. You will make one spade, two hearts, three diamonds and three clubs — enough for the contract.

As with many such contracts, if East does have a spade to return (perhaps he started with ♠J93), the defenders' spades will break 4-3 and pose no threat.

PLAN: Only East can gain the lead when I set up my extra tricks (in diamonds). I will therefore hold up at Trick 1, aiming to exhaust East's spade holding.

The situation changes completely when you expect the opening leader (West, in our diagrams) to gain the lead subsequently. Then you will want to win the first trick with the king, retaining your Qx as a second guard in the suit. That's the case in this amended version of the deal that we have just seen:

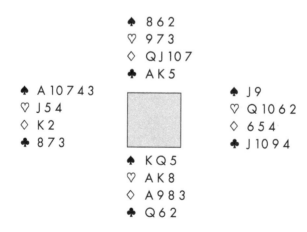

Now the diamond finesse is into the West hand. In other words, it is West who will gain the lead if the diamond finesse loses. So when West leads the ♠4 to East's ♠J, you must win the trick. Let's say you win with the ♠K. You cross to the ♣A and run the ◊Q to West's ◊K. You still have ♠Q5 in your hand; the suit is guarded when West has the lead. If West switches to some other suit, you will win and score at least nine tricks.

> **PLAN: Only West can gain the lead when I set up my extra tricks (in diamonds). I will therefore win with the ♠K at Trick 1, retaining my ♠Q5 as a second guard in the suit.**

Note that in the last two contracts, the plan would have been exactly the same if East had held the queen of the suit led and your stopper had been KJx. Again you would have a choice between winning with the king (retaining your Jx as a guard if West would gain the lead subsequently) and holding up (aiming to remove East's cards in the suit if he would then gain the lead).

Holding up from AJx

The situation is similar when you hold AJx in the suit that has been led. West leads a fourth-best spot card and East plays the queen or the king. Should you hold up or not? If East is likely to gain the lead later, you should hold up your ace until the third round, aiming to exhaust East's holding. If instead West is likely to gain the lead, you should win with the ace immediately, retaining your Jx as a second guard in the suit.

We will make do with just one example. Let's consider the case where it is East who may gain the lead:

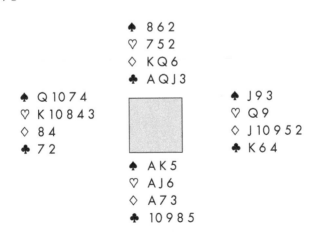

West	North	East	South
			1NT
pass	3NT	all pass	

West leads the ♡4 against your 3NT, East playing the ♡Q. You see these quick winners:

Top Tricks: ♠ 2   ♡ 1   ◊ 3   ♣ 1   **Total: 7**

You will need to play clubs to create the extra two tricks that you need and East may then gain the lead. You should therefore hold up the ♡A for two rounds with the aim of exhausting East's hearts.

East's ♡Q wins the first trick and he returns the ♡9. You cover with the ♡J and West wins with the ♡K, clearing the hearts as East discards a club. When you run the ♣10 to the ♣K, East has no heart to return. You win his return in some other suit and take your nine tricks.

> **PLAN: Only East can gain the lead when I set up my extra tricks (in clubs). I will therefore hold up the ♡A, to exhaust East's hearts.**

Suppose you swap the North and South club holdings, so that the club finesse would be into the West hand. The correct play in hearts would then be to win the first round with the ♡A, retaining your ♡J6 as a second guard in the suit.

Now for something a bit different — have you heard of the Bath Coup? It arises when your left-hand opponent leads a king and you hold up from an AJx combination. Look at the spade suit here:

```
              ♠ 7 3
              ♡ Q 10 5
              ◊ A Q 8 3
              ♣ A 7 6 4
♠ K Q 10 9 4                    ♠ 8 6 2
♡ 9 8 3                         ♡ A 7 4 2
◊ 6 2                           ◊ 9 5 4
♣ 10 9 5                        ♣ Q J 3
              ♠ A J 5
              ♡ K J 6
              ◊ K J 10 7
              ♣ K 8 2
```

West	North	East	South
			1NT
pass	3NT	all pass	

West leads the ♠K against 3NT and you see these quick winners:

Top Tricks: ♠ 1 ♡ 0 ◇ 4 ♣ 2 **Total: 7**

You can establish two extra tricks in the heart suit but you will need some protection against the spade suit when one or the other defender wins with the ♡A. This is easy to arrange. You simply allow West's ♠K to win the first trick, playing the ♠5 from your hand. West cannot continue the suit without allowing you to score two spade tricks, with the ace and jack. When he switches to some other suit, you can win and knock out the ♡A while you still have a guard in spades. Ducking from AJx when the king has been led is known as the Bath Coup. The technique was well known in the days of whist, more than a century ago.

> **PLAN: I will allow West's ♠K to win. He cannot continue spades safely, so I can win his switch and set up the hearts.**

Holding up with Kxx in the dummy

Suppose dummy holds Kxx in the suit that was led, while you hold xxx in your hand. It is rarely right to commit dummy's king on the first trick. Let's see a couple of deals where it will cost you the contract if you do so.

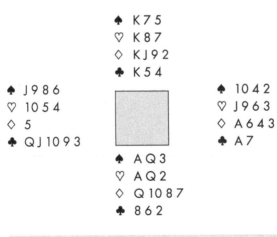

```
              ♠ K 7 5
              ♡ K 8 7
              ◇ K J 9 2
              ♣ K 5 4
♠ J 9 8 6                    ♠ 10 4 2
♡ 10 5 4                     ♡ J 9 6 3
◇ 5                          ◇ A 6 4 3
♣ Q J 10 9 3                 ♣ A 7
              ♠ A Q 3
              ♡ A Q 2
              ◇ Q 10 8 7
              ♣ 8 6 2
```

West	North	East	South
			1NT
pass	3NT	all pass	

West leads the ♣Q against 3NT and you see this winner situation:

Top Tricks: ♠ 3 ♡ 3 ◇ 0 ♣ 0 **Total: 6**

The diamond suit will provide the three extra winners that you need. In the meantime, you must do your best to avoid losing four or more club tricks and the ◇A.

Even though West may have led the ♣Q from ♣AQJ10x, there is absolutely no reason to play the ♣K on the first trick. You must play the ♣4 from dummy. When West continues with the ♣J, life becomes more difficult. If the cards lie as in the diagram, you will do well to play low from dummy, setting up the ♣K when East's ♣A appears. However, it is dangerous to play low from dummy a second time. That will allow West to score five club tricks when he began with ♣AQJ10x! In the long run it is best to play the ♣K on the second round. Here this will lose to East's ♣A. All is not lost, though. Because of your hold-up on the first trick, East has no club to play. You will win his major-suit switch and play a diamond. Because East, the safe hand, holds the ◇A (and has no club to play), you will make the contract.

> **PLAN: I will play low from dummy. If West continues with the ♣J, I will play the ♣K and hope that I can subsequently set up the diamonds without losing too many club tricks.**

(By playing the ♣K from dummy on the second round, it is true that you will go down when West has led from ♣QJ10xx and also holds the ◇A. However, in that case East could have beaten the contract anyway by overtaking the ♣Q with the ♣A and then clearing the club suit.)

On the next deal, dummy again holds Kxx of the suit that has been led, but the opening lead is a low card rather than the queen.

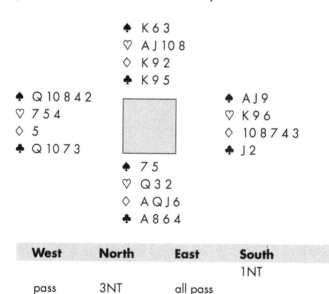

	♠	K 6 3
	♡	A J 10 8
	◇	K 9 2
	♣	K 9 5

West		East
♠ Q 10 8 4 2		♠ A J 9
♡ 7 5 4		♡ K 9 6
◇ 5		◇ 10 8 7 4 3
♣ Q 10 7 3		♣ J 2

	♠	7 5
	♡	Q 3 2
	◇	A Q J 6
	♣	A 8 6 4

West	North	East	South
			1NT
pass	3NT	all pass	

West leads the ♠4 against 3NT and these are your immediate winners:

Top Tricks: ♠ 0   ♡ 1   ◇ 4   ♣ 2   **Total: 7**

The heart suit will give you at least two extra tricks, but you must do what you can to avoid the loss of too many spade tricks meanwhile. As is nearly always the case, you should not play dummy's king (from Kxx) on the first round. If you do, and the cards lie as in the diagram, the defender will score the first five tricks in spades. You will be one down before your plane has left the ground.

You should play low from dummy and let's say that East wins with the ♠J. He cannot beat the contract! If he switches to one of the minor suits, you will win in your hand and run the ♡Q. Even though the finesse loses to East's ♡K, you will have nine tricks ready to go and the spade suit will be protected with East on lead.

Suppose instead that East clears the spade suit by continuing with the ♠A and ♠9 at Trick 2 and 3. You will win the third round with dummy's ♠K, cross to your hand with a diamond and run the ♡Q. East will have no spade to play when he wins with the ♡K, so again you will make the contract.

Finally, let's suppose that East makes the rather unusual play of winning with the ♠A at Trick 1 and returning the ♠J. You will hold up dummy's ♠K on the second round. You win the third round of spades, cross to your hand and run the ♡Q. Nine tricks are yours once again. So long as you play low from dummy at Trick 1, the best defenders in the world will not be able to beat you.

> **PLAN: I will play low from dummy. Whether or not East chooses to clear the spade suit, I will be able to run the ♡Q into the safe East hand.**

Holding up with AQx in the dummy

We will look at one more specific holding that dummy might hold in the suit that has been led: AQx. Although it is only one of many possible holdings, the principles involved will be the same for other combinations. Look at the next deal and decide what play you would make at Trick 1.

```
                    ♠ A Q 4
                    ♡ Q 8 6 2
                    ◊ J 9 8 4
                    ♣ K 6
    ♠ 9 3                                  ♠ K J 10 8 6 2
    ♡ J 9 7 5                              ♡ 10 3
    ◊ 7 6 2                                ◊ A 3
    ♣ J 9 4 2                              ♣ Q 10 7
                    ♠ 7 5
                    ♡ A K 4
                    ◊ K Q 10 5
                    ♣ A 8 5 3
```

West	North	East	South
			1NT
pass	2♣	2♠	pass
pass	3NT	all pass	

North bids Stayman, to look for a heart fit, and East overcalls 2♠. How will you plan the play in 3NT when West leads the ♠9? This is the top trick position:

Top Tricks: ♠ 1   ♡ 3   ◊ 0   ♣ 2   **Total: 6**

The diamond suit will provide the three extra tricks that you need, but you must take care not to lose a bundle of spade tricks along with the ◊A. What card should you play from dummy at Trick 1?

It depends on who holds the ◊A. If, for some reason, you thought that West held the ◊A, you would hold up the spade ace until the third round. West's spades would then be exhausted when he won with the ◊A.

Here East entered the bidding and it is therefore much more likely that he will hold the ◊A. Suppose you play the ♠Q from dummy at Trick 1. East will win and clear the spade suit; he will then score a total of five spade tricks when he wins with the ◊A. Down two! The same horrible result will occur if you play the ♠4 from dummy. West's ♠9 will be allowed to win the first trick and the spade continuation will set up East's suit.

To make the contract, you must rise with dummy's ♠A. When you play the diamond suit and East takes his ace, dummy's remaining ♠Q4 will act as a second stopper.

> **PLAN: I will win with dummy's ♠A and set up the diamonds.**

The situation may be different when West leads a low spot card through dummy's AQx combination:

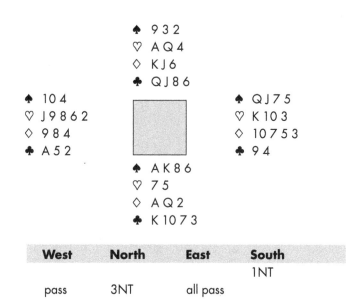

	♠ 9 3 2		
	♡ A Q 4		
	◇ K J 6		
	♣ Q J 8 6		
♠ 10 4		♠ Q J 7 5	
♡ J 9 8 6 2		♡ K 10 3	
◇ 9 8 4		◇ 10 7 5 3	
♣ A 5 2		♣ 9 4	
	♠ A K 8 6		
	♡ 7 5		
	◇ A Q 2		
	♣ K 10 7 3		

West	North	East	South
			1NT
pass	3NT	all pass	

How will you plan 3NT when West leads the ♡6? You have these top tricks available:

Top Tricks: ♠ 2   ♡ 1   ◇ 3   ♣ 0   **Total: 6**

The club suit will give you the three extra tricks that you need, but you must avoid the loss of four heart tricks when you establish the clubs. Which card will you play from dummy on the first trick?

As on the previous deal, nothing can be gained by committing dummy's ♡Q immediately. When the cards lie as in the diagram, East would win with the ♡K and clear the heart suit. West would then cash a total of four heart tricks when he came on lead with his ♣A. Nor is playing dummy's ♡A at Trick 1 a good move. When you subsequently knocked out West's ♣A and he played the ♡2, you would have no idea whether to play the ♡Q from dummy.

To avoid any such problems, you should play the ♡4 from dummy at Trick 1. East will win with the ♡10 but he cannot continue hearts without giving you an extra trick. Whichever other suit he chooses to return, you will set up the clubs while you still have a heart stopper in the dummy.

> **PLAN: I will play the ♡4, allowing East to win the first trick. I will win his switch and set up the club suit.**

Holding up in a suit contract

As we have seen, the purpose behind holding up an ace is to break communications between the defenders. This can prove useful in a suit contract, as well as in notrump. Try this one in 4♠:

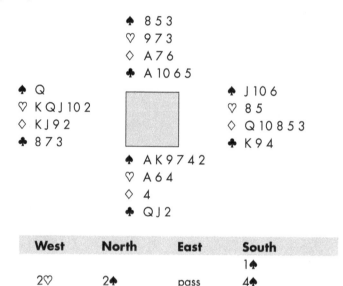

	West	North	East	South
				1♠
	2♡	2♠	pass	4♠
	all pass			

West leads the ♡K against your spade game and you see these potential losers:

Losers: ♠1   ♡2   ◇0   ♣1   **Total:** 4

What is your plan for this spade game? Suppose that trumps are 3-1 and the king of clubs is offside, putting your contract at risk. How can you give yourself a chance of making the contract?

The original declarer won with the ace of hearts and continued with the ace and king of trumps, discovering the 3-1 break. Everything depended now on the club finesse. This lost to the king and East then played the jack of trumps, followed by his remaining heart. West's two heart tricks put the contract down one.

To improve your chance of surviving against a poor lie in the black suits, you should hold up the ♡A at Trick 1. This is a familiar maneuver in notrump contracts, but it can be useful in suit contracts too. The hold-up is perfectly safe because if West holds six hearts, a heart ruff on the second round will not harm you; East will be ruffing a loser (perhaps from a natural trump trick, too). You win the second round of hearts, play the ace and king of trumps and run the club queen. See the difference! When East wins with the ♣K, he has no heart to play. You win his diamond return, give East his trump trick and eventually discard a heart on the fourth round of clubs.

PLAN: I will hold up the ♡A until the second round, play the ace and king of trumps and run the ♣Q. Eventually I will discard the remaining heart loser on the clubs.

Remember these points

- When you have a stopper of AJx and a low card is led to the king or queen on your right, you must consider carefully whether to hold up. When you expect the defender on your right to gain the lead, it is generally right to hold up. When instead you expect your left-hand opponent to gain the lead, you should win with the ace and retain the Jx as a second stopper.

- When dummy holds Kxx in the suit that has been led, and you have only low cards, it is rarely right to play the king on the first round.

- A hold-up can prove useful in a suit contract, as well as in notrump. The objective is the same — to break the communication between the two defenders.

Now try these...

A.

                    ♠ K J 6 2
                    ♡ 9 7 3
                    ◇ K J 8 6 2
                    ♣ A

♡K led

                    ♠ Q 5
                    ♡ A 8 2
                    ◇ A Q 10 9 7 3
                    ♣ 6 2

West leads the ♡K against 5◇. How will you plan the play?

B.

                    ♠ 8 5
                    ♡ A 2
                    ◇ A K J 10 5
                    ♣ K 9 5 4

♠10 led

                    ♠ A J 3
                    ♡ K 8 6 3
                    ◇ 8 3
                    ♣ A 6 3 2

West leads the ♠10 against 3NT, East playing the ♠Q. What is your plan?

C.

                    ♠ 10 2
                    ♡ A Q J 6
                    ◇ 9 8 4
                    ♣ Q J 5 3

◇K led

                    ♠ A
                    ♡ 5 2
                    ◇ A 5 3
                    ♣ A K 10 9 7 4 2

West leads the ◇K against your contract of 5♣. What is your plan?

D.

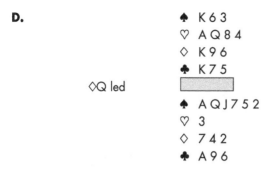

♠ K 6 3
♡ A Q 8 4
◇ K 9 6
♣ K 7 5

◇Q led

♠ A Q J 7 5 2
♡ 3
◇ 7 4 2
♣ A 9 6

What is your plan for 4♠ when West leads the ◇Q?

E.

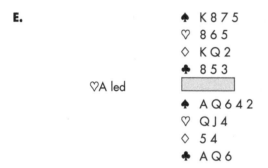

♠ K 8 7 5
♡ 8 6 5
◇ K Q 2
♣ 8 5 3

♡A led

♠ A Q 6 4 2
♡ Q J 4
◇ 5 4
♣ A Q 6

West, who opened the bidding with 1♡, leads the ♡A against your contract of 2♠. He continues with the ♡K and another heart, East ruffing. What is your plan when East switches to the ♣J?

F.

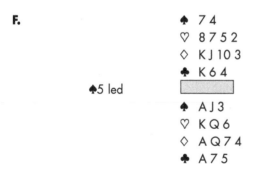

♠ 7 4
♡ 8 7 5 2
◇ K J 10 3
♣ K 6 4

♠5 led

♠ A J 3
♡ K Q 6
◇ A Q 7 4
♣ A 7 5

West leads the ♠5 against 3NT and East plays the ♠Q. How will you play the contract?

ANSWERS

A. You have one loser in spades and two in hearts (and one club loser which you can ruff in dummy). Suppose you win the first heart, draw trumps and knock out the ♠A. When East holds the ♠A, it is almost certain that he will have a heart left; on a heart return, you will lose two tricks in the suit before you have had a chance to take a discard on the spades. To give yourself some chance of making the contract, you should duck the first round of hearts. You win the next heart, draw trumps and knock out the ♠A. Now you will make the contract when East holds the ♠A and began with only two hearts.

PLAN: I will hold up the ♡A and win the heart continuation. I will then draw trumps and play a spade, hoping that East holds the ♠A and has no hearts left.

B. You have seven top tricks and can establish at least two more by finessing in diamonds, even if the finesse loses. What you cannot afford is that the defenders score the ◇Q and four spade tricks. So, you must hold up the ♠A at Trick 1. East returns the ♠6 and you play the ♠J, losing to West's ♠K. West clears the spades, but this removes East's last spade in the critical case where spades are 5-3. You can then finesse diamonds into the safe hand (twice if the first finesse wins). Whoever holds the ◇Q, you will make the contract.

PLAN: I will hold up the ♠A for two rounds and then finesse diamonds into the safe hand.

C. You have three possible losers, one in hearts and two in diamonds. Playing in 5♣, you should hold up on the first round of diamonds. You win the next diamond, draw trumps and finesse the ♡Q. If the finesse wins, you will return to your hand and finesse the ♡J to set up a diamond discard on the ♡A. If instead the heart finesse loses, you will still make your contract (thanks to your hold-up at Trick 1) when East began with only two diamonds and now has no diamonds left. You will be able to take a discard on the established ♡J.

PLAN: I will hold up the ◇A for one round, draw trumps and then finesse in hearts. I will make the contract when West holds the ♡K, also when the heart finesse loses but East has no diamond to return.

D. There is no chance whatsoever that a sane West has led the ◇Q against a suit contract from a holding headed by the ◇AQJ. You can bet your life savings that East holds the ◇A and you should therefore play low from dummy, both on the first and second round of diamonds. When East's ◇A is singleton or doubleton, which is quite a good chance when West has led from a sequence, he will be forced to play it on one of the first two tricks. Your ◇K will then be established and the contract will be safe. If East holds ◇Axx, the defenders will be able to take three diamond tricks. In that case you will win their return at Trick 4, draw trumps and finesse the ♡Q, hoping that the finesse will win and you can then discard your club loser on the ♡A.

> **PLAN: I will play low from dummy on the first two rounds of diamonds. If East's ◇A does not appear, and they take a third diamond trick, I will finesse the ♡Q to set up a discard for my club loser.**

E. You have lost the first three tricks and must hope to lose in addition only one club and one diamond. West, who opened the bidding, is very likely to hold the ♣K. If you finesse the ♣Q at Trick 4, West will win and clear the club suit, leaving you with six losers. Instead, you should rise with the ♣A, draw two rounds of trumps with the king and ace and lead toward the ◇KQ2. If West plays low and the ◇K wins, you return to your hand with a third round of trumps and lead another diamond toward dummy. If West rises with the ◇A this time, you will have a discard of one of your clubs on the ◇Q. If instead he chooses to play low for a second time, you will not lose a diamond trick.

> **PLAN: I will rise with the ♣A and play the king and ace of trumps. I will then lead twice toward dummy's ◇KQx to establish a club discard.**

F. To decide whether or not to hold up to create an extra stopper from AJx, you must determine which defender is likely to gain the lead. If it is East, you hold up; if it is West, you win immediately. On this deal, you will need to make a plan for the whole contract before playing to the first trick. You have seven top tricks and will need to score two heart tricks to bring the total to nine. This will require East to hold the ♡A and you should therefore hold up the ♠A for two rounds. You then cross to a diamond and lead a heart to the king. (If this loses to West's ♡A, you could not have made the contract anyway.) When the ♡K wins, you return to dummy with a diamond and lead a heart toward the ♡Q. When East takes his ♡A he will have no spade to return; that was the purpose of your hold-up play.

> **PLAN: I will hold up the ♠A until the third round and then lead twice toward the ♡KQx.**

17

PLANS THAT INVOLVE COUNTING

Would you make more contracts if you could see the defenders' hands? Of course you would! One of the most important skills for a top-class declarer is the ability to build a picture of the defenders' hands. In particular, you should seek to obtain a 'count on the hand'. What does that mean? It means that you gradually discover how many cards the defenders hold in each suit.

Counting the defenders' distribution

Counting the hand can often help you to decide how to take a particular finesse. Let's start with a deal where you can make 6NT, provided you can guess how the club suit lies:

```
              ♠ K 9 7 6 2
              ♡ 3
              ♢ A K 7
              ♣ K 10 8 6
  ♠ 4                          ♠ J 10 8 5 3
  ♡ A Q J 10 8 5 2            ♡ 9 7 4
  ♢ 9 4                        ♢ 10 8 5 2
  ♣ Q 7 4                      ♣ 2
              ♠ A Q
              ♡ K 6
              ♢ Q J 6 3
              ♣ A J 9 5 3
```

West	North	East	South
3♡	3♠	pass	4NT
pass	5♢	pass	6NT
all pass			

West leads a safe ◇9 against 6NT and this is the winner situation:

Top Tricks: ♠ 3   ♡ 0   ◇ 4   ♣ 2   **Total:** 9

You need three extra winners to bring the total to twelve. These are available in the club suit, provided you can guess (or calculate) how the suit lies. Suppose you had to play clubs immediately. What guess would you make?

West is likely to hold seven hearts to his partner's three. So, on the information available at the start of the hand, East has ten non-hearts to West's six. He is therefore likely to hold more clubs than West and the odds would favor playing East for ♣Qxx; you would cash dummy's ♣K and then finesse the ♣J.

You do not have to play clubs immediately! Instead you should play a few rounds of spades and diamonds, hoping to get a 'complete count' on the hand. When you play the ♠A and ♠Q, West shows out on the second round. You continue with your remaining diamond winners and West shows out on the third round. You are now practically certain that West's shape is 1-7-2-3. Since West has three clubs, you play the ace on the first round of the suit. When only small cards appear on the first round, you then lead a low club to dummy's ten. The finesse wins, just as you expected it would, and the slam is yours.

Suppose instead that West had followed to the second round of spades. You would play two more rounds of diamonds ending in dummy, and then play the ♠K. If West showed out on both the third diamond and the third spade, his shape would be 2-7-2-2. You would play for the drop in clubs (in other words, you would play the ♣A and ♣K, hoping to drop the queen). If instead you discovered that West started with three spades and two diamonds, his shape would be 3-7-2-1. You would cash the king on the first round of clubs and then finesse the jack. Do you see how wonderful 'counting the hand' is? You will 'guess' the clubs right every time, however the suit lies!

> **PLAN: I will win with the ◇A and play diamonds and spades to obtain a 'complete count'. I will then know how to play the clubs.**

Does counting the hand seem a bit like hard work? It is, yes, but a big payday can come at the end of it. Let's see another slam where you can save yourself a guess in one of the suits.

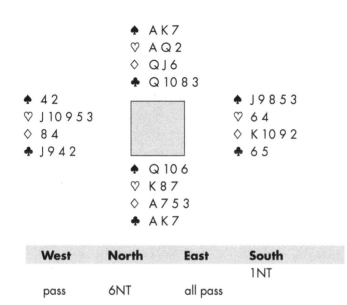

	♠ A K 7	
	♡ A Q 2	
	◇ Q J 6	
	♣ Q 10 8 3	

♠ 4 2
♡ J 10 9 5 3
◇ 8 4
♣ J 9 4 2

♠ J 9 8 5 3
♡ 6 4
◇ K 10 9 2
♣ 6 5

♠ Q 10 6
♡ K 8 7
◇ A 7 5 3
♣ A K 7

West	North	East	South
			1NT
pass	6NT	all pass	

How will you play the notrump slam when West leads the ♡J? You start with these immediate winners:

Top Tricks: ♠ 3   ♡ 3   ◇ 1   ♣ 3   **Total: 10**

First of all, you should try to establish two extra tricks from the diamond suit. What is the best way of doing this? You would like to score tricks with the queen and jack, as well as with the ace. As we saw way back on page 112, the way to attempt this is to lead toward the honors that you are hoping to score. You should lead toward the ◇QJ6, twice if necessary. In that way, you will score two extra diamond tricks when West holds the ◇K. If East holds the ◇K, you may find that diamonds divide 3-3 and again you will have two extra diamond tricks. If the diamond suit fails to provide both the extra tricks that you need, there will still be a chance of an extra trick in clubs.

So, you win the heart lead with the king and lead a diamond to the queen. Your first chance fails when East wins with the ◇K. You capture the heart return with dummy's queen and test the diamond suit by playing the jack and ace. No luck is forthcoming there either, the suit breaking 4-2. You now need to score four club tricks. To decide whether to finesse the ♣10 on the third round or to play for the drop, you would like to obtain a complete count on the hand.

Before tackling clubs, you play a third round of hearts. East shows out and you now have a count on both the red suits. You continue with three rounds of spades and West shows out on the third round. So, West began with 2-5-2-4 shape. He holds four clubs! You cash the ♣A and ♣K and lead a third round, the ♣9 appearing from West. Only one club is still out, the jack. Since you know that West began with four clubs, you finesse dummy's ♣10 with confidence. East shows out, as you knew he would, and the slam is yours.

Suppose instead that West had followed to three rounds of spades. Three spades, five hearts and two diamonds would leave no room for four clubs. You would then have known that the ♣9 was his last club and you would have risen with the ♣Q, dropping East's ♣J.

> **PLAN: I will lead twice toward dummy's ◇QJ6, scoring three diamond tricks when West holds the ◇K or diamonds are 3-3. Failing that, I will seek a complete count on the hand so that I can guess clubs correctly.**

Detective work to obtain a count

Sometimes you have to take some trouble to obtain information on the distribution. When you hold a suit of ♡A1085 in dummy opposite the singleton ♡3 in your hand, for example, you might ruff two or three rounds simply to see how the defenders' cards break.

On the next deal, a grand slam, you have a key guess to make in diamonds. Detective work will give you the information that you need.

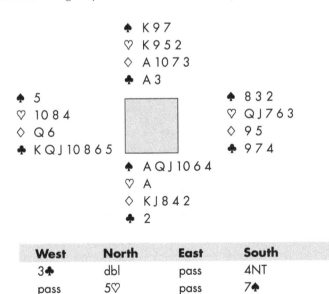

West	North	East	South
3♣	dbl	pass	4NT
pass	5♡	pass	7♠
all pass			

North's double is for takeout and South's 4NT asks for aces, the 5♡ response showing two. How would you tackle 7♠ when West leads the ♣K? This is the loser position:

Losers: ♠0 ♡0 ◇1 ♣0   Total: 1

It's simple enough, then — you need to avoid a diamond loser. If you can obtain a complete count on the hand (discovering whether a particular defender holds three diamonds, or that diamonds are 2-2), this will save you from having to guess in the suit.

You win the club lead in dummy and cross to the ♡A. You then play the ace and king of trumps, noting that West shows out on the second round. So far you place West with one spade, along with seven clubs for his opening bid of 3♣; you are about to discover how many hearts he holds. You play the ♡K and ruff a heart in your hand, everyone following. You then cross to the ♠9, drawing East's last trump, and ruff another heart in your hand. West shows out on this trick and you can place him with 1-3-2-7 shape. Diamonds are 2-2! You play the ◊A and ◊K, the defenders' cards breaking 2-2, and the grand slam is made.

Suppose West had shown up with only two hearts instead. His shape would then have been 1-2-3-7. Knowing that West held three diamonds, you would have played the ◊K on the first round and then finessed dummy's ◊10.

> **PLAN: I will play four rounds of hearts, ruffing twice in my hand. This will give me a count on the hand and I will know how to play the diamond suit.**

Obtaining a partial count on the distribution

The deals that we have seen so far showed counting the hand at its most precise. You were able to determine the precise shape of the defenders' hands and could then be certain to play the key suit correctly. Life is not always so perfect, as you may have discovered, and sometimes you can get only a rough picture of the defenders' shape — perhaps an exact count on just two suits. This may still be enough to increase your chance of playing the key suit correctly.

On the following deal you need to guess which defender holds the ◊J:

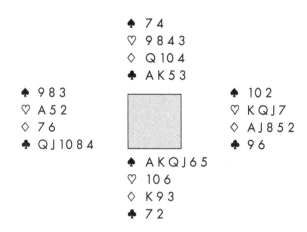

West	North	East	South
			1♠
pass	1NT	pass	3♠
pass	4♠	all pass	

West leads the ♣Q, won in the dummy, and East plays the ♣9. How will you play the spade game? You can see these potential losers:

Losers: ♠0 ♡2 ◊2 ♣0   **Total: 4**

You have a two-way finesse available against the ◊J. If you can guess that suit correctly, you will lose only one diamond trick and make the contract. How can you give yourself more than a 50% chance of guessing correctly?

The defender who started with more diamonds than his partner will be the favorite to hold the missing jack and you should therefore seek a count on the hand — if not a complete count, then as good a count as you can achieve.

Look at the club suit first. What is your best guess as to the number of clubs held by each defender? West has led the ♣Q. Such honor leads are nearly always the top of a sequence and imply some length in the suit. Here East has signaled his count with the ♣9 (a high card shows an even number of cards in the suit). By far the most likely lie of the clubs is that West holds five clubs and East has played high-low from a doubleton.

When you draw trumps, you find that West began with three trumps to East's two. So, you are inclined to place West with eight black-suit cards to East's four. This leaves East with nine red-suit cards to West's five. You have little idea how the heart suit lies but, even so, East is a 9-to-5 favorite to hold the ◊J.

You might as well exit with a heart, in case the defenders give you any more information there, but when East wins the first heart he returns the ♣6 to remove dummy's last entry. The time has come to guess in diamonds. You follow the 9-to-5 odds and finesse the ◊9. It wins the trick and you can then knock out the ◊A.

> **PLAN: The contract depends on taking the two-way guess in diamonds correctly. I will seek as accurate a count as possible before deciding how to finesse in diamonds.**

Counting points when a defender opens the bidding

When one of the defenders has opened 1NT you should count all the honor cards that he subsequently produces. This may allow you to deduce the position of an outstanding honor card. Look at this example:

```
                    ♠ 7 2
                    ♡ K J 5 4
                    ◇ J 10 4
                    ♣ A K 5 4
   ♠ Q 9                              ♠ 10 8 4
   ♡ A 9 2                            ♡ 8 7 3
   ◇ A K 7 6                          ◇ Q 9 5 2
   ♣ Q J 8 3                          ♣ 10 9 6
                    ♠ A K J 6 5 3
                    ♡ Q 10 6
                    ◇ 8 3
                    ♣ 7 2
```

West	North	East	South
1NT	pass	pass	2♠
pass	4♠	all pass	

West, who opened a 15–17 point 1NT, leads the ◇A against 4♠. East encourages with the ◇9 and West continues with the ◇K and a third diamond to East's queen. How will you play the contract? You have these potential losers:

Losers: ♠ 1   ♡ 1   ◇ 2   ♣ 0   Total: 4

The red-suit losers are set in stone, so you will have to avoid a trump loser. Normally, missing five cards to the queen, you would finesse the ♠J. On this particular hand, though, West's opening bid has told you that he began with 15 or more points. You can see 22 points between your own hand and the dummy. Only 18 points are left for the defenders and East has already shown up with the ◇Q. If East held the ♠Q too, this would leave only 14 points for West — not enough for his opening 1NT bid. So, after ruffing the third round of diamonds you should play the ace and king of trumps, hoping that the ♠Q will fall doubleton. The alternative play of crossing to dummy to finesse the ♠J is certain to fail.

> **PLAN: West's opening bid promised 15 of the opposing side's 18 points and East has already shown up with the ◇Q. I will therefore play to drop the ♠Q in the West hand.**

On the next deal, the information at your disposal is that East has opened with a one-bid in a suit.

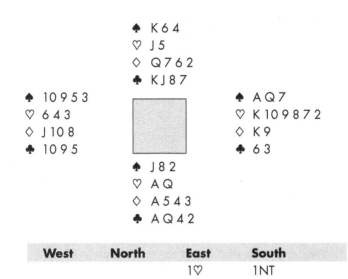

```
              ♠ K 6 4
              ♡ J 5
              ◊ Q 7 6 2
              ♣ K J 8 7
♠ 10 9 5 3                      ♠ A Q 7
♡ 6 4 3                        ♡ K 10 9 8 7 2
◊ J 10 8                       ◊ K 9
♣ 10 9 5                       ♣ 6 3
              ♠ J 8 2
              ♡ A Q
              ◊ A 5 4 3
              ♣ A Q 4 2
```

West	North	East	South
		1♡	1NT
pass	3NT	all pass	

You win the heart lead with the queen and see this top trick position:

Top Tricks: ♠ 0   ♡ 2   ◊ 1   ♣ 4   **Total:** 7

Two more diamond tricks will carry you to the victor's podium. With this combination you would normally cash the ◊A and then lead toward the queen, hoping that West held the king. Is that likely to be the case here, though? There are only 13 high card points missing and East opened the bidding. It's possible that East opened on 10 high card points, but the odds are strongly in favor of him holding the ◊K.

You play the ◊A and East follows with the ◊9. When you lead a second round of diamonds, West follows with the ◊10. You should follow the evidence from the bidding and duck in the dummy. East's ◊K does indeed appear and the game is yours.

> **PLAN: East is very likely to hold the ◊K after his opening bid. I will therefore play the ◊A and duck the second round.**

Counting points when a defender does not open

When a defender has the chance to bid but chooses to pass, this gives you information about his hand. If he chooses not to open the bidding, for example, he is unlikely to hold 12 points. If he chooses not to overcall at the one level and shows up with a suit of KQJxx, he is unlikely to hold another high card.

You can make good use of such a deduction on the next hand:

```
                    ♠ K 10 4
                    ♡ A 10 8 2
                    ◇ K 7 5
                    ♣ Q J 5
  ♠ 9 8 2                              ♠ Q 7 5 3
  ♡ K 4                                ♡ 6 5
  ◇ 9 6 3                              ◇ Q J 10 4 2
  ♣ A K 9 3 2                          ♣ 10 6
                    ♠ A J 6
                    ♡ Q J 9 7 3
                    ◇ A 8
                    ♣ 8 7 4
```

West	North	East	South
pass	1♣	pass	1♡
pass	2♡	pass	4♡
all pass			

West, who passed in the first seat, leads the ♣A and ♣K and then gives East a club ruff. How will you continue when East returns the ◇Q? You have lost three club tricks already, so this is the loser position:

Losers: ♠ 1   ♡ 1   ◇ 0   ♣ 3   **Total:** 5

You win with the ◇A and run the ♡Q successfully. You draw the last trump, West producing the ♡K and East discarding a small diamond. You now need to negotiate the two-way spade finesse successfully. Do you have any ideas?

West has already shown up with the ♣AKxxx and the ♡K. If he held the ♠Q in addition, he would surely have opened the bidding. So, you play the ♠K and then finesse the ♠J, playing East for the ♠Q. Not surprisingly, this finesse proves successful. It was not a 50% finesse on this occasion. With the evidence before you, it was more like 99%!

> **PLAN: I will take the trump finesse. If it is successful, West cannot hold the ♠Q or he would have opened the bidding. I will therefore finesse East for that card.**

Counting points when a defender did not respond

When a defender did not respond to his partner's one-bid, it is reasonable to assume that he does not hold 6 points. Keep a close watch on the cards that he plays. Once he has produced one big card, he is unlikely to hold another. Here is a straightforward example:

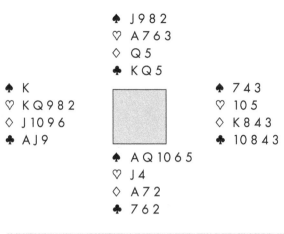

                    ♠ J 9 8 2
                    ♡ A 7 6 3
                    ◇ Q 5
                    ♣ K Q 5

    ♠ K   ♠ 7 4 3
    ♡ K Q 9 8 2   ♡ 10 5
    ◇ J 10 9 6   ◇ K 8 4 3
    ♣ A J 9   ♣ 10 8 4 3

                    ♠ A Q 10 6 5
                    ♡ J 4
                    ◇ A 7 2
                    ♣ 7 6 2

West	North	East	South
1♡	pass	pass	1♠
pass	3♠	pass	4♠
all pass			

West leads the ◇J against 4♠ and this is the loser situation:

Losers: ♠ 1   ♡ 1   ◇ 2   ♣ 2   **Total:** 6

You might as well try the ◇Q from dummy, but this is covered with the ◇K and you win with the ◇A. You have two certain losers in the red suits (only one diamond because you can ruff the third round) and must therefore hope to lose no trump tricks and only one trick in clubs.

You can reduce your club losers from two to one by leading twice toward dummy's honors, hoping that West holds the ♣A. Does West hold the ♣A? Yes! East has already shown up with the ◇K; if he held an ace too, he would have seven points and would have responded to his partner's opening bid.

What about the trump suit? Exactly the same reasoning applies. If East held two kings he would surely have responded to his partner's opening bid. You can therefore place the ♠K with West and your only hope is that the card is singleton. Nothing can be gained by finessing East for the ♠K. At Trick 2 you should lay down the ♠A. As it happens, your luck is in. West's king falls and you draw the remaining trumps. A club to the king wins and you will eventually reach your hand with a heart ruff to lead a second round of clubs toward dummy's queen. You lose one heart, one diamond and one club to make the contract.

> **PLAN: I will play dummy's ◇Q. If East covers with the ◇K he cannot also hold the ♠K. I will play to drop that card from the West hand. I can then lead twice toward the ♣KQx and ruff a diamond in dummy.**

Sometimes, the opening lead will give you an enormous amount of information — not only about the lie of the suit led, but also about some different suit that the defender chose not to lead. The next deal illustrates this idea:

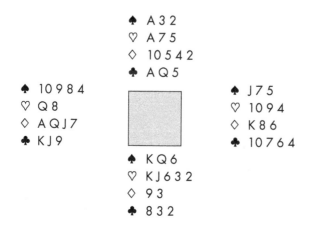

	♠ A 3 2	
	♡ A 7 5	
	◇ 10 5 4 2	
	♣ A Q 5	

West		East
♠ 10 9 8 4		♠ J 7 5
♡ Q 8		♡ 10 9 4
◇ A Q J 7		◇ K 8 6
♣ K J 9		♣ 10 7 6 4

	♠ K Q 6	
	♡ K J 6 3 2	
	◇ 9 3	
	♣ 8 3 2	

West	North	East	South
1◇	pass	pass	1♡
pass	4♡	all pass	

West leads the ♠10 against 4♡ and you see these potential losers:

Losers: ♠ 0   ♡ 1   ◇ 2   ♣ 2   **Total: 5**

If the hearts broke really badly, you might have more than one loser in the suit. The contract would be hopeless in that case, so let's assume that you have at most one potential loser there.

What deductions can you make from West's opening lead of the ♠10? Firstly, you can assume that East holds the ♠J. In addition, you can you tell something about West's diamond holding. If West held the ◇A and ◇K, he would surely have led the suit. So, East must hold either the ◇A or the ◇K! That is at least 4 points that you have identified in the East hand. If he held the ♡Q too, he would have had enough points to respond to the opening bid.

Amazing as it may seem, you can deduce from West's opening lead of the ♠10 that he must hold the ♡Q. After winning the spade lead, you should therefore play the ♡A and ♡K rather than taking a finesse. As it happens, West's queen is doubleton and the card falls. You draw the last trump and finesse the ♣Q successfully, making the heart game.

> **PLAN: After West's ♠10 lead, I can deduce that East holds the ♠J and either the ◇A or the ◇K. He cannot hold the ♡Q in addition, so I will try to drop the queen in the West hand.**

Remember these points

- To play most contracts to best advantage, you should keep track of the distribution of the defenders' hands.

- A defender who is long in one suit is likely to be shorter than his partner in the other suits.

- When you have a two-way finesse for a queen, try to discover which defender holds more cards in that suit. Unless the bidding gives evidence to the contrary, that defender is the favorite to hold the queen.

- Counting the high-card points for each defender can also provide important information.

- When a defender declines to open the bidding, he is unlikely to hold 12 points. When a defender does not respond to his partner's one-bid, he is unlikely to hold 6 points. Such inferences may allow you to calculate where a particular honor card lies.

Now try these...

A.

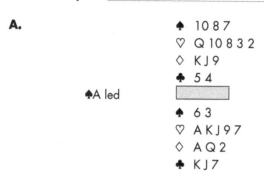

♠ 10 8 7
♡ Q 10 8 3 2
◇ K J 9
♣ 5 4

♠A led

♠ 6 3
♡ A K J 9 7
◇ A Q 2
♣ K J 7

You are first to speak and the bidding goes 1♡ – 2♡ – 4♡, with both defenders silent. How will you plan the play when West cashes the ♠A and ♠K and leads a third spade to East's queen?

B.

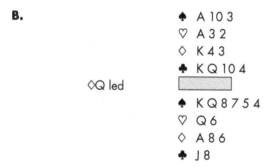

♠ A 10 3
♡ A 3 2
◇ K 4 3
♣ K Q 10 4

◇Q led

♠ K Q 8 7 5 4
♡ Q 6
◇ A 8 6
♣ J 8

You open 1♠ and West overcalls 2♡. How will you play the eventual contract of 6♠ when West leads the ◇Q?

C.

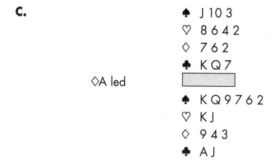

♠ J 10 3
♡ 8 6 4 2
◇ 7 6 2
♣ K Q 7

◇A led

♠ K Q 9 7 6 2
♡ K J
◇ 9 4 3
♣ A J

West opens a 15–17 point 1NT and you bid 2♠ on the South cards, ending the auction. West plays the ◇A and ◇K, continuing with a third diamond to East's ◇Q. How will you plan the play when East returns the ♡7?

D.

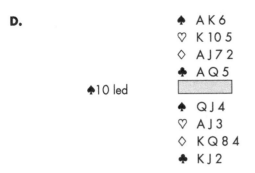

♠ A K 6
♡ K 10 5
◇ A J 7 2
♣ A Q 5

♠10 led

♠ Q J 4
♡ A J 3
◇ K Q 8 4
♣ K J 2

How will you plan a contract of 7NT when West leads the ♠10?

E.

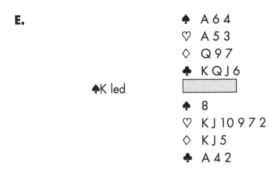

♠ A 6 4
♡ A 5 3
◇ Q 9 7
♣ K Q J 6

♠K led

♠ 8
♡ K J 10 9 7 2
◇ K J 5
♣ A 4 2

West opens 3♠ and you end in 6♡ on the South cards. What is your plan when West leads the ♠K?

F.

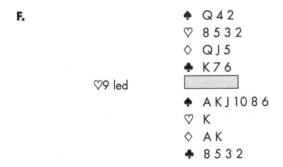

♠ Q 4 2
♡ 8 5 3 2
◇ Q J 5
♣ K 7 6

♡9 led

♠ A K J 10 8 6
♡ K
◇ A K
♣ 8 5 3 2

East opens the bidding with 1♡ and you end in 4♠. What is your plan for this contract when West leads the ♡9 to East's ♡A, dropping your ♡K, and East continues with the ♡Q?

ANSWERS

A. You ruff the third spade and draw trumps in two rounds, West showing up with a singleton. You need to escape for only one club loser. Should you play a club to the jack or a club to the king? The fact that East played the ♣Q suggests that West holds the ♣J. If West's hand is: ♠AKJ2 ♡4 ◇10543 ♣A932, he would have made a take-out double of your 1♡ opening. Not expecting West to hold the ♣A, you should lead low to the king.

> **PLAN: After drawing trumps, I will lead low to the ♣K. West would surely have bid something if he had the ♣A as well as his good spades and short hearts.**

B. Dummy's club suit will provide two discards for your red-suit losers, so the only risk to the contract is a 4-0 trump break. If you cashed the ♠K on the first round, you could pick up ♠J962 with West by finessing the ♠10. However, it is almost impossible for West to hold all four spades. He has indicated long hearts with his 2♡ overcall and suggested long diamonds with his ◇Q lead, which is likely to be from a sequence.

It is much more likely that East holds four spades and you can pick up this holding too. Win the diamond lead in your hand and cross to the ♠A. Let's say that West shows out on the first round. You continue with the ♠10, covered by the ♠J and ♠Q. Needing to set up discards for your red-suit losers, you now lead the ♣J. Whether West wins the first or second round of clubs, you will be able to reach dummy (with the ◇K if West ducked the first round of clubs). You will then finesse the ♠8, draw East's last trump and return to dummy with the ♡A to discard your losers on the established clubs.

> **PLAN: I will win with the ◇A and cross to the ♠A to pick up a possible ♠J962 with East. I will also set up the clubs, to discard my red-suit losers.**

C. You need to count the points that West has shown. He has at most 8 points in diamonds (the ◇AKJ) and 4 points in spades (the ♠A). To give him enough points for a 15–17 point 1NT, he must hold the ♡A. You should therefore play the ♡J when East switches to a heart; you will then make the contract when East holds the ♡Q.

> **PLAN: West is marked with the ♡A, to give him at least 15 points for his 1NT opening. I will therefore play the ♡J at Trick 4.**

D. You have twelve top tricks and will need to guess the two-way finesse in hearts correctly to make the grand slam. To give yourself the best chance, you must seek a count on the hand (or at least a partial count). You should therefore cash all your winners in spades, diamonds and clubs. The defender who has the majority of the hearts will be the favorite to hold the ♡Q. For example, suppose that West turns up with five clubs, two diamonds and at least three spades (both defenders following to three spades). West can then hold at most three hearts and may hold only two. East will have the majority of the hearts and you should finesse him for the ♡Q.

> **PLAN: I will play a total of ten tricks in spades, diamonds and clubs. The defender who holds the majority of the hearts will be the favorite to hold the ♡Q.**

E. You have a certain loser in diamonds, so everything will depend on picking up the trump suit for no loser. West's 3♠ opening suggests that he holds seven spades to East's two. Even though you have no count on the minor suits, you know that West holds only six non-spades, while East holds eleven. The odds are therefore 11 to 6 that East holds the ♡Q. After winning the spade lead, you should cash the ♡A (two low cards appearing) and then finesse the ♡J.

Another factor in favor of the recommended play is this: a player who opens 3♠ will usually hold a singleton in his hand. If West had held a singleton in diamonds or clubs, he might well have led it, hoping for a ruff. The fact that he chose to lead a spade instead is further evidence that he may hold a singleton trump.

> **PLAN: I will win with the ♠A, cash the ♡A and finesse the ♡J. East is shorter in spades and therefore likely to be longer in hearts.**

F. You should ruff the second round of hearts high, just in case the opening lead was a singleton. You then draw trumps. It makes little difference how the trump suit divides, because you will still have to avoid three losers in the club suit. The ◇Q will allow you to discard your fourth card in the suit. Normally you would lead toward the ♣K at some stage, hoping that West held the ♣A. That is very unlikely after East's opening bid, however. There are only 14 points missing, so East is a huge favorite to hold the ♣A. Your best chance is to duck the first two rounds of clubs, hoping that East began with a doubleton ♣A.

> **PLAN: I will ruff the second heart high and draw trumps. East's opening bid strongly suggests that he holds the ♣A, so I will duck two rounds of the suit.**

Master Point Press on the Internet

www.masterpointpress.com

Our main site, with information about our books and software, reviews and more.

www.teachbridge.com

Our site for bridge teachers and students — free downloadable support material for our books, helpful articles and more.

www.bridgeblogging.com

Read and comment on regular articles from MPP authors and other bridge notables.

www.ebooksbridge.com

Purchase downloadable electronic versions of MPP books.